A POLITICS OF UNDERSTANDING

Political Traditions in Foreign Policy
Kenneth W. Thompson, Series Editor

A POLITICS OF UNDERSTANDING

The International Thought of Raymond Aron

REED M. DAVIS

LOUISIANA STATE UNIVERSITY PRESS
BATON ROUGE

Published by Louisiana State University Press

Manufactured in the United States of America
First printing

Designer: Tammi L. deGeneres
Typefaces: Arno Pro, Franklin Gothic
Printer and binder: Thomson-Shore, Inc.

Library of Congress Cataloging-in-Publication Data

Davis, Reed M.

A politics of understanding : the international thought of Raymond Aron / Reed M. Davis.
p. cm. — (Political traditions in foreign policy series)
Includes bibliographical references and index.
ISBN 978-0-8071-3517-4 (cloth : alk. paper) 1. International relations. 2. Political science—Philosophy. 3. Aron, Raymond, 1905–1983. I. Title.
JZ1242.D39 2009
327.101—dc22

2009019029

The paper in this book meets the guidelines for permanence and durability of the Committee on Production Guidelines for Book Longevity of the Council on Library Resources. ♾

To Maggie

CONTENTS

ACKNOWLEDGMENTS

THIS WORK WOULD HAVE never seen the light of day had it not been for the support of several institutions and countless individuals. I am deeply indebted to those who read and improved the manuscript in its earliest manifestations, most notably Inis Claude, Hugh Davidson, and Michael Brint. My two anonymous readers from Louisiana State University Press also offered invaluable suggestions and improved the manuscript immeasurably. I hope they see the evidence of their helpfulness in these pages. I am also profoundly grateful for the unflagging patience and cheerfulness of John Easterly of LSU Press and the superior talents of my manuscript editor, Elizabeth Gratch. I also appreciate the support provided to me by the Miller Center of Public Affairs, the Institute for the Study of World Politics, and the Earhart Foundation. I also thank the *European Journal of Political Theory,* the *Review of International Studies,* and the *Political Science Reviewer* for permission to draw from material published earlier in their journals. But I owe more than I can say to Kenneth W. Thompson, whose ongoing friendship and encouragement have made everything—absolutely everything—possible.

My deepest debt of gratitude, however, goes to my family. My parents have been living examples of love and selfless devotion; I owe them all that I know and am. My children were a constant source of joy while I wrote this book. Now that they are old enough, I hope they read it. But my deepest, most heartfelt appreciation goes to my wife, Maggie, to whom this book is dedicated.

A POLITICS OF UNDERSTANDING

INTRODUCTION

THE 1930S WILL LONG be remembered as one of the ugliest decades of modern French history. Diplomatic humiliation abroad combined with unrestrained partisanship at home to plunge France into an era of almost unparalleled political turmoil. During this unhappy period, H. Stuart Hughes has reported, "the customary warfare among ideological groups mounted to an unprecedented shrillness as rival intellectual clans threatened to devour each other whole."[1] Struggling to moderate these quarrels, "the honest and rigorous social thinkers began to realize that a new kind of discourse was necessary—a discourse which would give a surer grasp of reality and translate more easily into the vocabularies in use outside France."[2] Although the call for a new grammar of politics reverberated through an intensely creative generation of French thinkers, few responded to the challenge as vigorously or as brilliantly as Raymond Aron.

Recognized on both sides of the Atlantic as one of the leading social theorists produced by France in the twentieth century, Raymond Aron poured his remarkable talents and energies into two closely related vocations. As a sociologist at the Sorbonne and the Collège de France, he wrote more than forty books and six hundred articles on a staggering variety of topics in philosophy, sociology, economics, military strategy, and international relations. As a journalist, first for *La France Libre* and later for *Le Figaro* and *L'Express,* he produced some four thousand columns of political commentary devoted to French and world politics. Taken together, Aron's scholarly and journalistic output constitutes a body of work that finds few equals in recent history. Indeed, many commentators have declared that France has not seen the like of Raymond Aron since the *philosophes,* those remarkable luminaries of the eighteenth century.

Coming of age during the interwar years, Aron was deeply shaken by the ideological clamor retarding rational debate. Determined to improve the quality of social and political discourse, he tirelessly reminded his audience that the pursuit of values must respect the contingencies of existence. Transforming the ideal into the real requires more than blind, single-minded determination; it requires, above all else, "an understanding of those conditions which are likely to set limits to what men can achieve." [3] Thus, in order to articulate realistic and attainable goals, modern men and women needed "faith without illusion." [4] In order to discern the moments when human will is able to intervene effectively in history, they needed a political science.

The purpose of this study is to review Raymond Aron's science of politics, particularly his theory of international relations. Because Aron advocated "a science for the politician and a politics based on science," I intend to explore not only the logical coherence of his science of politics but its practical significance for statecraft as well. In doing so, I hope to penetrate to the very heart and meaning of Aron's scholarship. As Aron himself tells us, "I found my way at about twenty-six when I chose the theme of my philosophic thought: the relations between action and history, and it is out of this query that all of my books have emerged." [5]

As perhaps the last great representative of classical French liberalism, Aron fashioned a science of politics in the grand style of Montesquieu and Alexis de Tocqueville, thinkers who tried to take in the entire sweep of whole societies without losing contact with the solid ground of actual experience. Consequently, Aron's political science (or what he often termed his "political sociology") is distinguished by two overriding features—a proclivity for normative analysis and a commitment to empirical proof. By referring to Aron's social science as "normative," I mean to suggest that his political sociology is both interpretive and descriptive, as much a philosophy of history as it is a science of society. Unlike a great deal of modern-day sociology (which the American philosopher Richard Rorty once lampooned as the expenditure of a fifty thousand–dollar grant to discover the address of a whorehouse), Aron's political sociology attempted to comprehend the whole of society, not just discrete fragments of it. Empirical research, Aron maintained, must in some way answer the larger questions of human progress and social justice if it is to retain its significance for human affairs. At the same time, however, he vigorously insisted that reflections on the whole must be disciplined by factual knowledge of the parts if these reflections are not to degenerate into speculative or metaphysical flights of fancy.

By pulling intentional realities and structural necessities into the same loose orbit, Aron's political science tried to hold the middle ground between an abstract idealism that stretches normative ideas beyond any prudent regard for the contingencies of existence and a narrow realism that denies that general ideas should play any role in informing judgment. In doing so, Aron's science of action claimed to present a fuller picture of reality, one that would allow citizens and leaders alike to make rational—or at least more plausible—political choices. Properly speaking, then, what Aron developed was not a political theory but a political science, a way of thinking about politics attuned to the need for making specific decisions in a given set of circumstances.

In constructing a political sociology alive to the possibility of moral action, Aron tried to breathe new life into democratic liberalism, a political tradition that many in France insisted was unable to meet the political and moral challenges of the twentieth century. Reviled by many of Aron's contemporaries for its egoism and possessive individualism, liberalism drew fire for its reputed tendency to weaken social cohesion and collective action. Consequently, in order to make liberalism credible, Aron infused his science of social action with a bracing measure of idealism, attempting to destroy many of the old shibboleths about liberalism in the process.

In judging the originality and utility of Aron's political science, and with it his reconfigured liberalism, I take the road less traveled. Of the two fundamental theoretical impulses that Aron grappled with, it has been his realism, or his insistence that moral ideas reckon with structural necessities, that has drawn the most comment, almost all of it heated. This should not be too surprising: In an age when political debate had reached a near-murderous pitch, Aron's insistence that we give ourselves over to those values that stand the best chance of being realized represented the kind of "bad faith" that moralists of his day utterly abhorred and furiously denounced. My interests, however, lie in precisely the opposite direction: I am concerned with evaluating the effects that Aron's idealism had on his science of social action. When the dialectical relation between realism and idealism is viewed from this direction, Aron's efforts to hold the middle ground appear in a new light. I contend that for all of his moderation and realism, Aron found it far easier to *imagine* a middle course than to call one into existence.

The central difficulty of Aron's political science concerns the erratic and unsteady course of its idealistic impulse. In seeking to apply a formalized ethic to political realities, Aron's idealism often overshot its mark and threatened to dissolve the very structural or historical necessities he relied on to justify a politics of moderate and prudent reform. Domestically, this had the effect of transforming Aron's liberalism into something approaching "fin-de-siècle republicanism," a peculiarly French form of political romanticism that regarded France as "a single being, compounded into a unique and morally unimpeachable whole." [6] Internationally, Aron's idealism had a similar effect. Although he acknowledged the importance of power in foreign affairs, Aron refrained from urging a policy predicated on the national interest. Instead, he argued that Western nations must come to stand for something abroad as well as at home, especially if the West expected to prevail in the cold war. This not only made for a rather confusing set of policy prescriptions, it also made Aron vulnerable to peculiar kind of political immoderation which, for all of his ingrained prudence, got the best of his better judgment from time to time.

In order to take the full measure of Aron's idealism, I chart the course of his dialectical logic as it emerges in his epistemology and works its way down the ladder of abstraction from epistemology to methodology and from methodology to theory. These three levels of analysis—epistemology, methodology, and theory—are part and parcel not only of Aron's political sociology but of any well-formed comprehensive science of social action. Our authority on this matter is Talcott Parsons, whose monumental work *The Structure of Social Action* Aron greatly admired. Theory, Parsons explained, "is confined to the formulation and logical interrelation of propositions containing empirical facts in direct relation to the observation of the facts and thus empirical verification of the propositions." Methodological considerations become relevant when we "inquire whether the procedures by which this observation and verification have been carried out—including the formulation of propositions and the concepts involved in them, and the modes of drawing conclusions from them—are *legitimate.*" These kinds of inquiries will necessarily spill over into the epistemological or philosophical ones because, "among the grounds, real or alleged, for believing or disbelieving in the validity of a scientific procedure, there will be some of a philosophical order, which must be philosophically considered."[7] Although these three sets of considerations are closely related, Parsons added, it is nevertheless important to keep them logically distinct.

These three levels of analysis are of such importance to my presentation of Aron's political science that I devote an entire chapter to each. Consequently, my first chapter is devoted to Aron's epistemology, the second to his methodology, and the third to his theory of international relations. My third chapter, an extensive analysis of *Peace and War: A Theory of International Relations,* may be regarded as the culmination of the first two chapters and an introduction to the fourth, which presents a detailed analysis of Aron's military strategy and foreign policy. The fifth and final chapter is reserved for a critical examination of Aron's thought as a whole.

Although I have chosen to present Aron's political sociology by proceeding from the general to the particular or from philosophy to politics, this should not be taken to mean that Aron charted his politics according to a fixed star plotted by his philosophy. Quite the contrary: Aron's philosophy of historical knowledge was dedicated to the proposition that there are limits to our knowledge of action and history, a proposition directly at odds with Marxist dialectics. In opposition to conventional Marxism, Aron argued that the intentional reality of human behavior sharply limits the utility of causal analysis. Given the fact that action can change the very conditions of its existence—and thus its very character—human behavior demands to be "understood" and not simply "explained." Social scientists, in other words, must try to retrieve the intentional determinants of behavior if they are to comprehend the meaning of an action properly. But, because two minds never "completely coincide," as Aron put it, knowledge can never be certain. And, if knowledge is inherently provisional or ambiguous, then political action must of necessity be measured and moderate.

The politics of understanding thus stands in direct opposition to what Aron termed the "politics of Reason," a politics that lays claim to a complete knowledge of the future.[8] For Aron the politics of Reason was nothing other than the politics of totalitarianism, a politics he fought his entire life. "In all forms of fanaticism," Aron wrote, "even those motivated by idealism, I suspect a new transformation of the monster."[9] Aron's reflexive suspiciousness is certainly understandable. Born in Paris on 14 March 1905, Aron was of that generation whose intellectuals "were students in the days that followed the First World War and [who] wrote their books in the years that preceded the Second. After 1945, they wondered how to avoid the third."[10]

Beyond that vast generalization Aron had little in common with the public intellectuals of his generation. Overshadowed and outnumbered by radical philosophers such as Jean-Paul Sartre, Maurice Merleau-Ponty, and Simone de Beauvoir, Aron did not receive the full measure of popular and intellectual recognition which he so justly deserved until the end of his life, when the language of violent revolution had spent its force and lost its appeal. Now that the ardor for revolutionary projects by the French intelligentsia has apparently cooled, Aron's moderate liberalism and political science are being rediscovered and reexamined. As many of Aron's former detractors now admit, it may have been better to be "wrong with Sartre than right with Aron" in the 1960s, but one can be wrong only so often before the glamour of romantic rebellion begins to wear a little thin. Sartre, one of his former admirers recalls, "was wrong about Hitler, wrong about the resistance, wrong about postwar Europe, wrong about the East-West struggle, wrong about totalitarianism, wrong about the future of France . . . [And] exactly where Sartre was likely to be wrong, Aron was likely to be right." [11]

Even now, however, more than two decades after his death, it is difficult to gauge the full significance of Aron's life and work. Unlike Sartre, Aron left no followers, no "school." In fact, Tony Judt has observed, Aron spent much of his life "largely excluded from the company of his peers." [12] Hastening to add that a portrait of Aron as an "outsider" should not be overdrawn (four thousand newspaper columns, forty books, and six hundred scholarly articles surely caught *someone's* attention), Judt nevertheless rightly insists on describing Aron as a "peripheral insider," as someone who was rarely considered by his fellow French *philosophes* to be "one of them."

What alienated the Left, of course, was Aron's implacable anticommunism. At a time when bien-pensants such as Merleau-Ponty were making the case for revolution and terror, Aron was denouncing the Soviet Union and its work camps, pleading all the while for France to choose liberal democracy and the Western alliance. Aron's embrace of industrial society and the West was not devoid of hesitations and qualifications, as we will see. Nevertheless, those in thrall to the prospects of violent revolution found Aron's defense of decadent Europe incomprehensible and unforgivable and for that reason dismissed him as nothing more than a relic of the old established order.

Aron fared better with the Right but not much. Not only did his articles and public comments sometimes grate on those committed to the cause of French grandeur, they also grated on its foremost herald, General Charles de Gaulle. Although Aron joined de Gaulle's political movement, Rassemblement de Peuple Français (RPF), in 1947 and wrote in support of de Gaulle "every time there was a crisis," he never hesitated to criticize the general—sometimes quite sharply—prompting de Gaulle to complain to André Malraux, "Aron was never a Gaullist." [13]

Aron was most often out of joint with the temper of the times because his critical impulses flew in the face of what many in postwar France wanted most—namely, a reassurance, a guarantee even, that human life *meant* something, that human beings were part of a coherent, purposeful universe. From a certain angle, then, de Gaulle's efforts to resurrect French greatness bore at least some similarities to Sartre's efforts to conjure up historical rationality: Both insisted that individuals found happiness and fulfillment, at least to some extent, in playing roles assigned by larger wholes. Both, in other words, believed that meaning and purpose demanded a collective will or personality strong enough to repress what Joseph de Maistre once called "the aberrations of individual reason." But these "aberrations," and not the collectivities from whence they came, were precisely where Aron mined for meaning. In fact, as Allan Bloom once observed, "Aron lived—and in all probability would have died—defending this unnatural spiritual asceticism, one of the most arduous of all, namely, the one that consists in believing in the rights of others to think as they please." [14] This is not, Bloom emphasized, the same thing as dying for God or one's country. Rather, it is the essence of the liberal conviction, and it defined Aron to the core of his being.

Aron's liberalism was grounded in the elementary principle of respect, a principle that Aron believed found its fulfillment in democracy and the rule of law. Yet Aron knew that in postwar Europe the battle for simple respect would be a hard one. After all, a democratic future is by definition an uncertain future, marked by all the compromises and hesitations one would expect from a form of government predicated on public criticism and the right to one's own opinion. Compared to ideologies that chased after "the vain gods of progress and history," [15] democratic liberalism was much more mundane; it had no transcendent cause to serve, "no credo to teach." [16] "We are under no illusions about the future," Aron once declared. "No spectacular or grandiose task opens up before us for the simple reason that neither conquest nor revolution are *within the range of the possible.*" [17]

Implicit in this call for a politics of lowered expectations was the recognition that social science should play some part in lowering them. "Intellectuals do not want to understand or change the world," Aron once lamented, "they simply want to denounce it."[18] To Aron's way of thinking, changing the world meant clearing the air of those "myths" or "illusions" that seemed to seize so easily the imaginations of French *litterateurs.* However inspired they may have been—and Aron frequently acknowledged that they were indeed stirringly creative—the arguments of thinkers such as Marx and Sartre simply had to be rebutted. Criticism, nevertheless, was not enough: Changing the world thus also meant staking out a social science that could "mark the points of application of human will." [19] Hope, Aron wrote, "is less a matter of exaltation than lucidity and courage." [20]

Sentiments such as these earned Aron a reputation for cold, clear-eyed realism. Although Aron maintained that democracy was capable of great moral accomplishment, he took equal pains to point out that moral progress was often slow and tortuously difficult. Reason "does aim at a certain universality," he declared, "but that universality is defined by the enlargement of consciousness through the criticism of itself and its institutions." [21] Knowing full well that self-criticism is hardly a natural reflex, Aron recognized that democracy required a citizenry that could occasionally summon political qualities that bordered on the heroic while despairing at times over the seeming inability of some countries—such as France—to engage in the sort of disciplined soul searching necessary to self-governance. ("The final question of the historical destiny of France is always the same," Aron once glumly observed. "How shall a people who rationalize their dreams and conceal their disabilities arrive at a recognition of reality?") [22] For Aron dreams and moral ambitions must always pass through the reality of constraining necessities: "To live and think historically is to recognize the servitudes of our condition and to work to enlarge, by action, the margin of our autonomy." [23]

Aron's realism thus demanded a capacity for skepticism and detachment, sensibilities that found few ready admirers in postwar France. The journalist Dominique Wolton, for example, probably spoke for an entire generation of younger French intellectuals when he recalled his youthful impatience with Aron's "apparent lack of enthusiasm or indignation" in the face of great historical moments. Wolton found one of Aron's pet phrases, "I am not the world's conscience," particularly off-putting because it expressed an attitude that "simply did not correspond to what one expected from an intellectual." [24] What one expected, apparently, was *engagement,* a spirited call to action in the name of high principle. Yet impassioned crusades of the sort launched by angry moralists such as Sartre or de Beauvoir left Aron unmoved. "A moment will always come," Aron wrote, "when the non-fanatic . . . will have to tell the fanatic of principles, 'This I can never accept,' and the fanatic of history, 'In periods of crisis, those who act out history do not obey the maxims of practical reason.'" [25]

Compared to the thunderbolts Sartre could hurl, this was pretty pallid stuff. A politics that hectored would-be revolutionaries for violating the maxims of practical reason struck many not only as bloodless but downright bleak. Even those who treat Aron with a measure of critical sympathy underscore the pessimism that seems to leaven his work. Roy Pierce, for example, believes that there is a "dampening quality" to Aron's oeuvre, while Tony Judt wonders if Aron perhaps took "excessive satisfaction in icy dispassion for its own sake."[26] Indeed, Judt observed, "there was . . . a self-inflicted discomfort in Aron's ultra rational approach to especially heated debates: he deprived himself of the pleasure of indulging his own human feelings."[27]

There is much to Judt's assessment. By all accounts Aron subjected himself to an absolutely merciless regimen of self-criticism, practically "punishing himself," as one friend put it, in order to banish bad faith and unwarranted supposition from his thinking. Attributing Aron's principled restraint to an overactive id, however, or to a debilitating preoccupation with the life of the mind would miss the moral point of it all. "One of the qualities I attribute to myself," he once declared, in a rare moment of self-revelation, "is the ability to understand others."[28] And this, he insisted, was possible only because he "had the capacity to be detached from himself." There is irony here: A man who stood repeatedly condemned for his coldness and distance was in fact irrevocably committed to a politics of understanding and to dialogue with the "other." Nicholas Baverez, perhaps the best of Aron's French biographers, sees this as a measure of Aron's greatness, observing that Aron sought "through action and discipline" to create a life that "could surmount solitude and the absurdity of existence."[29] Despite a prodigious written output, it was here, in his personal example, that some locate Aron's true significance. "The importance of Raymond Aron," Claude Lévi-Strauss once related to an interviewer, "transcends his works: the man was a model to me and I admired in him this extreme sensibility, willingly controlled and mastered, which seemed to attain a sort of asceticism that [Aron] found indispensable in order to attain the truth."[30] Bloom goes even farther. Raymond Aron, he declared, "was living proof that a democratic personality is possible."[31]

Some see the origins of Aron's capacity for self-restraint and reconciliation in the very circumstances of his birth and early childhood. Born into a well-to-do Jewish family of "intransigent French patriots," Aron described his upbringing as "classic," even "banal."[32] Although Aron's family felt no tension or contradiction between its Jewishness and its patriotism ("I do not believe,"

Aron wrote, "that they ever asked themselves the now fashionable question: Are we first of all Jews or Frenchmen?"),[33] Aron himself certainly did. A lifelong agnostic, he was nevertheless acutely conscious of the tension between his Judaism and his commitment to the principle of a rational, secular state, a tension, he confessed, that he never really resolved. Baverez believes that Aron's twofold commitment to the nation-state and to economic globalization had its origins here, as did his hope for European reconciliation especially between France and Germany.[34]

Indeed, it is not too much to think that Aron's interest in understanding the other and his preoccupation with reconciling universals and particulars of all sorts had its origins in this most personal of dualities, as may be apparent in a passage in which Aron commented on the "mystic unity" of Jews throughout the world. "I have not given up," he wrote, "the idea of a single destiny for the human race, nor have I given up the plurality of cultures, each one of which believes itself to be—correctly for those who are in it—irreplaceable. My attachment to the French language and French literature cannot be justified; it is, I live it, because it is identified with my being. Is my solidarity with Israel intellectual or organic? Perhaps both. In any event, this 'solidarity' does not rise to the level of the sacred or supernatural history, whose place is reserved for believers and to which I have no access."[35] Although Aron wrestled with his religion, he never personally suffered from it, recalling in his memoirs only one minor anti-Semitic incident in his youth. By all accounts his childhood was a happy one: Aron was close to his two older brothers, adored by his mother, and doted on by his father, himself a university professor. Friends recalled lively dinner table conversation at the Arons' home and summer nights devoted to bridge and tennis, the children taking full advantage of the father's insistence that no schoolwork be done after dinner; evenings were to be devoted to family conversation and recreation.

If any shadows fell across Aron's childhood, they were cast by his father, Gustave. Although Aron remembered his father as a happy man, "comfortable in his skin," he also knew that his father had suffered through a string of academically inferior teaching posts due to a second-place finish on the *agrégation,* the highly competitive French academic placement exam. Thus it was, Aron recalled, that his father gave him "a mission which weighed on my entire life, even more than my barely conscious intimacy with my mother during my earliest years."[36] Over the years, Aron wrote, "as my own aging allowed me to understand him, no longer as an all-powerful father but as a humiliated father, I felt myself to be the bearer of his hopes of his youth, entrusted with the task of providing him with a kind of compensation; I would cancel his disappointments with my success."[37] When Aron received an honorary doctorate from the University of Jerusalem, he paid tribute to his late father, which prompted a friend who heard the address to comment that, by honoring a parent, Aron had "given a lesson in Jewishness." Aron wondered if there was another explanation: "Perhaps I evoked the debt that had weighed on me for more than fifty years at this time, in this place, to convince myself that I had finally repaid it."[38]

As a boy, Aron certainly benefited from all that the French middle class had to offer. This meant, chiefly, that he was exceptionally well-educated. A precocious child, young Raymond distinguished himself early in school, winning a scholarship in 1924 to the most distinguished of France's grandes écoles, the Ecole Normale Supérieure (ENS). Few institutions of higher learning in France could match the intellectual stimulation or excitement of the Ecole Normale Supérieure. In his memoirs Aron recalled that he had never in his life encountered so much intelligence in such a small space. Among his classmates were Paul Nizan, the communist author of the 1930s; Daniel Lagache, who would become a renowned professor of psychology at the Sorbonne; the philosopher Georges Canguilhem, also a future professor at the Sorbonne; Albert Bédé, a professor of French at Columbia University; Louis Néel, a Nobel Prize–winning professor of physics; and, of course, Jean-Paul Sartre. In later years Aron was joined by the philosopher Maurice Merleau-Ponty, the writer Simone de Beauvoir, the Hegelian Jean Hippolyte, and the historian Henri Marrou. Among Aron's professors were the historian Elie Halévy, the social theorist Célestin Bouglé, and the philosopher Léon Brunschvicq, "a man who simultaneously instilled in you the meaning of the great philosophers and discouraged you from becoming one of them."[39] An altogether brilliant collection of individuals, Aron later wrote, "so much so that in all the other milieux I have known since then, I have retained a kind of nostalgia for the Ecole Normale."[40]

Aron performed brilliantly at the ENS, eventually earning top honors on the *agrégation*. Receiving a scholarship to study abroad, Aron chose to study and work at the University of Cologne, where he was an instructor and teaching assistant from 1930 to 1933. These were perhaps the most formative years of Aron's life because it was here, in Weimar Germany, that his capacity for critical independence began to take shape. A committed pacifist and socialist when he arrived in Germany, Aron had hoped to advance the cause of Franco-German reconciliation. Upon his arrival, however, he immediately recognized that Adolf Hitler's ambition made reconciliation impossible. In fact, Aron was one of the first in all of France to understand that the rising fortunes of National Socialism presaged an era of unprecedented barbarism in Europe, publishing his increasingly alarmed eyewitness accounts of German politics in two French leftist publications, *Libres Propos* and *Europe*. Although his light hair and blue eyes placed him beyond suspicion, it was not, as he recalled rather dryly, a very propitious time for a French Jew, "steeped in Kantian philosophy," to be living in Germany.

His encounter with Nazism so badly jolted Aron's Kantian sensibilities that it undid not only his pacifism but much of his socialism as well. Although he never entirely disavowed his leftism ("A Jewish intellectual of good will who chooses the career of letters . . . can hardly do anything but will himself, feel himself, to be on the left"),[41] Aron did renounce the soft, sentimental moralism that fed it. In Germany, Aron explained, "I had passed a threshold in my political education—an education that will last as long as I do. I understood politics as such, irreducible to morality . . . National Socialism had taught me the power of irrational forces; Max Weber had taught me the responsibility of each individual, not so much with respect to intentions as to the consequences of his choice."[42]

Transforming these sentiments into a working philosophy of history, Aron broke rather dramatically, but not completely, from the scientific pretensions of Brunschvicq and the ENS—indeed, from the whole of French philosophy at the time. During the early part of the twentieth century philosophy and the social sciences in France were guided almost wholly by a secular faith in science. Brunschvicq, for example, Aron's great patron and mentor, identified human progress with scientific progress, a view that prompted Aron to write, "Brunschvicq is our contemporary but he is the contemporary of Einstein, not Hitler."[43] The practical upshot of what many in Aron's generation took to be an overly simple scientism was an unshakable belief in the inevitability of human progress, a belief that Aron and his fellow *normaliens* found naive to the point of shocking.

In breaking from the influence of his elders, Aron fashioned a philosophy of history that stressed the contingency of existence, a turn that greatly agitated the older generation. What his teachers found so unsettling about Aron's conceptual universe was how little it promised. Concepts such as "objectivity," "progress," and "reason" were nothing more than theoretical possibilities to Aron, ideals that in themselves did nothing to dispel the specter of tragedy from history or, conversely, to ensure the progress of civilization. Aron never ruled out the possibility that human behavior could progress; he simply insisted that, given human freedom and the contingency of existence, there was no way to know that it *would*.

The misgivings of his professors were fueled, at least in part, by the fact that Aron was working with conceptual material virtually unknown in France. Ransacking whole libraries in order to discover all that was new in German philosophical and social thought, Aron carted off concepts from an astonishing range of thinkers, including Wilhelm Dilthey, Martin Heidegger, Heinrich Rickert, Othmar Spann, Max Weber, Wilhelm Windleband, and, of course, Karl Marx. Aron was also among the first in France to discover the phenomenology of Edmund Husserl, whose descriptive philosophy was deliberately opposed to Weber's causal methodology. Whereas Weber had believed that the chaotic, uneven texture of human history required social scientists to create arbitrary conceptual constructs in order to discover connecting causal threads, Husserl believed that philosophy could *describe* networks of meaning in order to discover the truth about the "life world." The difference between the two, as we will see, was traceable to a difference in first principles: For Weber the world was riven by power and conflict, while Husserl believed it was governed by reason and the unifying force of shared purpose.

Eventually fashioning a philosophy of history that moved between Husserl and Weber, Aron worked out what many considered to be the first expression of philosophical existentialism in France. It was Aron's insistence that human history is a three-dimensional one—"Man is in history; man is historic; man is history"—which landed him squarely in the vanguard of early existentialism, a position that was sealed with Sartre's pronouncement that Aron's philosophy of history provided the ontological setting for his own monumental work, *Being and Nothingness*. Somewhat uncomfortable with being tagged an existentialist—he never really knew what the term meant—Aron was always quick to remind his readers that the historicity of human existence did not preclude the existence of universal truth, a caveat that at least nodded in the direction of the idealism that sustained the older generation at the Ecole Normale Supérieure.

Aron broke with his mentors in yet another way, this time decisively. His own generation, Aron explained, simply "despised and detested" those of their elders who had condemned German culture because of World War I.

"One of our most violent reproaches against some of the preceding generation was the brainwashing that had taken place," Aron explained to Jean-Louis Missika and Dominique Wolton, a brainwashing that insisted that "one should no longer listen to Wagner because he is German." As for himself, Aron maintained that, "despite the 1939–1945 war, despite National Socialism, I never allowed myself to condemn a people and a culture because of political conflicts."[44] His years in Germany thus not only opened up whole new vistas of intellectual inquiry for Aron but provided him with his first practical lessons in "objective detachment" and the politics of understanding as well.

Returning to France in 1933, Aron threw himself into continued study and writing, hurrying to finish his books before war broke out. Despite his chastened socialism, his political involvement during the interwar years was limited largely to voting for Léon Blum's socialist Popular Front government and then sharply attacking it for its ignorance of elementary economic principles. By this time Aron had acquired a rather formidable understanding of economics, as evidenced by several articles on French economic policy published during the mid-1930s.[45] Aron also published two major studies on German sociology and German philosophy during that time, before finally defending his dissertation, later published as *Introduction to the Philosophy of History,* in March 1938, just a few days before the German invasion of Czechoslovakia.[46] Although he defended his dissertation to great public acclaim, Aron had to contend with a jury that was openly hostile, offended as it was by the melancholy overtones of Aron's approach to history and historical knowledge. In fact, one member of the committee, Paul Fauconnet, concluded his interrogation of Aron with these words: "I conclude with an act of charity, faith and hope: charity by repeating to you my admiration and my sympathy; faith in the ideas that you condemn; hope that the students will not follow you."[47] Earlier in the defense Fauconnet had declared that Aron's philosophy of history was so pessimistic that he judged Aron to be either possessed by the devil or in the grip of a pathological despair. An observer recording the proceedings noted that the members of Aron's jury behaved like hens "who hatch a duckling and then watch in terror as it moves towards the water, only to move with ease in an element unknown to them."[48] For his part Aron later recalled that he was "neither Satanic nor desperate [but] was experiencing in advance the world war that my judges did not see coming."[49]

It is important to note the historical significance of Aron's dissertation. Baverez argues that Aron's analysis of history and historical knowledge signaled a shift in intellectual paradigm comparable to the shift occasioned by the seminal works of Michel Foucault and Jean Hyppolite. As one of Aron's classmates explained, "This moment can be considered one in which, in the history of French philosophy, began the French philosophy of history."[50] Regrettably, however, few if any intellectual historians, either French- or English-speaking, have given Aron the credit he deserves here. One recent American study of postwar French phenomenology, for example, omits Aron's name altogether, while another major survey of postwar French philosophy scarcely mentions Aron's name at all.[51]

When France collapsed a year after Aron's dissertation defense, Aron, with his wife's blessing, made his way to London, where he hoped to join one of General de Gaulle's tank companies. Instead of being assigned a command, however, Aron found himself administering the company accounts. Yearning for a more substantial wartime role, Aron was eventually rescued by André Labarthe, an associate of de Gaulle. Labarthe, who had read the *Introduction,* was anxious to have Aron join the editorial staff of *La France Libre,* a French wartime periodical that Labarthe was launching with the general's support. Although Aron was still holding out hope for a command, he accepted Labarthe's offer, seemingly persuaded by a comment delivered by another editor at the meeting. "If you want a hero's death," the editor told him, "you'll have time for that. This war will not soon be over."

Aron's association with *La France Libre* was important for two reasons. First, it gave him a passion for journalism, one that lasted the rest of his life. Second, it marked the beginning of his relationship with de Gaulle, a relationship that was marked by alternating bouts of mutual irritation and respect. Aron frequently worried that de Gaulle's theatrics were sometimes detrimental to French national interests, while de Gaulle believed that Aron's commitment to French greatness was sometimes less than total. As de Gaulle explained in a lengthy letter: "I have read *The Great Debate* as I often read what you write, in various places, on the same subject. It seems to me that if you return to it so unceasingly and with such vivacity it is perhaps because you yourself are not fully satisfied by your own position. After all, all talk of 'Europe,' the 'Atlantic Community,' 'NATO,' 'arms,' etc. boils down to a single argument: yes or no—must France remain France? That was already the question at the time of the Resistance. You knew what my choice was and I knew that there will never be any rest for theologians."[52]

Aron's first, and only, exposure to public service lasted just a few months, when he was tapped by his old friend André Malraux, the new minister of information, to serve as his chief of staff. After de Gaulle resigned as French president in 1946, Aron then joined the staff of *Combat,* one of the most prestigious newspapers in Paris, where he was befriended by Albert Camus. *Combat* also lasted only a brief time, however, after which Aron chose to work at *Le Figaro,* one of the largest dailies in Paris. Aron's association with the paper was largely a happy one, lasting almost as long as the paper itself. The genial relations between Aron and his editors, however, were tested by the Algerian crisis. Aron's pamphlet calling for Algerian independence, *La Tragédie algérienne,*[53] created a furor in France, prompting the director of the paper, Pierre Brisson, to insist that Aron refrain from discussing the war in his articles. The uproar over Aron's defense of Algerian independence was so great that at one point Aron feared for his physical safety while speaking at a public meeting on the war in Paris.

It was Aron's journalism that propelled him to national recognition and made him a household name in France. Aron's success in attracting a national audience during the immediate postwar period was a little surprising. In a country where public intellectuals invariably emerged from literary circles, Aron distinguished himself by being among the first to combine social science and journalistic commentary. One cannot help but wonder how this leaning colored his role as a public intellectual. If Aron was not the "world's conscience," what was he? If Aron saw himself as both journalist and scholar, for whom exactly did he write?

Aron had a fairly clear conception of the role that intellectuals should play and the knowledge they should possess, a conception that was first sketched out in the opening paragraphs of an essay on economics drafted in 1937. Intellectuals, he argued, had not only the right but the obligation to intervene in political struggles. Nodding in the direction of French moralists such as Emile Zola, Aron acknowledged that intellectuals were called on from time to time to defend universal moral values, or what Aron termed "sacred values." Yet, Aron added, "it is not every day that a Dreyfus Affair comes along, justifying the invocation of truth against error." For that reason "in order for them to express their opinions daily as intellectuals, they should have some competence in economics, diplomacy, politics and so on."[54]

By insisting that intellectuals should know something, Aron consciously and immediately distanced himself from virtually every other public intellectual of his generation. As Tony Judt has pointed out, intellectuals in France have traditionally preoccupied themselves with "a search for truth in abstractions" and with "the exotic, the aesthetic and the absolute."[55] Aron, however, turned his attention to the more mundane problems of postwar reconstruction, freely digging into the messy, confusing realities of liberal democracy. This is not to say he shrugged off moral or philosophical engagement; given the energy he devoted to his critical analyses of Marx and Sartre, it is clear that such engagements were among his highest priorities. Rather, Aron simply refused to confine himself to such enterprises, insisting throughout his life that dealing with the practical necessities of human action had its own moral dignity.

Given his pragmatic bent, however, Aron chafed against the prospect of delivering his opinions from behind the insular walls of an ivory tower. Writing for *La France Libre* had given him a taste for being "close to the protagonists of history" and had momentarily turned his thoughts away from pursuing an academic career. In fact, Aron absolutely dreaded the thought of living the semi-secluded life of an academic. "At bottom," he recalled, "although I did not admit it to myself, the university as I had known it and as I anticipated it would be, bored me."[56] Populated as it is "by children and young people," Aron intoned, the academic world "is an insulated universe," one that "carries the risk of fostering a kind of puerility."[57] France was grappling with Herculean challenges in the immediate postwar period, and Aron found himself impatiently straining to be in the middle of it all. "I wanted to participate actively in the reconstruction of France otherwise than by an *Introduction aux sciences sociales* or a study of Machiavelli," he explained. "My country had been liberated, and everything remained to be done."[58] Nevertheless, despite the pressing problems facing postwar France, Aron repeatedly emphasized that the first calling of an intellectual was to serve truth and philosophy. To the degree that an intellectual serves truth, Aron maintained, "he serves society."[59]

Yet living in both worlds had its price; Aron frequently grumbled that he may have overreached in trying to live the life of a journalist as well as a scholar. Journalism requires different intellectual reflexes than scholarship, and Aron occasionally fretted that his journalistic commitments may have damaged his theoretical and philosophical gifts. "I was too obsessed by everyday realities," he once confessed, "to give my abstract books the breadth and dimensions they probably would have had if I had not chosen the easy course, that is, journalism."[60] In fact, Aron mused, "My scholarly books, I am sure, would have been different—perhaps better—if I had not been a journalist at the same time." Alternately commending and discouraging others from following the same course—on one occasion, within two pages of one another[61]—Aron summarized the dangers of living a double life: "I saw politics in action at much closer range than most political scientists—and I am glad of it—but political analysis *in vivo,* far from fostering philosophical reflection, paralyzes it. The philosopher, confronting politicians and journalists, has the feeling that he will be ridiculed, or that, like Plato's philosopher, he will tumble into the well."[62]

However these two worlds may have ultimately impinged on one another for Aron, it is clear that he wrote for an astonishing range of audiences and set for himself a breathtaking intellectual agenda, journalistic as well as academic. Indeed, one can distinguish several sorts of writings in Aron's corpus, each corresponding to a distinctly different audience. First, at the highest level of abstraction, there are Aron's philosophical polemics, directed against Marxism in general and Sartre and Merleau-Ponty in particular. Not that members of the Parisian intelligentsia much cared; few, if any, returned the favor by reading Aron with the same care and attention with which he read them. A prophet without honor in the philosophical circles of Paris, Aron was nevertheless received by intellectuals and philosophers beyond that world.

Second, Aron produced works of theoretical scholarship, books such as *Peace and War* and *Clausewitz,* in which Aron engaged not philosophers but scholarly specialists and perhaps—in the case of *Peace and War*—policy makers as well. Third, there are books that, as Aron explained, were devoted large to analyzing contemporary events, books that were marked by Aron's "attention to the present." This constitutes the largest bulk of Aron's writings and includes books such as *L'Homme contre les tyrans, De l'Armistice à l'insurrection nationale,* and *L'Age des empires et l'avenir de la France.* Many of these books (such as the three mentioned here) were compilations of journalistic essays as well as independent works of academic reflection. This category, both journalistic and academic, seems to have been targeted largely at policy-making elites but also includes members of the educated public. The eminent French economist Robert Marjolin once reported that Aron's writings on business and economic matters were highly influential among members of the French financial community and contributed significantly to the formulation of France's postwar industrial policy.[63] Moreover, an impressive array of statesmen and foreign policy leaders, American as well as French, not only knew Aron personally but read him quite frequently.[64] Indeed, near the end of his life and despite a long history of acute disagreements, de Gaulle referred to Aron as "mon cher maître."

Finally, Aron wrote for members of the educated public. In reflecting on the personal and intellectual qualities that a columnist or journalist should possess, Aron once observed during an interview that a journalist's "sense of responsibility" toward the public was perhaps the most important. "People are always saying how it is the newspaper owners who limit journalistic freedom," he said. "But what counts much more is concern for the public: the journalist is much less anxious about his financial masters than the reactions of the public."[65]

In sharp contrast to all this, the vast majority of postwar public intellectuals in France wrote for just two audiences, namely, themselves and a rather idealized body of "workers," a point Judt underscores in a stinging paragraph. "Most intellectuals," Judt wrote, "were astonishingly unfamiliar with opinion (and indeed life) outside of their own rather restricted social and cultural world. When they looked for workers, they found Communists. When they sought an echo of their views and the impact of their views, they found it in a plethora of journals directed primarily to them and them alone. Although they did not normally realize this, the intellectual community of Paris was almost as hermetic and divorced from the nation as that of London or even New York." This marginality, Judt adds, was proudly held aloft by French intellectuals and waved like a bloody shirt. In fact, many (like Sartre) "made a sort of self-lacerating virtue of their own isolation."[66]

Why did so many French intellectuals feel compelled to flee to "an illusory paradise buried in the foggy north or in the future"?[67] Because, as Aron explained, "France in its abasement no longer satisfies their appetite for greatness."[68] Realizing that France was no longer a power of the first rank, French intellectuals recognized that they were no longer playing to a global audience, at least not in the way they had been accustomed to during the decades leading up to the war. "From the moment that the French position ceases to have universal significance," Aron mused, "intellectuals seek a position neither Russian nor American, in hopes of thus attaining to universality."[69] Moreover, resigned to the apparent futility of striving for great power parity, postwar French intellectuals maintained that "attaining to universality" would henceforth be the work of history; thinkers such as Merleau-Ponty insisted that vast, irresistible currents of history, and not statesmen or technical specialists, were gathering themselves to sweep humanity into a glorious future. Under those conditions history simply needed witnesses and heralds, not social scientists.

In other words, under those conditions no other narrative mattered but the one constructed by intellectuals, a narrative that left just enough public space for intellectuals and the motive force of history but no one else. "Not one of the smallest paradoxes of the present situation," Aron wrote in 1950, "is a kind of 'de-politicization' of intellectuals taking place in a period of religious wars. The misconceptions under which they labor have brought certain intellectuals to a standstill in a kind of politics of abstention."[70] In contrast, by writing for so many different audiences, Aron was tacitly calling for a robust politics, one that accepted a pluralistic political world devoid of a simple, central story line narrated by history.

Although it is tempting to look for American intellectuals whose intellectual disposition and accomplishments match up with Aron's, searching for American analogues may, in the end, be a bit beside the point. As Richard Posner has observed, the greatest obstacle to attaining cross-cultural comparisons of intellectuals is that "public intellectual work, like most political work, tends to be local, focused on the political and ideological concerns of a particular society."[71] Aron, for his part, faced an entirely different challenge—and hence had a vastly different job description—than his American counterparts. Living in a country where public life teems with an almost endless array of special interests, American intellectuals are forced to elbow their way into the middle of the public square in the hope that they might make themselves heard above the cacophony that is American liberal democracy. In France, however, which has traditionally been uncomfortable with the very idea of liberal democracy or a public square in the first place, many intellectuals of Aron's generation saw themselves as philosophical "prefects" of a sort, functionaries of history whose primary calling was to superintend politics and public opinion. The sort of vigorous pluralistic universe Aron hoped to call into being could thus be possible, paradoxically enough, only if Aron and future generations of French intellectuals *refused* to be the "world's conscience." This is why, speaking to the French failure to develop a set of liberal democratic categories grounded in its own unique history and experience, Judt solemnly intones that "a refusal to occupy the post of the (engaged) intellectual may be the most positive of the steps modern [French] thinkers can take in any serious effort to come to terms with their own responsibility for our common recent past."[72]

By 1955 Aron's intoxication with politics and public life had faded, leaving him anxious to resume his academic career. By that year, in fact, Aron's intoxication with much of life had faded, having been crushed by the death of his two young daughters within months of each other in 1950. "There is no apprenticeship for sorrow," he wrote. "I was a bad student, slow and rebellious. I sought refuge in my work. The more I plunged into this illusory refuge, the more I lost myself. Aware that I was losing myself, I suffered more, beyond sorrow itself, from the wounds that time did not heal." Desperately searching for relief from his personal grief, Aron applied for a professorship at the Sorbonne and was appointed to a chair in sociology in 1955. He was not, as he later wrote, disappointed by the years he spent at the Sorbonne: "It did not restore what the year 1950 had forever taken from me but it helped reconcile me with life, with others, and with myself."[73] While at the Sorbonne, Aron quietly set for himself an intensely personal mission. "To the very end at the Sorbonne," he wrote, "I attacked my courses with a solid determination to conquer those hundreds of faces, those hundreds of young minds, some of whom were already won over; but others were rebellious and I dreamed of uniting them, through speech, into a welcoming community."[74]

Even after his appointment to the Sorbonne (Aron would be appointed to the Collège de France in 1970), Aron continued to write newspaper commentaries, leading a double life as scholar and editorialist almost until the day he died. Although his was an enormously productive career, it was hardly a secluded or serene one. Bitterly, even ludicrously, attacked by Sartre, pilloried by the Left, and occasionally heckled by protestors, Aron frequently found himself in the throes of public controversy. In 1967, for example, he publicly rebuked de Gaulle for comments that Aron felt "authorized" anti-Semitism, while in 1968 he enraged the Left for dismissing the student riots and demonstrations in May as nothing more than a pointless "psychodrama."

In 1977 Aron was felled by a stroke. Recovering to continue his lecturing and writing schedule, Aron planned to write two more volumes that would supplement *History and the Dialectic of Violence,* his study of Sartre, as well as a volume on Marx, which was published posthumously. But after 1977 Aron wrote that he questioned the time he had remaining and whether the "cursed clot" had left him enough strength to finish his projects. He had sufficient strength to keep up a steady stream of commentary, however, and to finish his magisterial *Mémoires*. On 17 October 1983, after testifying in court on behalf of his friend Bertrand de Jouvenal in a libel suit, Aron stepped into a waiting car and died.

Even in the space of this brief biographical overview, it is possible to catch a glimpse of the cantilevers and dialectical *buts* that constituted Aron's singular manner of engagement. As François Furet observed, Aron's politics, like his philosophy, centered on "the marriage of contraries": "He was on the left before the war but critical of the political economy of the Popular Front. Of the small number who made their way to London in 1940, he remained the exception: he alone was not a Gaullist. After the war, however, he became one but not until de Gaulle had left power. Breaking with Sartre on communism, he became a specialist on Marxism. An editorialist for *Figaro,* he spoke out against the war in Algeria. When de Gaulle returned to power, he offered only sustained critique."[75] Exactly how a balance was struck or a fine line was walked was often left to circumstance and personal choice, a method that sometimes mystified those who tried to sympathize or follow along.

There was something of the unpredictable in Aron's personality as well as in his politics. Although Aron's unflappable, methodical lucidity was universally recognized as his trademark, his discipline and self-control were sometimes tested by passions that his reason could not always contain. Writing for *Le Monde,* the Left-leaning Parisian daily, Pierre Vinsson-Ponté offered a fascinating observation:

> There remains in his character an element of anxiety, almost of agitation. Now aged 62, he has not lost the cold but twinkling look in his blue eyes; he still has the old liveliness of manner, the eager quickness and that mixture of profundity and lightness which softens the slightly stiff dignity of the *maître à penser* when university life keeps him in permanent contact with the young. But this depends on two conditions, both of which Aron fulfils: an optimistic temperament and a sense of humor . . .
>
> As a philosopher, thinker and historian, Aron is a liberal. As a writer, teacher and journalist, he is both tolerant and moderate. But he is in fact a man of passion, quick to anger and ready to surprise, to shock and disconcert . . .
>
> Despite everything, he still reacts on occasion like a thorough-

> bred harnessed to a heavy wagon. Frustration engendered in a vigorous mind that refuses to cross the frontier of action? Division, though a freely chosen one, between the role he has adopted and his real temperament? Here probably lies the source of a certain disabused bitterness and, above all, of that impetuous turbulence which still drives Raymond Aron on.[76]

Aron's philosophy, politics, and personality were thus bound by a common, dialectical thread, one that made the "marriage of contraries" a personal, lifelong project. I leave to future biographers the challenge of exploring the psychological wellsprings of it all. My aim here is more limited. I hope to illuminate the life of a mind by focusing, above all else, on its logic. In doing so, I hope to show that the work of Raymond Aron is still relevant for understanding the intractable problems and dilemmas of political life, especially in the international arena.

Readers interested in acquiring a more detailed knowledge of Aron's life and work would do well to begin with his autobiography, *Memoirs: Fifty Years of Political Reflection.* There is also Robert Colquhoun's useful two-volume intellectual biography, *Raymond Aron: The Philosopher in History* and *Raymond Aron: The Sociologist in Society.* Aron has been well served by his biographers and commentators. The best of Aron's French biographers is Nicholas Baverez, whose monumental study, *Raymond Aron: Un Moraliste au temps des ideologies,* provides an exhaustive and insightful overview of Aron's life and work. Two other excellent book-length studies are available in English, the first being Daniel J. Mahoney's work *The Liberal Political Science of Raymond Aron: A Critical Introduction,* which traces the fundamental motifs of Aron's philosophy of history to features of his political liberalism and to Aristotelian political science.[77] The second is Brian Anderson's book, *Raymond Aron and the Recovery of the Political,* which connects Aron's theory of knowledge, his ideological criticisms, and his peculiar brand of liberalism, which centers on what Anderson calls Aron's "antinomic prudence."[78] Other authors who have written excellent chapter-length studies of Aron are Tony Judt, *The Burden of Responsibility: Blum, Camus, Aron, and the French Twentieth Century,* and Roy Pierce, *Contemporary French Political Thought.* Judt has also written a highly acclaimed study of postwar French thought, *Past Imperfect: French Intellectuals, 1944–1956,* which provides a useful (but brief) discussion of Aron's place in the broader stream of postwar French political culture. Both Judt and Pierce have written introductions of recently reissued works of Aron, while Mahoney and Anderson are the coeditors of an ongoing series of newly translated books by Aron published by Transaction Press.

The present study is aimed at three broad, overlapping audiences. The first comprises those who are interested in theories of international relations. In recent years international relations theory has been stirred by several new debates, most notably those launched by "constructivism," a movement that seeks to rethink and reconstruct the theoretical foundations of international relations theory. Because *Peace and War* was itself an attempt to rethink the foundations of international relations theory, I outline the conceptual logic of *Peace and War* and then engage Aron in two debates, one with an older generation of thinkers such as Hans Morgenthau and Reinhold Niebuhr, Aron's contemporaries, and the other with the current and younger generation of international relations theorists, most notably Kenneth Waltz and Alexander Wendt.

The second audience includes those who are interested in what is generally referred to as "historical sociology." Although subject to a wide range of definitions, historical sociology can be defined, most simply, as "an attempt to understand the relationship of personal activity and experience on the one hand and social organisation on the other."[79] This approach is a theoretical project that was at the very heart of Aron's intellectual concern, as this study hopes to show. Indeed, if it is true that every thinker thinks but a single great thought, this concern for historical sociology is the thought from which everything else radiates in Aron. It should be noted that there are noted historical sociologists, such as Fred Halliday, who are calling for a historical sociology of international relations and who recognize the important contributions Aron has made in this regard. Third, this study is aimed at philosophers who are interested in what Aron termed "praxeology," that difficult, contentious area in which theory, ethics, and action converge. Aron had little taste for pure theory. To his way of thinking, as we will see, theoretical analysis should always be disciplined and tempered by the insights of statesmen and policy makers, or those who have actually borne the burdens of political leadership.

There is a final audience for which this book is intended, a much broader one than those listed here. By many accounts American political culture is becoming politically polarized to an unsettling degree. Although American political discourse is not as toxic as it was in prewar France, many scholars and commentators sense that the reflexive urge for moral clarity is today hardening into an ideologically inspired set of political and moral categories, categories that make political cooperation and consensus increasingly difficult both at home and abroad.[80] For those who are concerned that American (and the world at large) may be slipping its moorings in human reason, reading Aron can be a bracing experience. Aron was an apostle of moral reasoning, which is, above all else, a never-ending exercise in self-examination and self-criticism. If we Americans are to avoid falling into the same bitter partisanship that has historically plagued so many other countries (most notably France) we would do well to heed the personal example and intellectual counsel of Raymond Aron. Here is a philosophy, both personal and political, that has been forged in the searing fire of historical experience and for that reason worthy of sustained attention. Here, in other words, is a political philosophy devoted to calming the ideological passions that are apparently beginning to roil American politics.

His lifelong effort to view society in the round prompted Aron to expand his scholarly and theoretical horizons to an astounding degree. No narrow-minded specialist, Aron pushed himself to master whole academic disciplines. "What is the winner of the prestigious Goethe prize?" Ralf Dahrendorf once asked, obviously a little unsure himself. "A sociologist? A philosopher? A man of politics? A journalist? An historian? A political economist? These categories don't apply; as an individual, [Raymond Aron] has outgrown all categories."[81] Thus it was that Pierre Manent asked the inevitable question: "When a single soul is capable of accomplishing so much, one question naturally arises: are the many aspects of his work—philosophy, international relations strategy, sociology, journalism—the expression of a conception of the world that is fundamentally *one?*"[82]

I believe they are. At the center of Aron's sociopolitical thought there is a relatively simple "categorial framework" that bestows unity and coherence upon his entire life's work. *Categorial frameworks* (a term I borrow from Stephen Körner) describes comprehensive interpretations of the human condition that establish the basic distinctions and logical relations that are believed to inhere in reality. To use an older but perhaps more familiar term, a categorial framework is akin to a weltanschauung, or worldview, a quasi-theoretical construct that constitutes that center of thought and concern from which an individual's subsequent reflections draw their fire and acquire their force.

We first encounter such a framework in Aron's account of the manner in which we come to know ourselves, or, more exactly, our *past* selves. Aron's description of self-knowledge, which appears early on in his dissertation, is in essence a bare-bones account of the order inherent in reality and the process by which this order is apprehended. In reconstructing the logic that governed Aron's thinking, I begin with his epistemology, conventionally regarded as "the deepest form of overt assumption."[83] It is there that we first see the dialectical logic that stamps all of Aron's later reflections with its peculiar cast.

1 "To Grasp Truth and Reality"

Max Weber, Edmund Husserl, and the Philosophy of History

"**I LONG AGO RECONSTRUCTED** my intellectual biography," Raymond Aron wrote near the end of his life. "Before the class of *philosophie,* darkness; thereafter, light."[1] It would be difficult to exaggerate the extent of Aron's fascination with philosophical thought. Although he was interested in other subjects as a student at the Ecole Normale Supérieure (ENS), Aron was absolutely "transported" and "transfigured" by his courses in philosophy. Despite his passion for philosophy and his affection for the Ecole Normale, Aron was deeply disturbed by what he perceived to be a serious weakness in French philosophical thinking at that time. The philosophy taught in French universities, Aron complained, "taught us nothing about the world in which we lived."[2] Utterly indifferent to the harsh realities of political life, members of the French academy occupied themselves with theoretical abstractions far removed from the nonacademic concerns of their country, a turn of mind that scandalized the younger generation of students under their tutelage. "One cannot understand the rage—the nausea—of a young philosopher like Jean-Paul Sartre at France's intellectual establishment on the eve of the Second World War," H. Stuart Hughes explained, "unless one appreciates how smug and fatuous the entrenched dignitaries of the Sorbonne looked to those outside."[3]

This monumental indifference, together with the war itself, sparked a revolt in contemporary French thought that profoundly affected the course of Continental philosophy. As if to compensate for their predecessors' apparent historical ignorance, members of the French intelligentsia, inspired by the vast, syncretic systems of Hegel and Marx, now rushed to follow Sartre's lead in searching for a method of total historical knowledge. Starting from the assumption that history "is not a simple sum of juxtaposed facts," this historico-philosophical quest generated countless studies on the problem of historical understanding which, despite their diversity, had one thing in common—the desire to see history whole. Aron was thus tempted to represent this movement as a half-conscious "return to Hegel" in opposition to the "return to Kant" of the previous generation. For his part, however, Aron deplored this trend and turned back, as we will see, to the somewhat less elevated ambitions of Max Weber and Edmund Husserl for his hope and inspiration.

Because Weber's ideas gave shape and substance to much of Aron's early reflections on the nature of historical knowledge, any discussion of Aron's epistemology must take into account his "elective affinity" for Weber, whom Aron regarded as "the greatest of the sociologists." Often overlooked, however, especially by those who see in Aron nothing but a grim, unflinching realism, is the fact that Aron was severely critical of Weber. If the scope of this criticism is not fully understood, then the dialectical character of Aron's epistemology cannot be properly appreciated and assessed, because the "Weberian moment" in Aron's thought constitutes but one pole of his theory of knowledge. The other derives from the phenomenology of Edmund Husserl. Taken together, these two theoretical impulses set in motion the peculiar dialectic—and the peculiar difficulty—that resonates throughout all of Aron's work.

MAX WEBER

Unhappy with the narrowness of his philosophical training and finding the sclerosis of French political life difficult to contend with, Aron traveled to Germany in 1930 in search of fresh intellectual inspiration. Anxious to become both "an observer and an actor in history" but uncertain about how to do so, Aron struggled at the outset of his intellectual journey "to overcome a duality that was perhaps inevitable but one that made me suffer. On the one hand, I read Kant's *Critique of Pure Reason;* on the other, I observed Weimar Germany, where I had been living since 1931. Kantian philosophy fascinated the student and scholar in me but not the social and historical man who was painfully witnessing the rise of German National Socialism and the conditions that spawned a second European and world war."[4] It was Aron's discovery of Max Weber that resolved this crisis and made some kind of inner peace possible. His encounter with Weber hit Aron with all the force of a conversion experience. In Weber, Aron declared, "I discovered what I was looking for: in him was to be found a combination of historical experience, political understanding, a striving for truth, and, ultimately, decision and action. The decision to grasp truth and reality and at the same time to act in the world seem to me to be the two imperatives which I have tried to follow throughout my life—and I found these two imperatives in Max Weber."[5]

Weber's thought figured prominently in Aron's first two publications, *La Sociologie allemande contemporaine* and *Essai sur la théorie de l'histoire dans l'Allemagne contemporaine: La Philosophie critique de l'histoire.*[6] Although Weber's major historical and sociological works were fairly well-known in France by that time, what was not understood nearly so well, in Aron's opinion, were the leading motifs of Weber's philosophy. Consequently, Aron devoted almost all of his early commentary on Weber to Weber's theories of knowledge and action. These doctrines, Aron explained, cannot be understood apart from one another. "Weber's greatness consists first of all in the fact that he was, and aimed at being, a politician and a thinker at the same time, or more precisely that he both separated and united politics and science."[7] Following Aron's order of analysis, we begin our review of Weber where Aron began his, with a summary discussion of Weber's theory of knowledge.

Pushing the Kantian distinction between facts and values to the breaking point, Weber renounced all but empirical knowledge. Accordingly, theoretical thought no longer plumbed the true meaning of being but confined itself to ordering experience and establishing causal connections. The "intensive and extensive infinity" of reality, however, makes a fixed order indiscoverable; the unbridgeable gap between the conceptual and the real means that knowledge is inherently fragmentary, provisional, and incomplete. From Weber's perspective, then, as Julien Freund has explained, no matter what method we use, "we can only impose an order of relationships on reality, not exhaust it."[8]

By stripping history of rationality, Aron wrote, Weber made humanity a "free agent in the world of immanent experience."[9] In the absence of any empirical or metaphysical benchmarks, we suddenly find ourselves at liberty to interpret this world however we please. Relating history to values now means relating historical "matter" to the personal values of the historian, not to a universal system of values. The choice of the subject matter, the organization of data, and the construction of hypotheses all have their origin in what was for Weber a purely subjective decision.

It was on the basis of this decision that Weber invited theorists to form concepts; theoretical thought no longer grasped ready-made structure in history but, rather, by giving free rein to the imagination, fabricated blocks of meaning that created an object or field of investigation. Thus we encounter what is universally held to be Weber's greatest contribution to the social sciences, his theory of "ideal types." An ideal type, Weber wrote, "is formed by the one-sided *accentuation* of one or more points of view and by the synthesis of a great many diffuse, discrete, more or less present and occasionally absent *concrete individual* phenomena, which are arranged according to those one-sidedly emphasized viewpoints into a unified analytical construct. In its conceptual purity, this mental construct cannot be found empirically anywhere in reality. It is a *utopia*."[10] Ideal types are thus designed to grasp original as opposed to universal features of phenomena. How are these typical traits determined? In a word, freely. From the elements given in experience, we select a limited number that are important only by virtue of their relevance to values, that is, to our values. By combining characteristics that are more or less apparent in different instances, Aron explained, "we emphasize, eliminate, exaggerate and finally substitute a coherent rational whole for the confusion and incoherence of reality."[11]

As instruments of research, ideal types play a crucial role in the formulation of explanations and hypotheses. If historical explanation is ever to rise above the "vaguely felt," historians must at some point make use of rigorously defined concepts. This is the first and simplest function of ideal types—they define that which needs to be explained. Ideal types may also serve as imaginary backdrops or yardsticks against which an actual sequence of events may be measured. In this capacity they enable social scientists to speculate about the reasons for the gap between the real and the imaginary and, by so doing, contribute to the formation of hypotheses. In order to understand an economic collapse, for example, it is necessary first to construct an ideal type of normal market activity. By then comparing this utopian construct with the actual course of events, one can chart the extent and the causes of the disturbance.

Although historical explanation begins with concepts and definitions that are both partial and subjective, Weber did not conclude (as Carl Becker did a generation later) that "everyman" is "his own historian." For Weber historical interpretation could be verified by a calculus of probabilities that tracked the lines of causality connecting acts and events. Causality constituted the "armature" of history for Weber and made possible a logic of empirical proof that checked the free, undisciplined impressions of personal understanding. The freedom of interpretation which Weber permitted at the outset of historical investigation thus stopped short of anarchy. By insisting on the need for a method of causal reasoning, Weber made room for both subjectivity and objectivity, for "the will of the historian and the necessity of things," as Aron put it.[12] The cultural sciences are objective because causal reasoning must be conducted according to the laws of logic; they are subjective because it is the historian who defines his terms and establishes hypotheses.

Weber intended causal analysis to solve what is perhaps the most difficult problem in the social sciences, namely, ascertaining what went on in another individual's mind. Comprehending our own behavior is difficult enough; uncertainty is magnified almost beyond measure when we turn our attention to the innermost thoughts of others, particularly if the distance between observer and actor spans hundreds or even thousands of years. The motives that individuals attribute to their behavior may be pretexts or justifications or be altogether obscure even to the actors themselves. Faced with this ambiguity, how does the historian choose? How does one determine which relationship or motive is the real one? What we must grasp, Aron maintained, "is, above all, the intention, the combination of means in order to attain an end which is suggested or imposed by the circumstances."[13] This is a task for the historian because it demands the use of causal reasoning. It requires, however, causal explanation of a special order. The empirical understanding of human behavior demands a science of the singular capable of assessing the causal efficacy of specific intentional determinants. And, no matter how certain the intuition or how obvious the relation, interpretation does not become knowledge until it has been verified by causal analysis.

The discovery of causal factors depends on a series of mental experiments which consists, most simply, of asking, "What would have happened if . . . ?" Aron has explained that "the causal analysis . . . should proceed by means of an imaginary alteration of one of the elements and should try to decide what would have happened if this element had not been present or had taken a different form."[14] In the case of World War II, for example, we may freely imagine what would have happened *if* Neville Chamberlain had not been the prime minister of Great Britain or *if* Hitler had not invaded Poland or *if* France had not accepted the terms of occupation. If a hypothetical change fails to make a difference in the outcome of a series of events, then we may reasonably conclude that the factor in question had little or no causal significance.

This logical schema, Aron noted, has been sharply criticized because it obviously requires a knowledge of that which we can never know with certainty, namely, what did *not* happen. It is unnecessary, however, for historians to know with any degree of precision what might have happened; all that he or she needs to establish is that events would have in some measure been different had a particular fact been altered. Indeed, Aron declared, "if anyone claims that the particular historical event would not have been different, even in the event that a given antecedent had not been what it was, the burden of proof rests with him. The role of persons or accidents underlying historical events is the first, immediate fact, and it is up to those who deny this fact to prove that it is an illusion."[15]

Causality, however, is rather slippery terrain on which to peg a historical judgment. Causal regression inexorably leads historians back to the beginning of time, drawing them across a smooth, unbroken sequence of events offering no sure starting point or foothold. In order to resolve this difficulty, Weber applied the same principle to the selection of antecedents and the determination of regressive limits which he applied to the construction of objects. Devoid of normative criteria, history becomes intelligible only through the creative application of personal values; selecting the antecedents and determining the limits of causal regression, like constructing an object, turn on the interests and commitments of the observer.

Two corollaries flow from this interpretation of causality. First, causal relationships, marked as they are by the values of the social scientist, are always partial and incomplete. Because we arbitrarily define concepts and establish causal limits, the relations that may be confirmed do not exhaust the explanatory possibilities inherent in any given situation; as in the case of ideal types, other relations based on different values are entirely possible. Weber's study of Protestantism and capitalism provides us with a case in point. Recognizing that Calvinism can be characterized by several different doctrines or dogmas, Weber constructed an ideal type (or definition) that concentrated on only one theme—the election of the saints—and analyzed its effect on economic behavior. A different characterization of Calvinism, Weber emphasized, would have probably led to different conclusions, a point borne out by Werner Sombart's study of Calvinism some years later.

Second, causality must be expressed in probable and not necessary terms. The language of logical necessity, while of some use in understanding human events, is far too refined for the rich, earthy dialects of historical explanation. To explain an event by subsuming it under a general law distorts history because history, by definition, is always a succession of singular events. By recognizing an infinite plurality of antecedents (and so demanding a subjective moment of selection), Weber underscored the fact that chance and irrationality are powerful determinants of historical development. Although what Aron termed the "massive facts" of necessity endow human affairs with a certain measure of predictability, Aron, like Weber, also believed that "the facts which appear to us to determine certain consequences create in reality only an objective possibility." [16]

At this point Weber drew a distinction between the two modes of causality which Aron found to be immensely illuminating: Historical or accidental causality, the "analysis of the influence exerted by the various antecedents of a particular and unique event," was differentiated in Weber's mind from sociological or adequate causality, which Aron explained establishes "the regular connections between one term and another." [17] In order to illustrate the difference between these two kinds of causality, Aron offered the example of the Revolution of 1848. A sociological explanation of the event is one that concludes that, given the French political situation in 1848, revolution was probable; that is, any one of a large number of accidents could have triggered the violence. The causality between a situation and an event is adequate, Aron wrote, "when we feel that the situation made the event, if not inevitable, at least very probable." [18] A historical explanation is one that contends that the shooting in the streets of Paris was the real and fortuitous cause of the revolution. "Thus," Aron explained, "the two notions of adequate and accidental causality, of law and accident, are reciprocal, both being based on arguments of probability." [19] History and sociology therefore mark two avenues of approach to the study of human behavior which cannot exist one without the other. Historical comprehension "requires the use of general propositions and these demonstrated only by beginning with historical analyses and comparisons." [20] We have before us, Aron concluded, "a history which does not ignore regularities and a sociology which does not eliminate either accidents, or ideas, or human strivings. The historical world as a whole, with its dramatic character, can find a place within these categories." [21]

Although Aron eventually softened the harsher features of Weber's nominalism, he nevertheless shared Weber's conviction that the broad tendencies at work in every historical moment leave some margin for action allowing us to shape the future. This representation of history, Aron asserted, allowed Weber "to retain a sense of the nobility of the man of action." If events have been fated by some mysterious force to unfold as they have, then "politics would become a sorry business. It is to the degree that the future is uncertain, and that a few men are able to shape it, that politics is one of man's noblest activities."[22]

Despite his appreciation for the fresh, provocative lines of inquiry generated by Weber's epistemological and methodological innovations, Aron was quick to point out a serious flaw restricting the scope and utility of Weber's approach. Weber sought, above all else, to understand the meaning that men and women attributed to their conduct. By pulling the airy substance of collective concepts back to the hard earth of actual experience, Carlo Antoni has written, Weber intended to study those ideas where they were real, "in the hearts and minds of individuals."[23] From this vantage point it is possible to account for historical change, to explain how institutions, social mores, or normative realities have been shaped and handled by successive generations. Positive science, then, is an interpretation of "lived experience," of the subjective meanings that motivated individual behavior; positive science is not an analysis of the normative or "universal" meanings debated by philosophers and metaphysicians. These types of meanings are useful only as ideal types. They are not, Weber emphasized, useful as historical explanations.

But, if the social and historical sciences can remain true to their calling as empirical disciplines only by focusing on the subjective meaning of behavior, as Weber so resolutely maintained, then "the norm as norm or the truth as truth," as Aron put it, can never be the object of analysis: "The historian knows only the empirical validity of norms or truth, a validity which is reduced to facts and frequencies." In other words, if the objective meaning (or what Aron called the "true relation") functions only as an ideal type or an instrument of research, then "the truth serves only to reveal the error."[24] Aron thus argued that, "to maintain the absolute opposition between means and ends of positive knowledge, Weber was obliged not only to reduce science to a matter of causal connections, he also had to admit the fundamental irrationality of the given and the impossibility of discovering in it any intrinsic truth or intelligibility."[25] Weber's preoccupation with irrationality in history in short was itself carried to unreasonable extremes. Aron summarized it this way: "Faithful to the absolute separation of facts and values, to the postulate of a univocal reality, Weber would have demanded what at bottom is paradoxical—that the historian disregard, in past beings, the will for value or truth, without which the historian himself would not exist and the artist or the contemporary student would become unintelligible. This is an impossible ambition, for the historian passes as naturally from man to ideas as from ideas to man" (95).

Aron leveled a second criticism against Weber's theory of action, a doctrine that unfolds naturally from his theory of objectivity. To Weber's way of thinking, Aron wrote, positive science "reveals to us what we desire and what we *can* attain, but not that which we ought to strive for; it leads us to self-knowledge and to knowledge of the world. Beyond that is the sphere of desire and will."[26] Incapable of grasping the whole of reality, science leaves men and women to choose their fate and confines itself to predicting or analyzing the consequences.

The impossibility of scientific value judgments is due not only to the conceptual limits of science but to the nature of moral decisions as well. According to Weber, all values eventually conflict. And to Weber's way of thinking, Aron explained, the ultimate or fundamental antinomy is the antinomy between the morality of conviction and the morality of responsibility: "Either we swear to obey the law, whatever may happen, or we try our best to change the world in the direction we desire, to foresee the consequences of our acts in order to triumph over determinism and avoid bringing about, in the last resort, a situation contrary to that at which we aimed."[27] The ethics of responsibility in short is defined by its concern for *consequences* of action, while the ethics of conviction is defined by its preoccupation with the motivations or *intentions* of action. To symbolize the ethic of responsibility, Weber cited one of Machiavelli's favorite figures, the leader who risked sacrificing the salvation of his soul for the security of the city. To illustrate the ethics of conviction, Weber frequently referred to the Sermon on the Mount and the politics of the revolutionary syndicalists. Although he adopted the ethics of responsibility as his own, Weber granted equal legitimacy to the ethics of conviction: "Even if science should prove a particular aim to be impossible of attainment," Aron wrote, "even if it should show that circumstances make our revolt futile, man is still not deprived of his autonomy, for he is not obliged to seek success."[28]

Weber's philosophy of choice was intended to serve as a bulwark against the increasing rationalization of the modern world. The more organized and rational society becomes, Weber believed, the more we are condemned to experience what Marxists have called "alienation," the sense that we are enslaved by a whole greater than ourselves. Weber could see no escape from the inevitable advance of rationalization except by seeking refuge in the arbitrary and even irrational assertion of personal freedom. The liberty Weber proclaimed, Aron declared, "was to be exercised in the political sphere against bureaucratic crystallization, and in the sphere of morality by decisions in cases of moral conflict and ultimately by a personal choice of supreme values."[29] Politically, then, what must be preserved and encouraged are the great-party conflicts; Weber hoped that the free play of competition would produce charismatic leaders rather than petty, narrow-minded functionaries. Individually, Aron explained, Weber believed that we must "retain the right to a purely personal religion beyond bureaucratic rationalization."[30] We must be free, in other words, to find and serve our own gods.

However much Aron may have been fascinated by Weber's "ascetic heroism," the fact remains that he found Weber's philosophy irrational and nihilistic. If choice is completely subjective and arbitrary, Aron charged, then "one has no 'reasonable reason' for preferring one choice to another."[31] Politically, Aron abhorred Weber's naive obsession with charismatic leadership. Weber hoped that the charismatic leader would rescue the masses from the anonymous domination of the bureaucracy, Aron observed, but twentieth-century men and women "have learned to fear the promises of demagogues more than the banality of rational organization."[32]

Aron's conviction that thought must never abandon its quest for the truth of human existence testifies to his interest in another strand of German philosophy, namely, the phenomenology of Edmund Husserl. Although he had been disabused of his "Kantian optimism" by the events of the interwar years, Aron developed a philosophy of historical consciousness which allowed him to retain his faith in human reason, albeit in somewhat tempered form. More specifically, Aron attempted to create a philosophy of history which could reconcile the will-to-power with the will-to-truth. His critique of Weber, then, was not meant to repudiate Weber altogether but to clear some space for Husserl. Indeed, as Aron wrote many years later, "The phenomenology of Husserl, with which [Weber] was familiar . . . would surely have provided him the philosophical tool that he was seeking." This was because Husserl's phenomenology "would have helped him, in his analysis of understanding, to avoid oscillating between Jaspers' 'psychologism' . . . and the indirect paths of neo-Kantianism which leads to meaning only by way of values."[33]

Perhaps the best way to approach Husserl's phenomenology is by unpacking Husserl's slogan "Back to the things themselves." By calling for a study of "things themselves," Husserl signaled his allegiance to idealism, a philosophy that believes that the ultimate reality of the universe—and thus the source of all certainty—resides in the realm of essences or ideas rather than in the sensory data of the empirical world, which, Husserl felt, leads to "naturalism," or the notion that cognition is a purely biological phenomenon. If cognition is reduced to its purely psychic dimensions, he argued, then we cannot account for the realities of objectivity or reason. As Quentin Lauer explains, "The objectivity which [science] presupposes, without which it could itself lay no claim to being scientific, is essentially ideal and therefore a contradiction of naturalism's own principles."[34] Even worse, in Husserl's mind, was the fact that, because it does not rise above the contingent facts of experience, naturalism ultimately ends in relativism, which Husserl thought would lead to the undoing of Western civilization.

Husserl thus believed that consciousness and ideas possess their own form of being, a form utterly independent of the "facticity" of physical reality. Unlike Plato, however, he did not believe in the existence of a separate, transcendent world of universals; he was too much of a modern for that. Instead, he followed Kant here: Objective reality was simply that which was certified by true thought, or certified by that which met all the necessary conditions for a thought to be valid. Applauding Kant's "Copernican revolution," in which the objects of experience were forced to conform to the a priori concepts of reason rather than the other way around, Husserl nevertheless believed that Kant pulled up short of a completely rational philosophy by refusing to advance beyond a purely formal knowledge. For Kant "knowledge was guaranteed if its form was unimpeachable but that said nothing about its content." Husserl, however, "would find the entire content of reality in the phenomena themselves, thus rendering the contents of consciousness as known as are the *a priori* forms according to which they are known. There could be no need to even speak of things-in-themselves, since what things are is adequately revealed in consciousness."[35]

Husserl rationalized experience by attaching the objects of knowledge to cognition in an altogether novel way. The relation between consciousness and its objects would henceforth be by way of "intentionality," which means that the identity of objects would be disclosed by apprehending the meanings that a knowing subject bestows on them. We come to an objective understanding of that which is given to consciousness, then, only by analyzing the different acts of consciousness whereby an object is intended. "The essential is ideal," Lauer explains, "and the law of the ideal is in the act of consciousness wherein it is constituted."[36] Acts of meaning are not formless or indeterminate: They have an inner logic that makes all that appears in consciousness appear in a certain way. For Husserl, in short, "the essence of whatever is is ultimately ideally and objectively in the very subjective acts whereby what is is present to consciousness. It is a 'phenomenology' because it refuses to go beyond the only data available to consciousness, i.e., appearances. It is 'transcendental' phenomenology because all that is required can be discovered by reflection on subjective acts with their intentional objective correlates."[37]

Phenomenology, then, analyzes—or, better, describes—the constitutive elements of an intentional act, and it describes them from "within," or from what some phenomenologists call "the first-person point of view." Thus the difference between the aims of the natural sciences and phenomenology—whereas positive science tries to discover laws that determine how things behave, phenomenology tries to uncover the intentional structures that determine what things are in the first place. And this it does by expending immense amounts of intellectual energy on describing the minute, inner details of intentional acts. This, incidentally, is why Aron's first task in the opening pages of the *Introduction to the Philosophy of History* was to take stock of his consciousness as his consciousness encountered its own past.

Because the necessity that constitutes the objects of intentionality is a thoroughly rational one, a strictly scientific philosophy of the sort Husserl hoped to create involves describing an object that "is given to consciousness in such a way that the impossibility of its being given otherwise is seen."[38] How does one discover and describe the universals that one "sees"? By an act of what can only be described as "intuition." As Kolakowski explains it, "The eidetic insight . . . is not a procedure of abstraction but a special kind of direct experience of universals, which reveal themselves to us with irresistible self-evidence."[39] How do we know we intuit accurately or objectively? Here, Kolakowski points out, phenomenology really has no answer: "Either you have insight or you do not."[40] Lauer makes a similar point: "Logic or phenomenological method may be the means of assuring that I see correctly, but the ultimate court of appeal is still seeing—what I see to be absolutely necessary, I see to be absolutely true."[41] All that the phenomenologist has to go on really is what can only be described as the "quality," or the special sense of immediacy, of the original insight.

Husserl thus affirmed precisely what Weber had denied, namely, the existence of an immediate connection between consciousness and its objects, a connection made possible by the structure of intentionality. Because consciousness is always consciousness *of* something, Husserl believed he could traverse the "infinite distance" Weber had placed between subjects and objects. By bridging this gap, Husserl concluded that it was now possible for philosophers and social scientists to construct concepts that were rational and real and not, as Weber had maintained, arbitrary and artificial. Husserl's phenomenology and Weber's causal methodology thus rest on dramatically different assumptions about the world. Husserl's method of description rests on the conviction that the world is rational, meaningful, and coherent: We can avail ourselves of a descriptive social science because the truth of things, especially those given in the *lebenswelt,* is given immediately. Weber, however, saw a much different world; his universe is one in which the irrational, subterranean forces of power and conflict hold sway. Intelligibility, then, is something that has to be created and not discovered. Given that human will—and not reason—is the driving force of history, order must be imposed on human action and extracted by way of conceptual constructs, not intuited by way of insight. Aron's great accomplishment was to join both methods together, to create an approach to concept formation which wove together description and construction into a working, functional philosophy of history.

Aron's interest in Husserl leads to one of the more curious puzzles of Aron's scholarship. Throughout his life Aron frequently acknowledged his intellectual indebtedness to Weber and Husserl. Much has been written of his "elective affinity" for Weber, yet almost nothing has been said of his interest in Husserl. This is partly Aron's fault: Although Aron wrote a great deal about Weber, he wrote virtually nothing about Husserl. One searches in vain for an explanation of exactly what it was that Aron took from Husserl, but the only clue is a statement in Aron's memoirs that Husserl's phenomenological method taught Aron how to "meditate" on history and on the "immanence of meanings within human reality—a reality that has leant itself to deciphering." "I was less impressed by transcendental phenomenology," Aron wrote, "or the *epoché* than the method, the way of looking, of the phenomenologist."[42]

At the very beginning of *Introduction to the Philosophy of History* Aron declares that his study will not "measure historical knowledge by an a priori criterion"—Weber's mistake—but will instead use "a descriptive, or, if one prefers, a phenomenological method" (*IPH,* 9). Beyond this brief comment he says nothing about his method, apparently content to let his methodology reveal itself in the course of its application. That methodology is first revealed in his doctoral dissertation, *Introduction to the Philosophy of History,* to which we now turn.

INTRODUCTION TO THE PHILOSOPHY OF HISTORY

Aron's dissertation is, to say the least, a difficult work. Although it was generally well received in French academic circles when it was published (even the great Henri Bergson sent Aron a congratulatory note upon its appearance), virtually every reviewer commented on the difficulty the book poses for those who have no training in philosophy. In an otherwise sympathetic review Henri Marrou, the noted French historian, complained that he devoted an entire summer to a careful reading of the text but was only able to wade through it twice.

The purpose of the *Introduction* was to uncover "the limits of historical objectivity." Although Aron pointed out that his analysis "merges with the *critical* or *transcendental* question," he immediately added that, "instead of the Kantian formula: 'under what conditions is historical knowledge possible?' we shall ask: 'Is a universally valid science of history possible?'" This subtle reformulation of the problem, Aron explained, was intended to underscore the fact that neo-Kantian analysis was not "adaptable to the structure of the historical object" (*IPH,* 10). Unlike Weber—or any of the neo-Kantians, for that matter—Aron would not force his study of human history and historical consciousness to conform to a preconceived notion of what scientific knowledge was. "Quite otherwise," he declared, "we follow the natural movement which proceeds from knowledge of self to that of the collective development" (*IPH,* 9).

Aron stated the end of historical knowledge with perfect clarity: The goal of historical science, he asserted, is "*to understand the actors.*"[43] A historian "understands" when he or she has reconstructed the motivations and intentions that governed an individual's behavior. Understanding, then, is the knowledge of human life and action we acquire "as long as the latter remain intelligible without the elaboration of causal regularities" (*IPH,* 47). But the decisive question is this: How is the phenomenon of intelligibility characterized or explained? Dilthey, Aron noted, accounted for this intelligibility by relating parts to wholes, Weber and Jaspers accounted for intelligibility by relating means and ends, while others accounted for it by relating the sign to the object so signified.

How, then, should historians and philosophers explain intelligibility, "or, which amounts to the same, how define the concept of *meaning*, correlative of understanding (which is always grasp of meaning)?" Aron explained that he intended to "take the word in its broadest meaning: any ideal content, any object of an intentionality, will be for us a meaning. Neither the end, nor the value, nor the totality merge with the meaning, a concept superordinate to all contexts and all connections in which the mind recognizes itself. We speak of understanding when *knowledge shows a meaning which, immanent to the reality, has been or could have been thought by those who lived or realized it*" (*IPH*, 47). This definition, H. Stuart Hughes has observed, "is both profoundly true and profoundly unhelpful" because it simply "suggests what every historian worthy of his trade thinks he is doing when he tries to recapture the meaning of past occurrences."[44] In order to understand the reasons for Aron's rather loose, open-ended interpretation of intelligibility, we must review his effort to return "to the source of all understanding and meaning, namely, experience and reflection" (*IPH*, 47–48). It is there that one discovers the categorial framework—in the form of a model of self-knowledge—which informs not only Aron's epistemology but his subsequent studies in methodology, international relations, and military strategy as well.

In order to understand the relationship between understanding and meaning, Aron traced the manner in which an individual mind understands its past, for "consciousness of the past is a constituent part of the historical process itself" (*IPH*, 9). Reaching what appears to be the trite and self-evident conclusion that we can never resurrect even a fragment of our past in all its fullness, Aron underscored the existence of an unbridgeable gap between the *memory* of a decision and the *moment* of decision, a difference that suggests to Aron that the past can never be completely relived. Even if every nuance of a past episode were somehow conveyed to our present consciousness, Aron observed, "this miracle of resurrection would make knowledge in the proper sense useless, for we would again be the same self we had been" (*IPH*, 51).

Because one's past cannot be relived, it must be reconstructed. In Aron's opinion there are two ways in which to do this. The first is "to rediscover the goal or goals which motivated the action and later seemed to justify it." Aron termed the representation we fix in our minds before a decision—and which we later invoke to defend our action—"motifs." The second is to retrace "states of consciousness in order to follow the formation of the motif itself" (*IPH*, 53). These "states of consciousness"—"mobiles," in Aron's terminology—are psychological antecedents or determinants that may be said to "cause" our choice. The contrast between these two choices is clear: "The psychologist looking back, analyzes, not actions but states of consciousness. Involuntary signs interest him more than deliberate decision. Spontaneously, he explains from below: heroic courage by overcompensation, religious fervor by sublimation. The philosopher on the other hand reflects on fatality of character, he invites individuals to look ever ahead and, in sincerity, he sees the mark of liberty" (*IPH*, 58).

Both approaches are legitimate, but, considered individually, each fails to account for a part of reality. The crucial point, however, is that, even when taken together, both alternatives are equally parts of a whole, the totality of which exceeds the sum of its parts. Aron argues that self-knowledge "attains neither the whole nor the unity—or at least our self is a constructed unity, situated in infinity, like the unity of all objects. We perceive a series of inclinations which are ours: the self would be the fictive source of them. The more we extend our inquiry the closer we get to the totality without ever reaching it" (*IPH*, 55–56). Because the essence of all things, including human beings, is located at a point situated in infinity, there is a "gap," or a "break," between the intentional and the psychological dimensions of behavior which guarantees the irreducibility of one to the other. But there is at the same time a marked degree of interaction between the two. All self-knowledge, Aron declared, implies a certain idea of oneself. "And this idea is animated by certain assertions of value. Even those who claim to discover themselves passively choose themselves." In other words, the "knowledge of self develops according to a dialectic: between an ever-incomplete discovery and a never-triumphant decision, the individual defines himself by a double effort at lucidity and creation. Always menaced by Pharisaism or resignation, he can relax neither of the two tensions" (*IPH*, 57).

And here we reach the heart of the matter. By describing the knowledge of self as dialectical, Aron serves notice that at the center of historical knowledge, which, as we will see, is simply a form of self-knowledge writ large, lies the problem of the hermeneutical circle: "One's idea of his past is dependent on the manner in which that past determines his present . . . but, in our consciousness, our past depends on our present" (*IPH*, 55). Aron's analysis of self-knowledge thus reveals the fundamental indissociability of subject and object. All knowledge of self is "part of its object which it inevitably transforms, for the one who knows himself is already no more what he was before he became conscious of himself" (*IPH,* 49). The upshot of this introspective exercise is that all knowledge is in some measure "tied in with the intention of the spectator" (*IPH,* 55).

Is this to say that all knowledge is subjective and hence relative? Not exactly. Here Aron injects a crucial caveat: "This plurality of images, varying with the observer, will no doubt be admitted as evident *de facto* but paradoxical *de jure.* How can it be denied that there exists a reality, and consequently a true idea of each person? And yet, we should like to uphold the paradox. We know the essential character of an individual no more than we understand the ultimate intention of an act" (*IPH,* 68).

The structure of self-knowledge is now complete. Aron presents the self as a unified whole within which two contrasting elements—the intentional and the psychological—emerge from a common, unknowable source. The relation between these two modes of human experience is ambiguous and complex: The will does not create itself ex nihilo but "emerges gradually from the process of experience which it is capable of influencing because it is the expression of it as well as the judge" (*IPH,* 57). Intentionality is thus at one and the same time *conditioned by and independent of* psychological or causal factors, a state of affairs which suggests that self-knowledge culminates in the discovery of a riddle or paradox that reason can recognize but never resolve.

Aron's emphasis on the limits of reason, then, is altogether different than Weber's. For Weber choice and interpretation were frankly and unabashedly subjective; the incoherence of reality, together with the irrationality of values, makes it impossible to speak of a "fixed" reality or "true" ideas. Aron, however, attempted to affirm a subjective moment of choice without denying the existence of a priori realities. The issue, then, boils down to the nature of choice. On what grounds is it possible to affirm yet limit the freedom of interpretation? Aron's answer is forthright and unambiguous: "The selection we predicate is based neither on incoherence (Weber), nor on the infinity of the real (Rickert), but on the most incontestable fact: the interval which separates the historian from his object, the realization of consciousness from consciousness itself, and the observer from the party concerned" (*IPH,* 144). There is indeed a gap between the rational and the real, Aron maintained, but we have no right to conclude as Weber did that this break is *constitutive* of reality. History, in other words, is marked by continuity as well as discontinuity.

The inaccessibility of meaning, the fact that the unity of all objects is located at a point situated in infinity, thus implies that a historical object or history as a whole "acquires a unity . . . only in the mind which rethinks it, the mind of an historian or a historical personality."[45] Historians can bring out "the meanings of actions, institutions and lives," but they cannot discover "the meaning of the whole. History is not absurd, but no living being can grasp its one, final meaning."[46] This statement effectively sanctions not one approach to the study of history but many. History may be investigated at different levels with different techniques for different reasons; historians are free to see not one cause at work in history but several. The elusiveness of meaning, Aron concluded, suggests that "historical reconstruction must inevitably retain an unfinished character, because it never succeeds in unraveling all relationships or exhausting all possible meanings."[47]

What saves historical science from Weber's mad, chaotic scramble for knowledge is Aron's insistence that the indefinite regression of meaning should not be taken to indicate that the objects of history are "formless," as Weber had believed. Because Aron's schema of intelligibility postulates a partial relation between reason and experience, historians do not simply create meaning but, to a certain extent, discover it. We must remember, however, that this order or coherence is only partial: Aron may have punched a rather large hole in the barrier that Weber erected between facts and values, but he did not tear it down altogether.

Because Aron did not judge reality to be radically incoherent, he did not confine historical truth to the realm of subjective meaning; what is true or historically real now includes those objective or ideal meanings that Weber had consigned to the outer darkness of metaphysics. By pulling ideal meanings back into the purview of historical analysis, Aron, taking his cue from Husserl, effectively injected a measure of life and substance into what Weber had treated as "formless matter." In Aron's view historical objects are not constructed de novo by an act of creative imagination. Instead, different objects have different structural principles that must be respected when we account for that which we investigate: "The relations among persons or among ideas or those among the material factors that give unity to an economic system," Aron explained, "are not the same as the relationship within a political or cultural unit. [An] . . . ideal phenomenon such as religion has an entirely different structure and different principles of permanence and transformation than a material phenomenon such as the capitalist system."[48]

Historians, then, must take their bearing from the inherent order of the historical world. Even though a historian may sometimes give new names or apply new concepts to the periods, objects, or events he or she is studying, "he [or she] never creates a complex that has not at least been adumbrated by the past itself; he [or she] is always rethinking the complex that the records reveal."[49] This is the first step toward correcting Weber's relativism: "When we cease to interpret our knowledge of the past by the criterion of a transcendental ego that gives form to an inert mass of material, when we put the historian back into reality and take the structure of reality as the point of reference, then the whole sense of the relativist formula is transformed."[50]

In this context it is important to note that Aron identified three different categories of historical objects—ideas, institutions, and events. To the world of ideas belong "all natural objects on which the mind has left its stamp: printed books, carved stones, painted canvas" (*IPH,* 73). This class of objects forms the nucleus of what is conventionally regarded as "cultural history," that record of human expression as registered by the arts, the sciences, philosophy, and religion. To the world of events (Weber's world) belong those human actions that are "the result of a choice among several possibilities." An event may be defined most simply as the product of a human decision, "a response to a given situation."[51] And to institutions—the family, the state, an economic system—belongs properties of both ideas and events: "Social facts of the institutional type retain their privileged status as *psychic events;* they are comprehensible, they are not compatible with natural phenomena which would have to be classified according to regularities or reconstructed, but with human actions or words which must be interpreted like a literary or philosophical text." Institutions, Aron added, are both "rational and real" (*IPH,* 73).

In order to take the full measure of Aron's historical pluralism, we must recognize that he insisted on the reciprocal solidarity of ideas and events; both classes of objects and meanings exert a significant degree of influence upon each other. But in the final analysis Aron established a hierarchy that tilts the balance in favor of intentional or ideal realities. This approach does not necessarily elevate the world of ideal meanings to the status of a first cause or an unmoved mover. ("No philosopher," Aron wrote, "has ever been 'pure spirit' completely detached from his own time and his own country.")[52] It does, however, ascribe a degree of autonomy and independence to ideal meanings. Refusing to restrict the scope of historical or sociological interpretation, Aron nevertheless maintained that the study of causal origins cannot, by its very nature, discover "philosophical meaning." Social or historical conditions can explain "the manifold characteristics of different creations" but not "the secret of the masterpiece."[53]

The intelligible structure of history, then, taken as a whole, mirrors the intelligible structure of the self. In the history of philosophy, Aron wrote, "The real distinction is between ideal entities and real entities rather than between categories of behavior."[54] This distinction—which Aron elsewhere presented as a distinction between history conceived as a succession of *works* and as a series of *events*—clearly has its origins in the distinction between *motifs* and *mobiles.* Moreover, the unity of history, as in the case of the unity of the self, is located at a point situated in infinity: "In spite of the massing of evidence, total understanding . . . emphasizes the role played by decision. For the unity towards which we strive, the unity of an epoch or culture is nothing but the fictive source of works and actions which are all that is directly accessible" (*IPH,* 118). Historical reality, in short, contains a multiplicity of partial orders that do not combine into an overall, self-contained whole. For this reason history is "ambiguous and inexhaustible but not incoherent," a fact that justifies the plurality of historical interpretations but pulls up short of Weber's relativism.

This ontological description of the historical world, however, constitutes but one dimension of Aron's philosophy of history. The other is defined by its epistemological concern. "Ever since Vico," Aron explained, "all those who have reflected on history have in one way or another upheld a sort of kinship between the nature of reality and the mode in which reality is appropriated by consciousness."[55] This view suggests that the various levels of meaning that distinguish the various objects of analysis anticipate and correspond in some fashion to different levels of reasoning which distinguish the various moments of analysis. We will begin by analyzing understanding and explanation, heterogeneous forms of cognition which are, in Aron's opinion, the two basic modalities of knowledge.

Understanding, as we have seen, attaches a course of action to a human intention. Relating actions to intentions as means to ends, however, "usually turns out to be too simple" because a historian is inevitably drawn toward "other considerations that set the framework within which the act is reduced to a choice of means."[56] Historical inquiry must therefore place action within the context of a larger totality. In order to understand the behavior of a speculator, for example, we must have some knowledge of currency and the stock market, the organization of enterprise, and the legal norms that regulate speculation. Taking another of Aron's favorite examples, we can understand the behavior of a general in battle only if we know something about the organization of his army, the techniques and quality of his armaments, the knowledge he possesses of his enemy, the rules of battle, and so on. In historical matters, then, "the problem of intelligibility is related first of all to the totalities one is seeking to understand, from an individual life, to a battle, to a civilization, and finally the whole of history. In moving from elementary examples to even vaster ones, intelligibility slips from a practical meaning to a properly metaphysical one, from intrinsic understanding of man's behavior toward the ultimate meaning of the human adventure, accessible only to God or those who take themselves to be his confidants."[57] Given the fact that comprehension is drawn by its very nature to seek larger and larger wholes and contexts, a full knowledge of action would require the historian to view history "from the perspective of the sun," as Kant put it. Yet the possibility of scaling the walls of history in order to view it from the perspective of God or the Infinite is immediately precluded by the fact that historians are thoroughly historical beings. The finitude of the human condition thus presents an insurmountable barrier to understanding. Therefore, as one of Aron's commentators explained, historians are compelled "to discover a *substitute for comprehension,* which requires in effect a coincidence with an 'incomprehensible' totality."[58]

One such possibility immediately suggests itself—causal analysis. Causality intervenes "when comprehension has exhausted its resources."[59] The ultimately inaccessible character of historical wholes compels historians to reconstruct the objects of their analysis by locating those causal determinants responsible for historical change. Because causal analysis attempts to subsume the diversity of historical phenomena under general laws, placing an event in its context here means integrating it into the framework of a broader causal network.

Can such an attempt be successful? Is it possible to subsume the plurality of events and institutions under general laws from which historical development can be deduced or reconstructed in its entirety? This is, after all, the Marxist thesis. To such questions, and claims, Aron responded with an emphatic no. In order to demonstrate the limits of causal analysis, Aron resurrected Weber's interpretation of causal reasoning.

Like Weber, Aron distinguished between sociological and historical causality. "Historical research," Aron maintained, "sticks to the antecedents of a singular fact, sociological research to the causes of a fact which may be repeated" (*IPH,* 220). This difference in orientation does not mean that history and sociology exist in isolation from one another. Historical and sociological causality were for Aron, as they were for Weber, two sides of the same coin. Because the macroscopic regularities that preoccupy the sociologist are simply abstractions that ignore by methodological fiat the reality of individuals and accidents, the modality of judgment proper to sociological analysis must be one of probability, not necessity: "The causal relationship between an event and its antecedents, the responsibility particular to each one being evaluated by retrospective calculations of probability, involves a portion of uncertainty."[60]

It was precisely this indeterminacy that demanded in Weber's eyes a free act of creative interpretation. Because history has no inherent significance or order, meaning must be created by the social scientist. This is perhaps the single most important reason why causal analysis cannot replace comprehension as a mode of explanation: "Causal relations are dispersed, they do not fall into a pattern, so that they do not explain each other as do the classified laws of a theory in physics. Understanding makes up for this dual deficiency; it makes the regularities intelligible, it brings them together conceptually" (*IPH,* 205). Explanation, in other words, *presupposes* comprehension or interpretation. The most critical moment of causal research, Aron emphasized, revolves around the social scientist's choice of concepts and definition of terms. The relations one discovers in history "depend on the ideas used [and] on the division effected, which, conforming to certain regularities, do not eliminate the possibility of other relations and other interpretations" (*IPH,* 269–70).

But Aron did not follow Weber all the way in believing that causality confirms comprehension. To Weber's way of thinking "understanding puts the subjective questions, causality furnishes the objective answers." Aron, however, stressed the limits of causal verification: "Understanding, if it sometimes serves to introduce the search for determinism, is nevertheless independent when it is limited to reconstructing the events or narrating the sequence of facts. Since it is singular, it in no way borrows its validity from the verification of cause. So then, either it is of itself objective, or else it depends entirely on this decision which Weber strove to reject from the start. Even more, it would infect causality with its subjectivity, rather than acquire from it a total objectivity" (*IPH,* 269). By granting a measure of autonomy and independence to understanding, Aron transforms what initially appears to be a circular relationship between understanding and explanation—causality completes understanding when understanding has "exhausted its resources," while causality at the same time presupposes understanding—into a hierarchical or architectonic one.

From this perspective we discover that knowledge is composed not of two terms (understanding and explanation) but three: understanding, sociological causality, and historical causality. Moreover, we immediately notice that the intermediate term of this threefold formula, sociological causality, shares attributes of both understanding and explanation. Sociological causality, Aron explained, "is both comprehensive and explicative. It is comprehensive in that it reveals the implicit logic or rationality of individual and collective behavior, and it is explicative in that it establishes regularities, or rather places partial forms of behavior in contexts that give them meaning."[61] Because the abstract relationships fabricated by the sociologist depend on terms that "are more constructed than given," sociological causality necessarily presupposes understanding. And, because these abstract relationships represent only a partial image of the process of historical change, the work of the sociologist anticipates the work of the historian.

We here approach what is perhaps the most important and interesting feature of Aron's philosophy of history. By insisting on the primacy of ideal meanings—and, concomitantly, on the autonomy of understanding—Aron has ordered his three classes of meaning according to a sliding scale of indeterminacy. Very much like Montesquieu, Aron envisioned a hierarchy of beings or historical objects that are subject in varying degrees to the laws of necessity. In the case of events these laws are not of the same logical order as the laws of nature; a method of causal reasoning, however, can be applied to further our understanding of change and development. In the case of institutions the laws of causality also apply but not nearly to the same degree as in the case of events. Finally, when we reach the apex, ideal meanings, we have virtually—but not completely—abandoned the categories of necessity and contingency in favor of categories supplied by understanding. Conversely, if we proceed from the ideal meanings to events, we see that the increasing determinism narrows but does not eliminate the role of choice and interpretation. "A bare fact is nonsense," Aron maintained: "Selection and orientation have their function, even if it be small, in the narration of a single event."[62]

We are now in a position to describe more completely the relation between the objects of knowing and the process of knowing. Because each category of meaning contains elements of freedom and necessity, all of the objects of the historical world must be understood and explained. More specifically, Aron's philosophy of history requires the application of all three moments of analysis—understanding, sociological explanation, and historical explanation—to each of the three levels of analysis, being ideas, institutions, and events. This pattern of analysis constitutes the logical framework that governs not only Aron's philosophy of history but his entire life's work as well. It makes no difference whether Aron is analyzing problems in history, sociology, economics, military strategy, or international relations—these three basic categorical distinctions still obtain. All objects display the same threefold structure of meaning and thus require the same threefold process of analysis.

Before leaving Aron's philosophy of history, we must address one final epistemological issue, namely, the nature and scope of objectivity. Although Aron restored a measure of coherence and rationality to history, he nevertheless maintained that interpretation is still an essential element of knowledge. The postulate of partial coherence may shorten the infinite distance Weber placed between reason and experience, but distance remains nevertheless. What, then, guarantees the objectivity of judgment? How is it possible to bridge the gap between subject and object, especially after Aron has underscored the logical impossibility of the attempt?

Aron offered a twofold solution to the problem of objective knowledge. The first solution measures objectivity by one's willingness to accept a plurality of interpretations. Historical objects, by virtue of their "very texture," generate an almost endless number of interpretations that, when taken together, approximate the truth. Historical relativism, Aron insisted, is itself transcended as soon as the historian "ceases to claim a detachment that is impossible, identifies his point of view, and consequently puts himself in a position to recognize the points of view of others."[63] Even when they seem contradictory, Aron added, one must interpret the plurality of interpretations as "a sign not of defeat but of the richness of life." History does not "offer a final, universally valid account of societies, epochs and extinct civilizations for the very reason that they never had a unique and universally valid significance. The never-ending discovery . . . of the past is the expression of a dialectic that will last as long as the human race and is the essence of history."[64]

In itself, however, this is a rather shaky foundation on which to construct objective knowledge. As one of Aron's commentators observed, this solution "seems to presuppose that all interpretations are valid, thereby dissolving any difference between truth and error."[65] In order to shore up the foundations of objectivity, Aron added a second criterion of truth. "In order for history to be objective," he wrote, "it is necessary for us to believe in the existence of a universal system of values."[66] If all historical judgments bear the mark of a personal system of values, then the possibility of conferring a greater degree of truth on one interpretation over another depends on the existence of a transhistorical system of norms against which personal values may be measured and judged.

At this point Aron's solution to the problem of objective knowledge reveals its dependence on what Sylvie Mesure recognized as the "fundamental philosophical option," namely, "the Kantian thesis, according to which it is a certain representation of the end of history as the *Idea of Reason* which orients, in a regulatory fashion, historical knowledge."[67] "There is in Kant," Aron declared during an interview near the end of his life, "a concept to which I still subscribe: it is the idea of Reason, an image of a society that would be truly humanized."[68] Despite the senseless turmoil of the twentieth century, Aron never ceased "to think, or dream, or hope—in the light of the idea of Reason—for a humanized society."[69] For Aron, as for Kant, a truly humanized society is one that recognizes the freedom of the individual to enhance his or her own moral worth under laws hypothetically of his or her own making. The universal reign of law and the establishment of perpetual peace thus constitute "two representations of the Idea as the goal of history and as the realization of a rational humanity."[70] From this vantage point a historical reconstruction can be objective to the degree that it interprets the sequence of events as so many steps leading toward the fulfillment of this idea. Or, as Mesure put it, "An interpretation will be more objective when it is orientated by values capable of being shared by the whole of humanity."[71]

What saved Aron from the revolutionary optimism of the Marxists—and the nonrevolutionary optimism of nineteenth-century liberals such as Auguste Comte and Herbert Spencer, for that matter—was his unshakable conviction that the idea of the end of history was just that, an idea. As an idea, the end of history is simply an assumption or working hypothesis that is necessary for history and historical science to make any sense at all. As Mesure explains this point, a historian's effort "would be an absurd enterprise if the historian did not suppose . . . that the successive moments have between them a relationship of continuity which makes so many steps in a univocal direction readable in their succession itself: this direction, without which the very will to separate the meaning of events would be aberrant, is only in its turn thinkable . . . from the idea of a virtual outcome, thus of a goal of history from which each event would appear as a step toward this accomplishment."[72]

Transforming the end of history from a working hypothesis into a rational certainty, however, is equally absurd for doing so immediately destroys history. If the end of history becomes "progressively necessary," Aron explained, then "history is definitely eliminated, since the present state could have been encompassed at one stroke by a powerful mind. [O]ur perspective would disappear . . . and the science of the past would become useless at that moment when history would come to an end by being dissolved in suprahistorical truth" (*IPH,* 125). Because this eschatological perspective functions only as a regulatory ideal, the process by which history realizes its end must necessarily be represented as unachievable. A purely formal idea of the end of history, Aron wrote, "will carry no conviction (and does not claim to do so) but at least suggests the basic antinomy between the rational mission of man and brute existence. History exists only because of this contradiction. Either pure mind or blind impulse, it would be equally lost in a continuous state or a lawless sequence" (*IPH,* 316). History and historical knowledge therefore require an "inaccessible paradise" in order to be possible.

By arguing that the meaning of history can neither be known nor realized, Aron effectively removed all possibility of discovering historical truth in history. Beyond science, he explained, "philosophical reflection is possible . . . but this reflection is itself a function of history."[73] Because we are historical beings, possession of the whole truth can be granted to no one, a fact that lies at the root of Aron's pronounced aversion to totalitarian ideologies. Although we will reserve a more detailed discussion of the manner in which Aron related knowledge and action for the next chapter, here it is worth noting in passing that Aron's preference for what he called "the politics of understanding"—a politics governed by tolerance and compromise—has its origins in his epistemological conviction that knowledge is partial, incomplete, and uncertain. Similarly, his condemnation of the "politics of Reason"—a politics based on the conviction that one is "the confidant of Providence" and thus knows the future in its entirety—is justified by the same epistemological modesty.

For some this philosophical agnosticism was simply too much to bear. Aron's epistemological reserve was held in contempt not only by Marxists, who claimed to know the laws of history in their entirety, but by existentialists as well, who claimed to know no such thing. Although existentialists such as Sartre and Merleau-Ponty were utterly indifferent to the socioeconomic theories of Marxism, they were greatly intrigued by Marx's emphasis on revolution as a means of advancing social justice and personal liberation. In their view the problem with a Kantian philosophy such as Aron's was its uncertainty: The stringent limits that a Kantian ethics placed on theoretical thought made it difficult to deduce specific moral choices from general moral maxims. For de Beauvoir, Merleau-Ponty, and Sartre a Kantian reign of reason was conceivable not as the result of moral choice but of revolution. Such a revolution, Tony Judt has explained, "would not only release the intellectual from the discomfort of a contingent existence but would itself change the rules of the game."[74]

Although Aron harbored no animosity toward de Beauvoir, Merleau-Ponty, and Sartre—along with André Malraux, they had all founded the journal *Les Temps Modernes* and at one had time had been good friends—he was plainly angered by revolutionary talk of this sort. "Revolutionaries tend to exaggerate both the margin of their freedom and the power of their destiny," he declared. "Uplifted by their faith beyond the humdrum lessons of wisdom, they expect perpetual peace to flower from unlimited violence. They proclaim the inevitability of their triumph because the cause which embodies so much hope cannot fail." Tragically enough, however, "there is no law, either human or inhuman, which can direct the chaos of events to a definite end, be it radiant or horrific."[75]

Much of Aron's criticism of the radical Left was directed at his old friends Sartre and Merleau-Ponty. Although Aron and Sartre had been close during their years at the ENS, they drifted apart as they grew older, with Sartre eventually turning on Aron just as he had turned on countless others, attacking him on several occasions with unbridled ferocity. Given the closeness of their friendship at the ENS, Aron was at a loss to explain the personal edge to Sartre's attacks, other than to say that Sartre had always been something of a "nasty kid" and to suggest that for men of his generation "it seemed impossible to sustain friendships when political choices did not always coincide."[76] Although these attacks were surely quite wounding to Aron, he simply shrugged them off, refusing to stoop "to the low and vulgar level" of Sartre's ad hominems. "It was up to my friends to defend me, if they felt it necessary," Aron later wrote, "and it was up to Sartre's friends, if they were concerned with his dignity, to warn him against his passions."[77]

Aron may have responded to Sartre's personal attacks with studied indifference, but he attended to his philosophical works and polemical writings with great care—more care, in fact, than many of his friends thought Sartre's works deserved. The most glaring weakness of Sartre's politics, in Aron's opinion, was it abstractness, its taste for a "philosophy of history that soared high above reality and the problems that political leaders had to resolve." Almost contemptuously dismissive of the problems confronting existing societies, Merleau-Ponty and Sartre wanted "to dream about a different society, boundless, universal." [78] In the end, Aron explained, "Sartre was often lost in political affairs, precisely because he was essentially a moralist," albeit a rather unconventional one.[79] Indeed, Sartre's moralism was so unconventional that it allowed him to regard the Soviet gulag as simply an unpleasant historical necessity, "the price that had to be paid for a better future." [80]

Aron also thought Sartre's efforts to graft existential humanism onto Marxist dialectics was doomed from the outset. "A follower of Kierkegaard," he insisted, "cannot be a follower of Marx." [81] Although Sartre tirelessly repeated that he believed Marxism to be the "unsurpassable philosophy of our time," he was deeply unhappy with the materialist foundations of Marxism. To Sartre's way of thinking materialism failed to account not only for the reality of human consciousness but also for the very dialectic driving history. As Aron explained it, Sartre believed that the dialectic "is by nature a movement of ideas: it implies synthesis and totality, a further stage which at once surpasses and preserves the previous state, a kind of appeal of the future or a tendency of totality to realize itself. The dialectic, thus defined, appears as immediately irreconcilable with the order of spatial and material relations to which some would reduce it." [82] It is futile to claim, as most Marxists do, that organic and social complexity arises from inert material. Sartre believed that a hierarchy of this sort is neither incoherent nor incomprehensible, but, as Aron explained, Sartre did wonder how it was possible to account for "the progressions from the inferior to the superior type, unless one has begun with a contradictory notion of matter, surreptitiously introducing the superior terms into the initial [term]." [83]

Ultimately, Aron argued, Sartre's lifelong effort to reconcile human freedom with historical reason ended in failure. "If authentic reality is made up only of men, their actions, their sufferings or their dreams," he wondered, "how can their individual existences, each of which is unique and irreplaceable, be totalized?"[84] Moreover, Sartre equivocated before what is perhaps the most fundamental question of revolutionary Marxism—namely, will the revolutionary end of capitalism be the existential end of all forms of human alienation? Marx clearly believed it would. Given the unconditional and indeterminate nature of Sartrean freedom, however, it is impossible to know; Sartre's philosophy "suggests instead an endless alternation of alienation and revolution."[85] Ironically, Aron noted, there is nothing in Sartre's philosophy that rules out the possibility that "revolutionary *praxis* is finally incarnated in the will of a single man." Despite its commitment to freedom, "the Sartrean philosophy of violence risks teaching the same lessons as do the philosophies that Sartre, the man, detests."[86] In the end, Aron wrote, both Merleau-Ponty and Sartre "confused a particular aim with the end of history—a confusion that fosters fanaticism since it transfigures combat between classes and parties into the struggle, less eternal than final, between good and evil."[87]

But, if there is no final answer *in* history, what hope can we have *for* history? Aron's own response is clear: "I believe I have shown the necessity of rediscovering a faith in man and [in] seeking to understand our historical situation."[88] Yet Aron's faith in humanity is a far cry from the robust confidence that Enlightenment philosophies are made of. "Man is a reasonable being," Aron liked to say, quoting his old friend Eric Weil, "but it has not been demonstrated that men are reasonable."[89] If we are not to despair, we must assume, or better hope, that men and women will someday become reasonable. For the moment, however, we must recognize that our hold on reason and rationality is a precarious one: "Human life is dialectic, that is, dramatic, since it is active in an incoherent world, is committed despite duration, and seeks a fleeting truth with no other certainty but a fragmentary science and a formal reflection" (*IPH*, 347).

Because his theory of knowledge pulled the rug out from under the feet of those who stood on the conviction that history offers a guarantee of human progress, Aron was rebuked time and time again—particularly by those on the Left—for his "nihilism." For his part Aron freely admitted he was something of a historical pessimist: The rising tide of National Socialism, the misery of the Great Depression, and the horror of the Holocaust all combined to cure him of his youthful optimism. After witnessing these tragedies firsthand, Aron wrote: "I ceased to believe that history always obeys the imperatives of reason or the wishes of men of good will. I lost faith [but,] not without effort, kept hope."[90]

Yet this rather stark assessment of history and the human condition is not Aron's final word; as we have seen, he never stopped hoping that men and women might someday stumble across the hidden pathway that leads to peace and freedom. In fact, the entire sweep of Aron's scholarship can be interpreted as a lifelong search for evidence that the struggle to realize what he called "the essential values" is not in vain. Is history teaching us to become more reasonable? Are men and women making *any* progress in the age-old quest for freedom and fraternity? These are the questions that preoccupied Aron and run "like a red skein" throughout all of his writings.

More specifically, Aron searched for progress in the light of what he considered to be the two dominant facts of the modern age, industrialization and nuclear weapons. By a sort of "cunning of history," Aron observed, nuclear weapons and industrialization have converged to make war less rational than before. Are we entitled to believe, then, that we stand on the threshold of a new era? I propose to divide this question into two others. First, what are the consequences of industrialization for the social order, and, second, what are the consequences of nuclear weapons for the prospects of peace? Although I have arranged the chapters of this study according to an abstract logic that proceeds from the general to the particular, or from epistemology to policy, it is very much in keeping with the spirit of Aron's work to combine an analysis of the substantive problems of history with an analysis of the formal problems of knowledge because an answer to the question "What must I do?" is inseparable from an answer to the question "What can I know?"

As we will see, what we must do is not altogether certain because what we can know, at least in Aron's account, is not altogether clear. Although Aron never wavered in his conviction that reason must respect the constraints of historical necessity, he never squared that conviction with his equally firm commitment to the *autonomy* of reason, a shortcoming that left him defending the logically obscure proposition that reason is at one and the same time independent of and conditioned by the forces of historical necessity. What, after all, is the logical sense of somehow "shortening" the infinite distance Weber postulated between reason and experience while insisting that infinite distance nevertheless remains? It is there, in the double impulse between freedom and necessity, that we see the origin of the restless ambiguity that frequently plagued Aron's efforts to come to grips with the more immediate and concrete problems of his time. Unable to reconcile the moral demands of reason with the necessary constraints of history, Aron frequently found himself restlessly shuffling between one theoretical impulse and the other in a never-ending effort to keep both tethered to a politics of prudential and incremental reform.

Declaring that freedom and necessity connect "at a point in infinity" only begs the question. How does this abstract proposition bear on matters of practical choice? An inaccessible paradise may be a kingdom fit for philosophers. Whether it can be made hospitable to statesmen and political leaders remains yet to be seen. What are its consequences for statecraft and leadership, especially when confronting the daunting problems of the twentieth century?

2 "That Cool Distiller of Passion and Interest"

Sociology and the Meaning of Industrial Society

DRY AND HIGHLY ABSTRACT, Aron's dissertation was nevertheless a necessary first step toward his goal of understanding history-in-the-making. "The mere story of events teaches us nothing," he once remarked, "unless it is given form and meaning by reference to concepts."[1] If Aron is correct on this point, then we must have recourse not only to a method that generates the concepts we need but, at an even higher level of abstraction, to an epistemology that sanctions the methods we use. And therein lay the purpose of the *Introduction:* "To establish the truth of the most general propositions from which a methodology would be developed." Another book was necessary, however, "to advance from principles to their application" (*IPH,* 10).

Unfortunately, this book was never written. Consumed by his journalistic responsibilities and worried that he would spend the rest of his life writing introductions to the social sciences, Aron lost interest in exploring the more formal dimensions of knowledge. It was not until 1955, the year he received an appointment to a chair in sociology at the Sorbonne, that Aron resumed his efforts to advance from the first principles of the *Introduction*. Being more anxious, however, to address the problems of modern societies than to treat with the problems of methodology, he confined his methodological comments to several essays on Montesquieu and three short chapters introducing a series of volumes which has since become known as "The Sorbonne Trilogy." Originally delivered as a series of lectures at the Sorbonne, the Trilogy is a comparative analysis of Soviet and Western societies focusing on three dimensions of the social order—the economic (*Eighteen Lectures on Industrial Society*), the social proper (*La Lutte des classes*), and the political (*Democracy and Totalitarianism*).[2] Aron had hoped that he would someday return to the project and refine his theses but never found the time to do so. Consequently, he consented to its publication rather reluctantly, acutely conscious of "the imperfections resulting from the very conditions which gave rise to [these] short essay[s] on a very large subject."[3]

In turning his attention to industrial society, Aron had deliberately broken with tradition at the Sorbonne by making room in his lectures for current events, or for "five-year plans, agricultural collectivization, and the Moscow trials," which is why he worried from time to time that his sociology was just a cut above the journalism he had been engaged in for fifteen years. Nevertheless, he added, "the evocation, in a Sorbonne amphitheater, of the concentration camps or the confessions of Lenin's companions brought so-called academic sociology closer to everyday political concerns."[4] In reflecting on the reception that greeted the lectures that would become the Sorbonne Trilogy, Aron related that "a number of students, Marxists or *marxisants,* were waiting to trip me up. I arrived with a reputation of a man of the right and a journalist; I had to tame the Marxists, to convince them of my knowledge, make myself recognizable by all as a fully competent teacher. In [*18 Lectures on Industrial Society*], I more than once was less than candid about my judgment of the Soviet Union. To demonstrate my objectivity, I had to grant the regime to which I was opposed the benefit of the doubt, to show it some indulgence. I sincerely believe I achieved my aim."[5] In recalling his years at the Sorbonne, Aron could not refrain from pointing out that "Khrushchev's speech to the Twentieth Congress dates from 1956, the year of my first course." This meant, of course, that Aron's lectures on industrial society "were confirmed by the general secretary of the Communist Party of the Soviet Union."[6]

Despite Aron's reservations, the Sorbonne Trilogy is important to this study for two reasons. First, because it attempts to "clarify the problems which direct empirical research and comparative analysis," the Trilogy contains a *discours de la methode* for the social sciences and thus provides the methodological foundation upon which *Peace and War,* Aron's theory of international relations, was erected (*EL,* 4). Second, the Sorbonne Trilogy heralds a shift not only in the level of analysis but also in the subject of analysis. The appearance of this three-volume work marks Aron's return to sociology for the first time since the publication of his graduate school study, *German Sociology.* This change is of monumental importance for Aron's theory of international relations because *Peace and War* is an exercise in what Aron termed "political sociology," a phrase that suggests that political analysis is in some measure dependent upon sociology for its concepts and principles.

My overarching concern in this chapter is to describe the essential elements of Aron's method for the social sciences. In moving from epistemology to methodology, we move from the ends of knowledge to the means used to define the objects of analysis and to comprehend the whole. I intend to show that Aron's methodology is fired by the same dialectical impulse between reason and experience—and thus plagued by the same sort of difficulties—which fires his epistemology.

Because Aron chose to explain his method primarily by way of illustration—that is, by applying it directly to a specific set of problems—we must cull the elements of this method from a few short essays on Montesquieu and from the brief prefatory remarks introducing the Sorbonne Trilogy. In doing so, we will discover that the Trilogy is not a disconnected collection of sociological insights, as some have maintained, but an intelligible whole, the internal order of which not only reflects the critical logic of the *Introduction to the Philosophy of History* but anticipates the internal order of *Peace and War* as well.

In the course of this analysis we will also discover that the Sorbonne Trilogy is a work of practical importance. Like Weber, Aron advocated a science for the politician and a politics based on science. Deploring the fragmentation and petty empiricism that marks so much sociological research today, Aron tried to breathe new life into the discipline by connecting it to the "important questions," the larger issues of politics, ethics, and social action. At the same time, deeply distressed by the political turmoil created by the wake of World War II, Aron tried to calm the passions of ideological debate by subjecting the ideological objects of those passions to the rigors of empirical evaluation. And it was for this sort of analysis—distinguishing the desirable from the possible—that Aron became known among his contemporaries as "that cool distiller of passion and interest into order and light."[7]

SOCIOLOGY AND THE PROBLEM OF ORDER

At the outset of his opening lecture on the nature of sociological inquiry, Aron introduced a distinction between two theoretical attitudes which immediately calls to mind the distinction between critical and speculative philosophies of history. Sociology, Aron maintained, is analytic as well as synthetic in character and may therefore be represented as a discipline that incorporates features peculiar to both economics and philosophy. The analytic quality of economic analysis resides in its commitment to the scientific method in order to understand *one* aspect of social life. Because analytical knowledge is by definition that knowledge that is gained by breaking an object into its component parts, the scope of economic analysis is confined to a comparatively narrow and isolated range of social phenomena, namely, economic behavior.

This determination to be scientific is perhaps the first mark of the sociologist. Because of its analytic orientation, sociology, like economics, is initially led to consider a limited range of institutions and behaviors that Aron defined negatively as "those phenomena not studied by other disciplines" (*EL,* 21). Sociologists thus direct their attention to matters such as the family, stratification, and the kinds of social relations generated by economic forces, topics generally neglected by the other social sciences.

There is a synthetic dimension to sociological analysis, however, that compels the sociologist to imitate the philosopher's attempt to understand not one aspect but the whole of existence. Although sociology initially considers limited segments of collective life, social phenomena such as the family and class relations reflect to some degree the character or ethos of the particular society in which they are located. It is impossible, Aron argued, "to study social stratification (the distribution of individuals among sub-groups or within a hierarchy) without considering many different aspects—economic, political, and religious. If these phenomena, which are essentially sociological, are examined more carefully they are seen to be characterized by their global nature. They may be regarded as universal social phenomena" (*EL,* 21). Sociology cannot limit itself, however hard it may try, simply to establishing the facts. On this point, Aron noted, Comte was right: One can understand a part of society only by inserting it into a more comprehensive whole. Sociological research on the psychology of factory workers, for example, "means nothing" unless broader factors are taken into account "such as the role the factory plays in the surrounding area, and in the branch of industry involved; the status of ownership of the means of production; the relations between industrial workers' organizations and so forth."[8] Because reflection on the whole is an inescapable part of the sociologist's task, comprehensive considerations are as indispensable to the truth of analytic sociologies as they are to critical histories.

Given this fact, every sociologist must be prepared to answer what Aron considered to be the first and most fundamental question in sociology—namely, what is social? What is the common denominator that binds together every society and marks them as different species of the same genus? Broadly speaking, Aron explained, two answers to this question are possible: "In every group we see either relations between persons, or a distinct unity created by the collective life. The social *par excellence* can be understood either by the analysis of interpersonal events or by the intuition of wholes."[9] Microscopic and macroscopic perspectives are thus equally characteristic of the discipline and represent two forms of the sociological attitude.

Aron clarified the difference between these two directions of thought by comparing the individualism of Georg Simmel and Leopold von Wiese with the universalism of Othmar Spann. Individualism, or the microscopic perspective, regards individual action as the building block of social reality. Because it reduces social institutions (or "wholes") to the reciprocal relations between individuals, the microscopic perspective relies heavily on the techniques and principles of causal analysis to grasp the meaning of social behavior. Universalism, or the macroscopic perspective, accepts the Aristotelian teaching that the whole precedes the parts. Accordingly, universalism relies on the principles of interpretation, or "understanding," to grasp the structures and connections embedded in social reality. In attempting to construct a unified account of the social, then, sociologists are confounded by the same dichotomy between reason and experience, or unity and diversity, which plagues historians when they attempt to construct a coherent, intelligible account of individual behavior. Regarded separately, each approach overlooks a part of experience; taken together, they stake out the boundaries of social reality, thereby suggesting that the truth of the matter lies somewhere in between.

Attempting to join these two doctrines together, Aron argued that sociologists must recognize the existence of partial order. Between the absolute unity of an ideal society and the infinite diversity of empirically observable customs and institutions, Aron maintained, lies the plurality of an "intelligible" order. Social life "appears neither incoherent nor completely ordered; it contains innumerable semi-organized parts, but no obvious total order." The postulate of partial unity means, on the one hand, that the sociologist lifts out the order contained in the object of analysis. On the other hand, because this unity is only partial, order cannot be understood in only one way: "The sociologist brings out the categories and regularities of his subject, but he always makes a choice between these categories and regularities" (*EL,* 28). The whole of society, then, "constitutes an undifferentiated whole over which different conceptualizations give us partial views."[10]

The impossibility of locating a clear, well-defined nucleus of social reality, however, does not reduce sociological inquiry to a methodological free-for-all. By describing social wholes as partially ordered realities, Aron has immediately dispensed with two methods of causal analysis: The synthetic method of historical materialism, which attempts to reconstruct the whole of society on the basis of one primary factor, the economic, and the analytic methods of most modern-day sociologists, which dissolve social reality into an almost infinite number of causal relations. There is, Aron assured his readers, an "intermediate solution," namely, the interpretive method of Montesquieu. "In language that is not really clear and is often ambiguous, [Montesquieu's *Spirit of the Laws*] gives the essentials of the method of thinking a sociologist would need if he rejected both the completely synthetic claims of Marxist sociology and the type of pure analysis I have just described" (*EL,* 50).

Montesquieu's method of analysis bears close examination because it clearly prefigures Aron's. Although there are striking similarities between the sociologies of the two men, Aron claimed flatly that his thinking "owes nothing" to either Montesquieu or Tocqueville (*MC,* 2:viii). The parallels between the methods of Montesquieu and Aron are so close, however, that one cannot help but wonder whether *The Spirit of the Laws* was not in some way the prototype or at least the inspiration for the Sorbonne Trilogy.

MONTESQUIEU AND *THE SPIRIT OF THE LAWS*

In *The Spirit of the Laws,* Aron explained, Montesquieu's goal was to make social reality intelligible by replacing the apparently incoherent diversity of morals, customs, laws, and institutions with a conceptual order. Although this ambition is a properly sociological one, the steps required to make the transition from meaningless fact to intelligible order are far from self-evident. Weber, for example, hoped to effect the very same transition, but his political sociology is radically different than Montesquieu's. What, then, is the nature of the intelligibility that sociologists seek? On what level and with what tools does the sociologist discover an intelligible order? In Montesquieu there are two answers to these questions, Aron observed, and thus Montesquieu's answers are not contradictory but are, rather, two stages in the same process.

The first step is to recognize that history is not simply a tale of sound and fury signifying nothing: "Beyond the chaos of accidents, there are underlying causes which account for the apparent absurdity of things."[11] This, Aron declared, is Montesquieu's "first truly sociological idea" (*MC,* 1:15). Accounting for what may seem to be an accidental sequence of events by referring to an underlying stratum of general causes, however, does not necessarily imply simple determinism; Montesquieu, like Tocqueville, recognized that there are limits to sociological explanations. For Montesquieu "great events are explained by great causes but the details of events are simply events, that is, they are not deducible from the structural facts of the society in question" (*MC,* 1:264).

Aron found Montesquieu's second step "more interesting and perceptive" than the first—namely, that one must compress the almost infinite variety of customs and ideas into a relatively small number of types. Here Montesquieu sought to uncover the essence or principle that makes each social type what it is. Perhaps Montesquieu's most interesting discovery in this regard was the discovery that everything in a society—climate, religious belief, population size, political constitution—is interconnected. Although it is to Montesquieu's credit that he did not suggest that there is one element that strictly determines the others, Aron explained, Montesquieu did establish a connection between the form of government on the one hand and social mores on the other. Each form of government, in other words, has an essence that constitutes not only its own originality but also the originality of a society as a whole. By analyzing the forms of government, then, "Montesquieu gives us a concept of *intelligible wholes* or of the *significant relations within a whole.* It is impossible to analyze a society without referring to significant wholes, i.e. to the system constituted by the connected behavior of men in the political or economic order" (*EL,* 53). The diversity of customs and mores may thus be organized in two ways: "On the one hand, by ascertaining the causes underlying the particular laws observed in a given case; on the other, by discovering the principles or models which form an intermediate level between meaningless diversity and a scheme which is universally valid. We make *development* intelligible when we reveal the underlying causes which have determined the general direction of events. We make diversity intelligible when we organize it within the compass of a small number of types or concepts" (*MC,* 1:16).

Montesquieu reduced social diversity to manageable proportions by isolating three types or forms of government—the republican, the monarchical, and the despotic. After distinguishing among these three forms, Aron hastened to point out the monumental significance of Montesquieu's typology, for it marked a rather dramatic departure from the traditional or Aristotelian classification of political regimes. For Montesquieu democracy and aristocracy were two species of the same genus; both were republican forms of government. Aristotle, however, classified them as separate types altogether. In Montesquieu's opinion, Aron explained, Aristotle failed to comprehend the true nature of monarchy for the simple reason that monarchy had begun to reveal its potential as a regime only during the postclassical period.

There is an additional and more important reason for this departure from Aristotle's analysis. In Montesquieu the differences between and among the various forms of government reflect the differences between and among the different forms of society. Aristotle had articulated a typology of political forms which he assumed was universally valid but which really applied only to the Greek city-states. Because monarchy, aristocracy, and democracy constituted the three forms of political organization peculiar to the Greek city-states, it was perhaps inevitable that Aristotle would distinguish types of government only by referring to the number of individuals who possessed the sovereign power. This type of analysis, however, "really implied that these three forms of government were, in modern terms, the political superstructure of a certain type of society" (*MC*, 1:21). Montesquieu's contribution was "to combine the analysis of the forms of government with the study of social organization in such a way that each regime is also seen as a certain type of society" (*MC*, 1:22).

Montesquieu combined this novel approach to social organization with what Aron implied was a relatively novel tool of investigation, namely, causal analysis. Although Montesquieu's analysis of causal determinants appears to be rather crude and unsystematic, Aron noted that Montesquieu clearly divided causality into two categories, physical and moral. Under the heading of physical causes falls the influence of territorial size, climate, soil, and geographical milieu. Under the heading of "moral causes" Montesquieu listed such factors as religious belief and the manner in which trade and labor are organized. These causes, Montesquieu believed, all play a role—some to a greater or lesser degree than others, depending on the vagaries of history and geography—in determining how a nation comes to feel and behave.

Taken together, all of these causes contribute to forming what Montesquieu called "the general spirit of a nation," an obscure and difficult concept that Aron took to be directly analogous to the notion of "culture" as understood by American sociologists and anthropologists. The general spirit, Aron explained, "is not a partial cause comparable to the others, but a product of that totality of physical, social, and moral causes." It is a product that "enables us to understand what constitutes the originality and unity of a given collectivity . . . We can proceed from the diversity of causes to the unity of the general spirit without the latter excluding the former" (*MC,* 1:45). In Montesquieu's sociology, Aron added, it is of the utmost importance to recognize that the general spirit is inextricably bound up with the notion of the "principle" of government: The principle is the "sentiment" that maintains or upholds a given regime, and this sentiment is in turn related to a people's way of life as this ethos comes to be expressed through its institutions.

It is here, in Montesquieu's account of social wholes, that we discover one important reason for Aron's abiding interest in the great French thinker: The relation between the form of government and the spirit of a nation is of the same dialectical order as the relation between *motifs* and *mobiles.* The behavior of collectivities, like the behavior of individuals, is at root governed by the incessant and complex interaction between intentional and causal realities. In the final analysis, however, the way men and women govern themselves was "the essential phenomenon" for Montesquieu. He constructed his social types with politics as his point of reference because, like Aristotle, he believed men and women were essentially political creatures.

Although Montesquieu attempted to create a science of society, Aron explained, "he did not take the extreme position of accepting causal explanation as sufficient, but rather opposed to the positive laws, which he explained in a determinist fashion, the laws derived from an analysis of human nature which state the truths of human justice" (*EL,* 51). These truths precede the written laws of society and express those obligations of justice and equity which follow from a recognition of the natural dignity of all men and women. There are, then, three kinds of laws that operate in the sphere of human events: "Beyond the positive laws decreed by various societies, beyond the causal laws which establish relations among these positive laws and the influences operating on them, there must be laws-as-commands which are universally valid, whose legislator is unknown unless it be God himself" (*EL,* 54).

We have now reached the reason for Aron's entire excursus on Montesquieu. These rational laws lie at the foundation not only of Montesquieu's moral judgments but of his scientific method as well, for it was between the suprahistorical laws of justice, which Montesquieu deduced from the first principles of human nature, and the positive laws of society, which he explained causally, that Montesquieu located an intermediate concept, namely, the forms of government. By placing this concept midway between philosophy and science, Montesquieu demonstrated the possibility of a method that joins philosophical interpretation with empirical analysis. Through interpretive analysis, Aron explained, we know what a democracy must be—a regime in which social inequalities must not be too great. Yet because men and women are "intelligent"—a word Montesquieu used which Aron took to be synonymous with the word *free*—they can make decisions or promulgate legal codes that make it impossible for the regime to function. When such poor judgment is exercised, Aron added, it does not mean that we cannot find causes for these decisions. It does mean, however, that, when applied to free-willing and morally responsible beings, judgments of causality can never be more than judgments of probability.

The method of interpretive analysis, in sum, "sets up a kind of ideal type of the functioning of a regime. By comparing this ideal type with reality, we can see that the spirit of a regime is not always respected and that accidents may change the way it functions in particular instances" (*EL*, 53). The logical structure of *The Spirit of the Laws,* Aron concluded, now becomes intelligible. Beginning with the contrast between positive laws and normative realities, Montesquieu introduced the forms of government which are the intelligible wholes established by interpretation and observation. Montesquieu next demonstrated what each type of government implies for various social structures and forms of behavior. Finally, Montesquieu studied the strictly causal relations between a society and its environment. In this way, Aron wrote, "one could determine concurrently the supra-historical laws bound up with the nature of man, the intelligible laws arising out of the structure of a given regime, and the causal relations resulting from the connections between climate, geography, population, and group organization. Finally, one could discover the effects of accidents, i.e., the intervention of unexpected events which disrupt the coherent organization of society" (*EL,* 53).

In this summary overview of Montesquieu's sociology we discover the three essential "elements," or "steps," which constitute the distinctive method of interpretive sociology. First, the sociologist constructs different types, or systems, of behavior, which reveal what Aron called the "underlying," or "implicit," logic of behavior. Second, the sociologist enumerates the general causal determinants that play a role in shaping this underlying logic, or rationality. Finally, by arranging different social structures in a historical sequence, sociologists establish a framework of analysis for historical study and understanding. Only to the degree that sociology achieves these three objectives, Aron concluded—"the definition of the social, analysis of the social consensus (to adopt Auguste Comte's phrase), classification of the diverse historical forms of social structures and relationships"—can sociology "reconcile the two aims, scientific and synthetic, which characterize it" (*EL,* 22).

THE SORBONNE TRILOGY

With these methodological comments in mind, we now turn to the sociological task of the Sorbonne Trilogy—namely, assessing the effects of industrialization on social equality. The problem that Aron set for himself "emerges where Tocqueville's problem meets that of Marx" (*EL,* 34). Tocqueville and Marx, Aron asserted, posed an almost identical sociological problem, "or at least it is not impossible to combine the problem of the two thinkers" (*L,* 40). Both men recognized that the advent of industrial society created a new kind of social inequality and conflict, one in which the working class was pitted against an entrepreneurial class. Marx, of course, predicted that this conflict would intensify to the point of revolutionary upheaval. Tocqueville, however, while freely acknowledging that men and women worked for employers "whom they did not know and often hated," believed that this struggle would diminish over time. Taking stock of this conflict a century later, Aron asked: "What has become of this economic and social inequality? How far has the development of industrial societies tended to weaken social and economic differences, or conversely, to reinforce them?" (*EL,* 41). Defining the problem a bit more precisely, he wrote: "Given that we observe as a major fact in present-day societies, whether Western or Soviet, that science is being applied to industry and that this involves an increase in productivity and growth in the resources of the community and per head of the population, what are the consequences of this for social order?" (*EL,* 41–42).

At the heart of the problem of the modern social order, Aron observed, "I perceive an antinomy between the fact of differentiation and the ideal of equality."[12] Because industrial societies generate social functions that vary greatly in their complexity and value, industrial societies inevitably generate political, social, and economic inequalities. But at the same time, Aron noted, "the immanent purpose of politics is to lead men to participate in their community." This is the fundamental contradiction of social life "for which all regimes seem to provide an imperfect solution." There is therefore no society,

Aron wrote, that "does not attempt to bring about this participation of all men in political life; yet there is none either which can guarantee to all equality in the work they perform or in the prestige they are accorded. All societies and regimes are attempts to reconcile hierarchy with equality, the hierarchy of power with the equality of human dignity" (*EL*, 265). Aron is quite willing to admit that a definitive solution to the problem is conceivable, at least in principle. To believe otherwise, to maintain that we are in the presence of an utterly irresolvable antinomy, is to commit Weber's mistake of believing that values are inherently incompatible. Nevertheless, even though Aron accepted the possibility of reconciling principles that stood flatly opposed to one another, he repeatedly urged his readers to accept the practical necessity of "imperfect reconciliations."

But, if all regimes provide imperfect solutions to the problem of reconciling hierarchy with equality, how do we discriminate or choose among regimes? Do the shortcomings of Western-style democracies and the failures of Eastern-style governments mean that both types of regimes are flawed but equally legitimate solutions to the problems of governance and order? Aron's reflections on this problem constitute what is perhaps his most lasting legacy to the social sciences. "Aron's greatest contribution to contemporary political thought," Roy Pierce explained, "is his effort to link science to choice, political sociology to political decisions."[13]

As we have seen, Aron accepted Weber's proposition that scientific knowledge promises only limited access to the truth, but he did not follow Weber all the way in completely divorcing the world of choice from the world of science: "The fact that action is . . . of a different essence than knowledge can be agreed upon without our necessarily having recourse to the radical heterogeneity of fact and value."[14] Although Aron agreed with Weber that science cannot supply us with one "truth of action," he firmly maintained, in opposition to Weber, that science can

> judge those individuals who are arbitrarily fascinated by one aspect of the real, or who are inclined, by fanaticism, to sacrifice everything to value. In other words, Weber refused to recognize a reasonable politics based on a balanced analysis of the social order because he wanted to reserve the rights of the ethics of conviction, to elevate the pacifist or revolutionary trade unionist who is unconcerned with the consequences of his acts to the same level of dignity as the responsible states-

> man; and finally, in the name of the contradiction of ultimate ends, he wanted to "save" ideologists, although science is particularly suited for unmasking ideologies.

Instead of justifying the "legitimacy of commitment," Aron immediately added, "our intention is to lay the foundation of the legitimacy of scientific criticism."[15] Sociological analysis is thus not only a means of discovering the range of behavioral probabilities peculiar to different types of social wholes but, as Pierce has observed, a guide to political choice as well. According to Aron, reasonable choice begins with an objective analysis of the probable consequences of action, or, in this case, of different sociopolitical regimes. If we are attempting to choose between or among social systems, we must first have recourse to a typology of systems in order to understand the kinds of social wholes we are confronting. Accordingly, we ask the same question of Aron that he asked of Montesquieu: By what tool is meaningless diversity transformed into intellectual order? What, in other words, is the plan of the Sorbonne Trilogy?

Industrial societies, Aron wrote, "like complex societies generally, have three main forms of social differentiation—through the division of labor, through the hierarchy of wealth, power and prestige, and through the plurality of groups which are formed and come into conflict with each other within the society as a whole" (*EL*, 232). There are, in other words, three fundamental aspects of modern social reality: The economic, the social, and the political. Few sociologists would find fault with this rudimentary classification—the division of social reality into these basic elements is a rather common one. Debate is joined over Aron's next step, describing the relations between and among the various levels of modern society, because Aron, like Montesquieu, ascribed a measure of primacy and even autonomy to politics. "In our century," Aron declared, "everything happens as if, within the kinds of society called industrial, it is politics which determines the different variations."[16] In Aron's scheme the different species of industrial society owe their originality to their political systems. Clarifying his point, Aron explained that "all cooperation between men implies authority; now the method by which authority is exercised is the essence of politics. Politics is the major feature of the entire community because it conditions any cooperation between men."[17] Politics, then, exercises a degree of "causal primacy" over the rest of society. More than any other aspect of collective behavior, it is politics that grounds or determines a society's way of life.

Aron granted a measure of existential primacy to politics as well: "In relation to man, politics is more important than economics, by definition, because politics is concerned more directly with the very meaning of existence."[18] Politics may for this reason be regarded as the "interpretive aspect" of social life, or that dimension of collective association in which men and women give meaning to their existence as a whole. This should not be taken to mean that politics is free from conflict; Aron never turned a blind eye to the violent passions that lurk beneath the surface of even the most orderly political systems. But we delude ourselves, he maintained, if politics is defined solely by the struggle for power. "Anyone who does not see that there is a 'struggle for power' element is naive; anyone who sees nothing but this aspect is a false realist."[19]

The autonomy and primacy of politics, however, is only a partial one. Aron repeatedly insisted that he was not exchanging a doctrine of political determinism for a doctrine of economic determinism. Politics is primarily an ideal phenomenon existing "only in and through intentions; it is refracted differently in every consciousness and only attains intelligibility in and through the consciousness of the political scientist."[20] No single theory of politics, then, can identify "a list of variables as causes which we only have to mechanically pass in review: in a concrete case, the causes do not form a system, none is closed in upon itself."[21] The sort of primacy or autonomy Aron had in mind, therefore, was a very limited one.

In contrast to the essential indeterminacy of politics stands what Aron termed the "quantitative determinacy" of economics. As that aspect of social life which is concerned with the production and distribution of material goods and services, economics is located closer to the plane of necessity than is politics. Comparing the French and the industrial revolutions, Aron noted that the French Revolution was essentially a political or an ideal phenomenon; that is, it was precipitated by the human commitment to a normative principle regarding the best form of social organization. The industrial revolution, on the other hand, was an economic phenomenon driven by the forces of necessity, forces that, precisely because they are beyond human control, "continue to shield the major activity of our time [i.e., industrialization] from any conscious organization."[22] Because economic life is governed predominantly by the laws of necessity, economic problems are more amenable to quantitative analysis and resolution than political ones. Economics, in short, "which springs from the essential poverty of the species, constitutes the solution to the problem of man's relationship to nature."[23] Politics, "which originates in the inequality of men in society and the plurality of sovereign collectivities, constitutes a solution to man's relation with man."[24]

Occupying the middle rank in Aron's great chain of being is the social proper, a dimension of collective existence which exhibits properties of both freedom and necessity, or politics and economics. Like Marx, Aron regarded social life as an arena of conflict and struggle. Industrialization inevitably begets a stratified society in which groups may be roughly divided—very roughly, Aron emphasized—into "the maxima and the minima, the haves and the have-nots."[25] These groups do in fact press conflicting socioeconomic claims, particularly in regard to issues such as economic growth and the distribution of incomes. Yet for Aron, unlike Marx, the socioeconomic groups created by the economic forces unleashed by industrialization are not the only groups that constitute and affect social reality. In Aron's opinion "it is the structure of ruling categories, and not class relations, that determines the essence of social regimes."[26] Social behavior, in other words, is decisively affected by the kind of political regime controlling the levers of power. The state cannot eliminate the feeling of otherness and alienation if the disparity among incomes or living conditions is too great, Aron admitted. "But the right or prohibition of class organization, determine, in part, the degree of reality of that evanescent phenomenon known as 'class-consciousness.'" Thus, "a sociology of classes divorced from the sociology of political regimes has become the absurdity of our time."[27]

After explaining what features or properties all social wholes have in common, Aron then identified the major variable that enabled him to distinguish different species of the same genus. Given his emphasis on the significance of political life, it comes as no surprise to discover that, in constructing his social types, Aron attributed supreme importance to one feature of the political regime in particular—namely, the nature of the party system. When one party has a legal monopoly on the exercise of power, there exists what Aron termed a "monopolistic party system." When two or more parties have the legal right to compete for the exercise of power, there exists a "constitutional-pluralist system." The Soviet Union and China obviously fall into the first category, the Western democracies in the second. Describing the behavioral possibilities of each type of system consists of analyzing the consequences that the decisive fact of the party system implies for each of the three dimensions of social wholes. How are these consequences determined? By applying each of Aron's three methodological steps to the modality of social life under consideration: For each system an ideal type is constructed, causal determinants are listed, and actual historical developments are charted.

After analyzing the behavioral properties associated with each regime on each level of analysis, Aron then compared the two systems on the basis of the degree to which they consistently adhere to or fulfill the values they espouse, a step strictly prohibited in Weber's methodology for the social sciences. On this level of comparison Aron saw a yawning gap between the monopolistic and the constitutional-pluralistic party system. Constitutional-pluralistic regimes are imperfect, Aron maintained, "because they contain either too great a degree of oligarchy or demagogy and invariably suffer through the difficulty they have in being effective."[28] Aron termed these flaws "imperfections of practice." As Pierce explains, they are "imperfections in the implementation of the system which are not intrinsic to the system itself."[29] The imperfection of the monopolistic party system, however, is of a different order. If we imagine a homogeneous society without conflicts of interest among different social groups, then "the monopoly of the party is no longer indispensable." But, Aron added, "if public opinion is forbidden to express itself freely, if uniformity of thought is maintained, the society is no longer homogeneous. From the moment when society is no longer homogeneous, the group which imposes its will by force can carry out a task, which is in itself admirable, but it can no longer claim that it has established democracy. In the end it comes down to the question of how to have a perfect society; it contradicts itself when it puts forward the one-party regime as the realization of democracy."[30] The imperfections of the monopolistic party regimes are thus inherently imperfect.

Aron never claimed that sociological analysis could tell its practitioners exactly what to do. He did claim, however, that empirical analysis could tell men and women what was *reasonable* to do. From Aron's perspective a reasonable choice is one in which various courses of action are judged not simply by the intentions or the will of the chooser (as Kant had maintained) but also by their consequences. It is unreasonable to ignore or overlook consequences; to do so would be to act dogmatically or arbitrarily. An individual does not act irrationally, then, by choosing a flawed or imperfect regime if the regime's shortcomings have no bearing on the individual's goals or values. "It is possible," Aron maintained, "that, in certain circumstances, this essentially imperfect regime may be preferable to the effectively imperfect regime."[31] But, as Pierce noted, an individual "does act unreasonably if he chooses it because of a goal which it proclaims but which it is intrinsically unable to achieve."[32] The values on the basis of which one makes one's choice, in other words, must be related in some degree to the contingencies of existence.

Aron, therefore, attempted to occupy the middle ground between Weber's notion of free, arbitrary moral choice, on the one hand, and the positivist belief in scientifically demonstrable moral choice, on the other; sociological analysis requires one to weigh the advantages and disadvantages of different regimes, while moral reasoning requires one to take the findings of empirical analysis into account. Because a judgment of what is desirable is conditioned by—but not limited to—a judgment of what is possible, we may compare the nature of a reasonable choice to the nature of self-knowledge: In both cases there is a dialectical relationship, or what Aron called simply a "coming-and-going" between intentional and empirical realities which affects the final judgment.

One may wonder, however, whether Aron has here hit upon the judicious combination of idealism and empiricism which he was aiming for or whether he in fact fell rather heavily between the stools. A methodology that can mark out both the "range and meaning" of the political options available to modern industrial societies, Pierce observed, clearly "suggests that science, by confirming the claims of an ideology, can also justify it." If it is only those institutions implied by constitutional-pluralist regimes that support freedom, Pierce reasoned—parties, elections, parliaments—then liberals seem to be justified in "attributing as much value to those institutions" as they do to freedom itself.[33]

Yet this argument runs afoul of a cardinal tenet of Aron's critical idealism—namely, the notion that freedom is a purely formal reality that can never be completely incarnated in a specific set of institutions or actions. Readers thus find Aron straining to qualify, even disavow, the normative judgments of his own social science. Declaring, for example, that Western observers were right in prophesying that democratic institutions were "destined for the same triumphal progress across the globe as motor-cars or electricity," Aron nevertheless insisted that Westerners would be wrong to attribute "universal significance to the ideologies which glorify these institutions."[34] But, as Pierce observed, this conclusion is no more satisfying than the first because Aron "believes that the constitutional-pluralist system, with the institutions it implies, is the only system which will actually express those formal values once traditionalism is overwhelmed by the forces of modernization."[35] Thus, rather than achieving some sort of balance between the empirical and the normative, here Aron's dialectical logic forces him to hesitate between the equally unpleasant alternatives of dogmatism and relativism.

Whatever its shortcomings, Aron's doctrine of reasonable choice at least has this benefit: It immediately undercuts Weber's glaring and dogmatic contrast between the ethics of conviction and the ethics of responsibility. Although Aron made it clear that Weber never equated the ethics of responsibility with a vulgar Machiavellianism, Aron also hastened to add that Weber's refusal to discriminate among values or political ends forced him "to run the risk of justifying on the one hand the false realists who scorn the moralists' reproach, on the other the false idealists who condemn indiscriminately all policies which do not conform to their ideals and who end by contributing consciously or otherwise, to the destruction of the existing order, to the advantage of blind revolutionaries or tyrants."[36] If the power of the nation, whatever its culture or regime, is the supreme value—and it most certainly was for Weber—then "what reason have we for saying 'no' to what Weber would have rejected with horror?"[37] Despite this trenchant criticism, Aron did not dismiss Weber's distinction altogether; rather, he simply eased the pressure Weber had applied in pushing this antinomy to its point of maximum theoretical clarity. In politics, Aron wrote, "in action, we are divided between two attitudes . . . an attitude which I shall call instrumental . . . seeks to bring about results consistent with our objectives . . . and another attitude, which I shall call moral, which very often drives us to speak and act without concern for others or for the effects we have on events . . . Reasonable action is inspired by both these attitudes, but it was not without purpose, and I believe it illuminating, to have stated in all their severity the ideal forms of those two attitudes between which each of us wavers" (*MC,* 2:256). Between these extremes there is room for compromise, for a decision guided by reason rather than iron will or fanaticism.

Yet compromise requires moderate conditions of choice, and extreme situations in which compromise becomes difficult, if not impossible, are hardly exceptional circumstances in politics: "The risk of such a situation increases as soon as there is a conflict . . . Now Max Weber judged, not without reason, that politics is essentially conflict between nations, and between individuals."[38] But what Weber failed to see, Aron pointed out, was "the gap . . . between the power of arms and the prosperity of nations," an oversight that had its origins in the fact that Weber was "too much of a Marxist . . . too pessimistic in his interpretation of modern society." Because capitalism for Weber was simply another manifestation of the all-embracing process of rationalization, a process that threatened to rob human life of its freedom and vitality, he completely misjudged or ignored "the prospects of well-being for the masses thanks to the increase of productivity, or the reduction of class conflicts and perhaps of international conflicts in an age in which wealth depends on efficient labor and not on the dimensions of territory" (*MC,* 2:301). What Weber overlooked, in other words, was the possibility that industrial society could generate, at least in part, the moderate conditions of choice so essential to "reasonable" politics.

As one of the earliest advocates of industrialization in postwar France, Aron placed a high value on the benefits of economic growth. Only an industrial society, he maintained, can eventually provide the conditions of a decent life for everyone. Technological progress promises to liberate humanity from servile work and, in so doing, soften class conflict in the process. "American prosperity," Aron once declared, is in fact "the best guarantee of obtaining the objectives the European Left has always advocated."[39] Aron thus saw an integral connection between material gain and social progress: By reducing economic and social inequalities and by enlarging the equality of opportunity, industrial societies advance the cause of egalitarianism and so contribute to the creation of a peaceful and moderate social order.

Unlike Comte or Spencer, however, Aron refused to proclaim the coming of an industrial millennium in which all of the crises of modern society would be resolved by the irresistible logic of technical rationality. Despite his willingness to trumpet the benefits of modernity, he nevertheless warned that industrialization frequently bestows mixed blessings on its practitioners. Not only does industrial progress often produce ugly and undesirable side effects—Aron was always quick to underscore the environmental costs of industrialization, for example, as well as the alienation, or "anomie," which results from assuming one's place in a specialized division of labor—but, perhaps even more significantly, industrialization by its very nature generates hierarchies of power, prestige, and wealth, realities that fly in the very teeth of egalitarianism.

But between the folds of compatibility and contradiction lies the possibility of compromise because neither equality nor industrialization can exist without the other. Just as industrialization contributes to the creation of equal conditions by raising the standards of living and lowering the barriers to opportunity, so too does industrialization presuppose equality. Beyond a certain level of inequality, Aron explained, there no longer exists the human communication necessary to establish or preserve any society, industrial or otherwise.

Like history, then, social life is suspended between the poles of two opposites-in-relation. Because either extreme—absolute equality or absolute hierarchy—destroys true community, humanity must learn to live with "half-truths," or with the knowledge that there are limits to what may be accomplished in the name of higher values. In this vein it is worth noting that Aron's political sociology was not directed toward achieving a definitive or permanent solution to the problem of reconciling hierarchy with equality but toward reconciling "the partisans of hierarchy with the equalitarians."[40] In entering the debate over hierarchy and equality, Pierce explained, Aron's intention "was to argue that industrial society is hospitable to both principles, provided they are not pushed to their extremes, which represent opposing concepts of the good life and are ultimately incompatible." A reconciliation of these opposing outlooks, Pierce added, will not happen automatically: "It can only come about if the partisans of equality and of hierarchy abandon unconditional ideological attachment to these values and exercise 'reasonable cooperation.'"[41] Or, in Aron's words, "Industrial society *may* teach people to be reasonable if it ceases to be regarded as the instrument of a beast of prey."[42]

The man of action who commands Aron's respect and admiration is thus the man of restraint and accommodation. "The judgment of historical man can never be pure," Aron wrote, "because it is always the result of compromise."[43] Or, as he observed on another occasion, "Man without God risks his life for impure causes and cannot avoid doing so. He knows that humanity can create itself only through doubt and error. He acts not out of a will to be God but out of a wisdom that willingly falls short of the absolute."[44] The politics of reason is thus characterized by tolerance, patience, and, above all else, sympathetic understanding, or the ability to put oneself in another's shoes. Understanding was in fact the virtue, or quality of mind, which Aron tried to bring to bear on everything he wrote, both as a scholar and as a journalist. "I have done my best," Aron once declared, "to elicit the example of an effort, one that must always be renewed, to understand others and myself."[45] This does not preclude "the taking of a stand," he explained, but it does temper the Pharisaic impulse to assume that one is always right or that others—even Marxists—are always wrong.

Aron's notion of moderate, prudent, and reasonable action stands in sharp contrast not only to Weber's idea of choice but also to his idea of charismatic leadership. On this point Aron's attitude toward Charles de Gaulle is instructive, for it was the style of de Gaulle and the form of the Fifth Republic which most closely approached what Weber had so desperately hoped would emerge in Germany. How did the politics of understanding take to the politics of grandeur? At first, not well at all. In an article entitled "In the Shadow of the Bonapartes," a thinly veiled riposte to de Gaulle and Gaullism written during the summer of 1943, when de Gaulle's popularity was growing, Aron analyzed and lamented France's historic infatuation with a peculiar form of authoritarianism, one that "filled the void left by the disappearance of kings and the powerlessness of parliaments."[46] Whatever its short-term appeal, Bonapartism is, as Aron saw it, ultimately rent by an internal contradiction that will destroy not only the regime itself but the nation under its leadership: "It drains sovereignty from the people that it pretends to lead. It constrains and reduces to extreme servitude the people who are allegedly sovereign by reducing plebiscites to farces, by making into law the whims or good pleasure of one individual. Far from genuinely uniting groups and parties, it allows all the divisions in society to subsist by hiding them for a time and limits itself to superimposing the arbitrary on chaos." Because this regime has no authority other than "popular acclamations," Aron added, "le César" is driven by an insatiable need to refire the source of his authority and to that end tirelessly undertakes new adventures: "Condemned to subordinate interests of his country to the transitory needs of his rule, he ends by ordering strategy according to the needs of demagogy." In this way "the adventure of one man culminates in tragedy for a nation."[47]

Over time, because his worst fears were never realized, Aron softened his judgment of de Gaulle. In fact, he came to see in de Gaulle the promise of a republic that could rise above the "regime of the parties" and, in so doing, attain the stability and legitimacy that had eluded France for so long. Reversing his earlier assessment that the president offered little more than authoritarianism with a human face, Aron argued that the party that de Gaulle created in 1947, the Rassemblement du Peuple Français (RPF), was a necessary response to the growing threat of communism in France and to the increasing instability of French political institutions. In fact, alarmed by the growth of the Communist Party in France and, some speculate, wearied of being the perennial intellectual and political outsider, Aron came full circle and joined the RPF in 1947, a move that shocked his friends.

Although Aron had reservations about the wisdom of de Gaulle's foreign policy, he was for the most part supportive of de Gaulle's domestic leadership. Indeed, Aron once described de Gaulle's presidency in words that surely left those familiar with "Shadow of the Bonapartes" in open-mouthed wonder. Of de Gaulle's tenure during the immediate postwar period, Aron concluded that legality was as important to the president as authority. Conceding that de Gaulle had no taste at all for the "games, poisons and enchantments of the regime of the parties," Aron nevertheless insisted that de Gaulle had no interest in unlimited power either. "Far from dreaming of personal power," Aron wrote, the French leader "cherishes the ambition to give France durable institutions at long last."[48]

Yet, for all of his support and respect, Aron was never an "orthodox" Gaullist, if by "orthodox Gaullism" one means a degree of personal devotion to the general which approached "a kind of feudal tie." Despite the personal distance between himself and de Gaulle, Aron believed that France was deeply indebted to its leader. It was de Gaulle and de Gaulle alone, Aron once declared, "who preserved our freedoms and set himself between confusion in men's minds and chaos."[49] It may someday happen that de Gaulle's regime will develop into a democratic one, Aron wrote in the immediate postwar years. But for the moment "it is the work of a single man, admittedly a great man." Nevertheless, Aron concluded, "I persist in hoping that France will someday be capable of governing herself, otherwise than by unconditional faith in a prince, even if one sometimes rejoices that the 'cunning of reason' could have made a worse choice of the Prince."[50]

In this grudging tribute we catch sight of what is fundamentally wrong with charismatic leadership—it disdains "ordinary *legalité*" in favor of what Aron termed "mysterious *legalité*."[51] And ordinary *legalité* lies at the heart of what in Aron's opinion constitutes an authentically democratic regime. In Aron's words, "For peoples as well as individuals, liberty is not recognized by the more or less illusory consciousness that individuals have of it, but by the respect for the laws, which leads to respect for persons."[52] This is why classical liberal thought placed such emphasis on the separation of power; such a division, Aron observed, constitutes "the rampart of legality *par excellence,* the obstacle that the prudence of the legislators must raise up against the arbitrary." In fact, political philosophers such as Montesquieu believed that the separation of powers was not simply a check "against abuse and illegality" but was in fact "constitutive of liberty itself."[53] For Montesquieu (as well as for Aron) liberty was defined above all by "the reciprocal limitation of powers, as a guarantee of legality," and this existed only in moderate, limited regimes.[54]

Stripped of its great powers, great leaders, and great doctrines, democratic society thus appeared to Aron exactly as it had appeared to Tocqueville—a shallow, restless tumult devoid of brilliance or grandeur. "Doomed to moderateness," to use Aron's phrase, democracy is by its very nature subject to the law of mediocrity. Yet for Aron this was but a small price to pay for the matchless privilege of living in an open society devoted to tolerance and the preservation of critical freedom. And if tolerance is born of doubt, Aron added, then "let us teach everyone to doubt all the models and utopias, to challenge all the prophets of redemption and the heralds of catastrophe." If only they can eliminate fanaticism, then "let us pray for the advent of the skeptics."[55]

This passage from *The Opium of the Intellectuals,* one of Aron's early works, dropped like a bombshell over the heads of the French intelligentsia. Indeed, the book as a whole, Aron recalled, created a furor in France. To the French intellectual Aron's defense of mediocrity and his call for skepticism signaled a crisis of faith and a loss of hope. Far better to live with passion, the Left believed, to commit oneself unreservedly to the cause of the Revolution, than to accept the gradgrind realities of an industrial society. Far better, in other words, "to be wrong with Sartre than right with Aron."[56]

Although such criticism dogged Aron all of his life, he never wavered in his conviction that the politics of understanding was a politics of lowered expectations. Ever suspicious of those who spoke of wholesale social reconstruction ("those strange builders who begin by destroying"), Aron placed his confidence in a progress of incremental adjustment, in measured change wrought by the slow, hard work of negotiation and compromise. The refusal to be moved by the rhetoric of those who propose sweeping reforms or dramatic changes, Aron insisted, "does not lead to insipid pragmatism or lessen the value of intellectual controversy. On the contrary, it encourages a return to rational discussion of problems which, in any case, must be solved pragmatically, and lays bare the eternal and conflicting aspirations in the hearts of men and in the turmoil of history."[57] Aron freely admitted that, in comparison with those on the radical Left, or even in comparison with many "liberal Americans," he was indeed a pessimist: "I do not believe that it is an easy task to shape either human nature or human society."[58] Aron explained, however, that pessimists of his sort do in fact "seek constantly to improve society [but] in a piecemeal fashion. The only thing is that [we] have no global solution, whereas those with a reputation for optimism generally believe in a system that could never exist."[59]

To "moderate pessimists" such as Aron the only kind of regime compatible with such scaled-down expectations of history and human nature is a pluralist one, or one in which different and conflicting interests struggle peacefully for political, economic, and social power. Although such a politics sought to protect and advance individual freedom, Aron was well aware that pluralism was not without its costs: "It maintains an atmosphere of division and discord in the body politic, it blurs the sense of communal responsibilities and jeopardizes internal peace and friendship." Nevertheless, "in spite of everything," pluralism must be promoted because it is "a means of limiting arbitrary power and ensuring a legal expression to discontent, and [stands] as a symbol of the lay impartiality of the State and the autonomy of the human mind."[60]

Have these piecemeal reforms added up to anything? Is humanity making any progress in its slow crawl toward the end of history? If democracy is indeed a gamble, as Aron once suggested, or a "wager on the capacity of man to learn and understand,"[61] can it be said with any confidence that democracies are winning the bet? Or that men and women are making headway in their efforts to learn and understand?

For all of his pessimism Aron was surprisingly sanguine about the future. "World opinion today," he wrote, "understands more clearly than ever before the facts of modern economic life and its potentialities for peace."[62] The possible causes of class conflict, for example, "now seem less important than the things that make for interdependence."[63] There is nothing earth-shaking or even new in this idea, Aron admitted; after all, liberal economists have been patiently explaining for more than a century how trade benefits all parties. What is new, however, is the fact that these convictions, "formerly held by only a few, are now spreading," thanks to recent knowledge and experience. In Germany the price of defeat in World War II "has been, not poverty, as hitherto, but prosperity."[64] World War II may have cost Europe as a whole its colonies, power, and diplomatic prestige, but it "has achieved an unprecedented level of production and productivity." At the same time, "ideologies are also becoming discredited and tending to lose their emotional effectiveness." Economists have learned to control economic cycles with greater skill and, by so doing, have drained ideological invective of much of its force. In the West, Aron added, "and perhaps even in the Soviet Union, men no longer think of one regime as being imperialist or exploiting, and another as being peaceful and just. All regimes are thought of as imperfect and none is immune from injustice, none is subject to the law of impoverishment."[65]

Given these trends, what may we now hope for? What, in other words, does continued progress demand of human action? Those familiar with Aron's broadsides against utopian optimism or who see in Aron only a dark, brooding pessimism will undoubtedly be caught short by his answer. "In tranquil and happy epochs," he declared, "millennialism teaches us never to be satisfied with the results so far obtained."[66] Although "the promise may be all but destroyed" by the requirement of tranquillity Aron placed on it, Pierce observed, this statement nevertheless signals a concession to millennialism that even Albert Camus, "the philosopher of revolt," might have been unwilling to grant.[67]

Indeed, for all of his forceful polemics against those "with a reputation for optimism," in his own thinking Aron gave optimism rather wide berth. In encouraging his fellow citizens to stay the liberal democratic course during the postwar period, for example, he promised a rather heady payoff should they succeed in doing so. In the Old Continent, Aron wrote, "the scale of greatness remains that of the national states. Always of the second rank when compared to the colossus [of the United States and USSR], France will recover a radiance and an influence of the first rank on the condition that, by its interior stability and its prosperity, it creates a political and spiritual center around which will gather the smaller nations."[68] This stirring, almost breathless description of the future—which immediately calls to mind Victor Duruy's ringing declaration that "France is the moral center of the world"[69]—is remarkable not just for what it expects from French foreign policy but for what it demands of French domestic politics as well. "A great nation," Aron declared, "lives and prospers only by the constant and mysterious inspiration of a great idea," or by what Aron elsewhere termed a "task" (*un projet*). "Does France still have a task?" Aron asked in the immediate aftermath of World War II. "This is not only the decisive question," he added, "it is, one could say, the *only* question." France did indeed still have a task, and a rather lofty one at that: "The French idea," Aron maintained, "is to protect what is human at an hour when all conspire to deliver society to the inhumanity of enslaved masses and the pyramids of steel."[70]

In attempting to infuse French national politics with this rather bracing measure of moral concern, Aron clearly drew not from the precepts of classical French liberalism, a philosophy that accepts the permanence of the struggle for power, but from the tenets of French republicanism, a philosophy of public virtue and a self-sworn enemy of liberalism. In France, Tony Judt observed, it was fin-de-siècle republicanism that "first deployed to the full the idea that France *stood* for something, proselytizing an idea of civic virtue and implicitly denying any potential or actual differences or divergences in the nation itself." If there was a goal to which this strain of republicanism aspired, Judt added, "it was thus the creation of 'Frenchness,' an identity whose self-ascribed moral superiority would compensate for the gloomier aspects of recent history."[71]

But how this kind of idealism comports with the sort of pluralism Aron hoped would take root in France is far from clear. What is clear, however, is that these two impulses are at odds within Aron's own work. Spurring France on to become the "spiritual and political center" of Europe immediately after the war, Aron seemed to sour on the idea in the 1950s, when he wrote that "the longing for a purpose, for communion with the people, for something controlled by an idea and a will," is, quite frankly, "not for us."[72]

Aron's ambivalent idealism manifested itself again when he became engaged in the "end of ideology" debate that gripped intellectuals on both sides of the Atlantic at mid-century. Although the anti-ideologists (whose number included Daniel Bell, George Kennan, Seymour Martin Lipset, and Arthur Schlesinger Jr., among others) formed no single school of thought, they generally agreed that social action should be governed wherever possible not by the abstractions of ideological thinking but by the more modest propositions of the social sciences. "Few serious minds," Daniel Bell had written, "believe any longer that one can set down 'blueprints' and through 'social engineering' bring about a utopia of social harmony." Given the dismal performance of totalitarian regimes, Bell added, "the ladder to the City of Heaven can no longer be a 'faith ladder' but an empirical one: a utopia has to specify *where* one wants to go, *how* to get there, the costs of the enterprise, and some realization of and justification for the determination of *who* is to pay."[73] The good society at work was thus a relatively unexciting and unimaginative affair. As Aron envisioned it, an open, or "nonideological," society was one in which citizens, aided by the findings of policy analysts, would come together to pass judgment on a multitude of partial and ad hoc policy proposals and decide on small but important matters such as the price of farm subsidies or the increase in wages for public employees.

Even in *The Opium of the Intellectuals,* however, which was widely regarded as something of a manifesto for the anti-ideology movement, Aron was nagged by doubts and anxieties over the pragmatic, nonideological incrementalism that marks pluralist regimes. "The substitution of scientific thought for religious truth," he observed, "cannot but entail a spiritual crisis: it is difficult to be satisfied with a provisional truth, incontestable but limited, not guaranteed to console."[74] By 1960 Aron's idealism was in full voice. As Tracy Strong points out, Aron complained that many of those who rushed to embrace or tout the end of ideology did so to escape the responsibilities of action. "Under pretense of escaping from ideology," Strong observed, "such men have merely uncritically embraced the dominant one and called it reality."[75] For that reason Aron believed that ideology remained a necessary motive force for action.

Despite his open concern over the costs of living in an industrial society, Aron firmly believed not only that the costs were far outweighed by the benefits but also that those benefits were being globally distributed. Does this mean that the industrial society that Comte foresaw has finally come to pass, that humanity has become "socially uniform" and "diplomatically unified"? Unfortunately, Aron concluded, this judgment is exceedingly premature. Even if industrial societies do come to resemble one another, "there is no guarantee that they will get on with each other."[76] As Aron explained:

> It is what men hold sacred that divides men most. A pagan or a Jew who remains unconverted to Christianity is a challenge. Can the man who knows nothing of the God of the Salvationist religions be a fellow-man, or is he someone with whom we can feel nothing in common? Whatever our answer, it is with him that the new "spiritual community" must be established—as the superstructure, or the foundation, of the material community now arising from the scientific, technical and economic unity that historical necessity is imposing on men who are still more conscious of what divides them than of what unites them.[77]

In the end, then, industrial society does not guarantee either human happiness or social unity. An industrial social order confines itself simply to meeting the material conditions of well-being and leaves the responsibility for discovering personal meaning and significance to individual choice. This is, to be sure, a rather modest and sober reading of modern society; one will find no trumpet call to grandeur in Aron. Nevertheless, there can be dignity and decency in the modern industrial world, and for Aron that is greatness enough.

3 *Peace and War*

The Descent to Theory

LIKE SO MANY OTHERS of his generation, Raymond Aron found himself drawn to the study of international relations by the ineluctable force of World War II. Writing as a journalist-in-exile during the war for *La France Libre,* a monthly news and cultural review published in London, Aron applied his enormous erudition and a recently discovered talent for journalism to the pressing task of analyzing current events. Together with André Labarthe, Robert Marjolin, and Stanislas Syzmonyk, Aron served on the editorial staff of *La France Libre* for five years, turning out more than one hundred articles on politics, economics, and various military campaigns conducted during the war.

Despite the brilliant success of the review, Aron was plagued by a nagging sense of ignorance and inadequacy. What right did he have, he asked himself, to pass judgment on international relations before and during the war when he really knew next to nothing about the problems of global diplomacy, the balance of forces, or military strategy? Thus, it was "remorse or at least regret," Aron explained, which prompted his decision to take up the problems of war and peace.[1]

Although Aron produced several interesting and provocative studies on international relations during the years shortly after the war, they were nothing more than exploratory excursions into the field, potshots at the topic written while he was actively engaged as a journalist for *Le Figaro.* Once back in the university, however, he braced himself for a more systematic study. "As a commentator on international events for *Le Figaro,*" Aron related, "I felt the need to study both the military and historical context of the decisions that, as a journalist, I was supposed to understand and interpret."[2] The result was *Peace and War: A Theory of International Relations.*[3]

Peace and War is a work of heroic proportions. Comparable in scope and profundity to Hans Morgenthau's *Politics among Nations* and Quincy Wright's *Study of War, Peace and War* immediately established Aron as a leading figure in the field of international relations. Like many substantial works, *Peace and War* is heavy sledding. Its difficulty lies not in Aron's prose—one reviewer, in fact, breathing an audible sigh of relief, pointed out that in place of the difficult language of the *Introduction,* Aron had substituted a "prodigiously lucid and limpid style which is so effective in the communication of his thought"[4]—but in the scope and conceptual complexity of Aron's presentation. Not only is the book lengthy (it runs to some eight hundred pages), but it also seems to lack a center of gravity or a fundamental idea that would bestow a systematic coherence upon the work as a whole and enable readers to keep their bearings while tracking the lines of what seems at times to be an endless maze of arguments and observations. Stanley Hoffmann, a former student of Aron, spoke to this issue in his lengthy analysis of *Peace and War.* Aron's theory of international relations, Hoffmann wrote, "is not a synthesis centered on a major demonstration or flowing from major hypothesis—neither the subject matter nor the method lend themselves to such treatment; it is a mosaic construction of partial analyses often filled with doubt and negation." But, Hoffmann was quick to add, "I say mosaic and not motley, for there is a unity provided by Aron's very conception of his purpose: to understand in all its aspects the logic of one specific form of behavior."[5]

In *Peace and War* Aron attempted to construct a comprehensive theory of international relations, one that would explain the logic of interstate relations, cast light on the moral problem in statecraft, and sketch out the elements of a workable foreign policy for the West. Its practical turn is particularly significant. Although Aron never claimed as much, some commentators believe that for all of its abstractness, *Peace and War* was written primarily for American statesmen as they attempted to steer the United States and the Atlantic Alliance through the turbulent years of the 1960s and 1970s.

My task in this chapter is to illuminate how the logic of Aron's categorial framework gave form and substance to this project—in particular, whether it allowed for greater consistency in addressing the problems of foreign policy than it did in approaching the problems of domestic policy. In *Peace and War,* as in all his major works, Aron tried to strike a balance between two conceptual opposites; satisfied with neither realism nor idealism, at least in their conventional formulations, he tried to establish a via media between the two. Unfortunately, the middle way Aron crafted does more to exacerbate the dilemmas and harsh realities of statecraft than it does to alleviate them.

I begin by searching for a definition of *theory*. *Peace and War* is, after all, a theory of international relations and stands, in fact, as the only claim to theory Aron ever made. How, then, did Aron use this term?

"WHAT IS A THEORY OF INTERNATIONAL RELATIONS?"

It is surprisingly difficult to understand exactly what Aron meant by the word *theory*. There is, first, the problem of his rather confusing terminology. Theory, as Aron used the term, is both a level and a moment of analysis. As a level of analysis, theory implies a body of knowledge establishing the logical connections between propositions of empirical fact. Situating theory as a link in Aron's conceptual chain thus seems easy enough: It hovers below method but above concrete fact. As a moment of analysis, however, theory refers to something else entirely. In Aron's philosophy of the social sciences it also refers to the first step, or moment, in developing a theory—that of defining concepts and locating an object of analysis.

Second, even as a level of analysis, Aron nowhere offers a definition of theory which systematically distinguishes theory from model, hypothesis, or any other related type of conceptual abstraction. Although he began his article "What Is a Theory of International Relations?" with the promising complaint that few words in the social sciences are used as carelessly as the word *theory*, Aron ended the piece by declaring that analyzing the difference between terms such as *general theory* and *model* would entail an excessively long digression "in view of the aims of this short essay" and by wondering if theory is not, after all, simply the "critical or questioning equivalent of a philosophy."[6] In the same article Aron also offered a brief definition of theory which so blurred the elementary distinction between theory and method that it is virtually impossible to distinguish between the two. In order to understand the structure and significance of theory in Aron's thought, we return to our first level of analysis, epistemology, and thus to a fundamental theme of this study—namely, that knowledge can never be separated from its object.

As we have seen, a cardinal tenet of Aron's epistemology is that knowledge cannot be defined by a priori criteria. Aron's study of historical understanding, for example, did not measure historical knowledge against "a type of knowledge proclaimed in advance as the only truly scientific one" but followed instead the "natural movement" that proceeds "from knowledge of self to that of the collective development" in order to discover precisely what kind of knowledge history itself affords. In doing so, Aron tacitly suggested that Aristotle's timeworn rule still remained essential: One should expect no more precision than the subject matter can bear. From this it follows that the meaning of theory is dependent to some degree upon the meaning of its object. We cannot determine the structure and function of economic theory, for example, until we have first determined the nature of economic behavior. Similarly, we cannot establish the nature and purpose of a theory of international relations until we have first determined the nature of international relations.

The scope and structure of theory, however, is not accounted for by referring solely to material criteria, that is, by referring simply to the object of the analysis. There are abstract, logical criteria to consider as well. *Peace and War,* Aron explained, was in fact written "to illustrate a method, applicable to other subjects, which shows both the limits of our knowledge and the conditions of historical choices" (4). Theory, then, stems from the application of a methodology just as methodology derives from the application of an epistemology.[7] We immediately see that the structure of theory, like the structure of all intentional objects, is thoroughly dialectical.

In the field of international relations two very different intellectual paradigms, behavioralism and traditionalism, contend with each other in staking out the range and function of theory. As descendants of positivism, behavioralists apply the techniques and methods of modern science to the study of international relations. Although the quest for vast, overarching laws of behavior has long since gone out of vogue, the determination to affirm only that which can be empirically verified has not. Traditionalism, by contrast, of which Aron offered the work of Hans Morgenthau as a prime example, relies on interpretation as a source of knowledge. The difference between these two approaches to international relations, he explained, freely quoting Morgenthau, can be compared to the difference between a snapshot and painted portrait: "The photograph shows everything that can be seen by the naked eye. The painted portrait . . . shows something that the naked eye cannot see: the human essence of the person who is portrayed" (*PW,* 3).

Rather than opt for one approach over the other, Aron declared, *Peace and War* would "clarify" and "transcend" the debate because these two approaches to theory are not contradictory but compatible: "Rational schematics and sociological propositions constitute successive moments in the conceptual elaboration of a social universe" (*PW,* 3). This insistence on distinguishing and combining rational schematics and sociological propositions clearly has its origins in Aron's basic epistemological distinction between understanding and explanation and thus anticipates further refinement. Thus, it comes as no surprise to read that Aron would in fact proceed "from formal theory, to the determination of causes, and then to the analysis of a specific set of circumstances" (*PW*, 3–4).

These three moments of analysis define the principal topical divisions of *Peace and War.* To formal theory belongs the section on theory (subtitled "Concepts and Systems"); to the determination of causes belongs the section on sociology ("Determinants and Constants"); and to the analysis of a specific set of circumstances belongs the section on history ("The Global System in the Thermonuclear Age"). There is also a fourth section, "praxeology," or the theory of action ("The Antinomies of Diplomatic-Strategic Conduct"). Because these three moments of analysis are obviously indebted to the three methodological objectives outlined in the last chapter, we need not repeat the discussion relating these three moments of analysis to the structure of self-knowledge. What needs to be established at this point is the relation between these three moments of analysis and the nature of international relations. Let us turn, then, to Aron's discussion of international relations as a field, or an object of investigation.

RATIONAL THEORY: DEFINITIONS, CONCEPTS, AND SYSTEMS

Rational theory, or theory as a moment of analysis, encompasses the theoretician's efforts to define a field, fabricate concepts, and construct coherent blocks of action, or systems. Applied to international relations, these three intellectual exercises can be resolved into three questions that Aron raised in the introductory chapter to *Peace and War:* "Does the study of international relations involve a proper focus of interest? Does it aim at collective phenomena, human behavior whose specificity is recognizable? And does this specific meaning lend itself to theoretical elaboration?" In defining and delimiting the field of international relations, Aron observed, social scientists must contend with one irremediable difficulty: "'International relations' have no frontiers traced out in reality; they are not and cannot be materially separable from other social phenomena" (*PW*, 4). For this reason any definition of *international relations* inevitably involves a measure of uncertainty and ambiguity. Offering a definition that at least has the appeal of common sense, Aron asserted that international relations are "relations among nations," nations here being understood as "any political collectivity that is territorially organized." Although this definition presented difficulties that Aron was quick to recognize ("Are we to include in the relations among political units the relations among individuals belonging to those units? Where do political units, that is, territorially organized collectivities, begin and end?"), he nevertheless maintained that relations among states, "i.e., strictly inter-state relations, constitute international relations par excellence," treaties being an "indisputable example" of these relations (*PW,* 5).

Interstate relations present one original feature that distinguishes them from all other forms of social intercourse: "They take place in the shadow of war or, to use a more rigorous expression, relations among states involve, in essence, the alternatives of war and peace." This characteristic also distinguishes inter- from intrastate, or domestic, politics. Adopting Weber's definition of the state as an institution that possesses the "monopoly of legitimate violence," Aron argued that international relations is marked precisely by the absence of a comparable institution. There is an "essential difference," then, between foreign and domestic policy: "Politics, insofar as it concerns relations among states, seems to signify—in both ideal and objective terms—simply the survival of states confronting the potential threat created by the existence of other states. Hence the opposition common in classical philosophy: the art of politics teaches men to live in peace within collectivities, while it teaches collectivities to live in either peace or war" (*PW,* 6–7). Because each collectivity is the arbiter of its own interest, Aron maintained, states confront one another as if in a state of nature.

This definition immediately puts distance between Aron's theory of international relations and that of conventional realism. By insisting on an "essential difference" between international and domestic politics, Aron has kept his theory of international relations free from the "essentialist prejudices" of more traditional realists such as Hans Morgenthau. Unlike Morgenthau, for example, who held that "the idea of interest is indeed of the essence of politics and is unaffected by the circumstances of time and place,"[8] Aron viewed human action through the refracting prism of a very specific circumstance indeed, namely, state sovereignty. In doing so, he clearly suggested that the discovery of originality or difference in human action is of greater theoretical significance than the discovery of universality.

By proceeding in this fashion, Aron created a little more breathing space for the twin ideas of freedom and progress than was allowed for by "pessimistic" theorists of Morgenthau's sort. If Morgenthau is right—if, in other words, human nature being what it is, the stuff of politics remains constant across time and space—then there is indeed little moral progress to hope for in history. But, if human action is held to vary with its environment, then the hope persists that the character of action can be changed simply by altering the conditions of its existence. Aron's unwillingness to ascribe a universal or univocal meaning to politics thus testifies to his conviction that men and women can, to a vague but significant degree, remake themselves and the societies to which they belong.

Emphasizing the "essential" disconnectedness of phenomena, however, comes perilously close to affirming Weber's teaching on the original formlessness of matter. If human action is as variable as Aron here suggests—domestic and international politics are described, we must remember, not simply as different but as *essentially* different—then the prospects for a comprehensive theory of human action are dim indeed: Given the fluidity of behavior here assumed, theory degenerates into little more than a collection of descriptive snapshots to be discarded as time and circumstance change. Apparently sensing as much, Aron checked himself. After declaring for an essential difference between domestic and international politics, he then qualified his initial judgment by referring to that difference as a political one ("Politics, insofar as it concerns relations among states"). This may have rescued Aron from the relativistic quagmire that bogged down Weber, but it also left Aron embroiled in a considerable logical puzzle of his own: If the difference between domestic and interstate politics is an essential one, how can that difference also be thought of as simply two manifestations of the same thing?

Returning to the state of nature, we note that, strictly speaking, interstate relations are carried on not by people but by groups of people. How, then, does one make state action intelligible, that is, explicable in terms of human dispositions or intentions? As Gustav Bergmann explains the problem: "Groups, not being people, are not accessible to empathy. Yet they consist of people who are. Thus groups might become accessible if one could find a way of coordinating to each group a representative person, i.e., a person such by understanding it empathetically one could successfully predict the behavior of the group."[9] With this general principle apparently in mind, Aron explained that "interstate actions are expressed in and by specific actions, those of individuals whom I shall call symbolic, the diplomat and the soldier." These two individuals, Aron added, "no longer function as individual members but as representatives of the collectivities to which they belong: the ambassador, in the exercise of his duties, is the political unit in whose name he speaks; the soldier on the battlefield is the political unit in whose name he kills" (*PW,* 5).

Here we arrive at what is perhaps the most important element in Aron's conception of interstate relations—diplomatic-strategic behavior does not have an obvious or constant objective, but the risk of war forces it to engage in a never-ending series of power calculations. Aron's theory of international relations "starts from the plurality of autonomous centers of decision, hence the risk of war, and from this risk deduces the necessity of the calculation of means" (*PW,* 16). International political action, to use Weber's terminology, thus appears to be "zweckrational" action; that is, action driven by the rational consideration of means in order to attain a given end.

Aron's acceptance of Weber's means-ends schema does not mean that his interpretation of international relations is an essentially Weberian one. Although he accepted the fact that states pursue a plurality of ends, Aron refused to concede Weber's fundamental point that these ends are irreconcilable or incompatible, a point of great import for Weber's interpretation of international relations. In Weber's view the incompatibility of values means that states, as the embodiments of different cultural values, inevitably find themselves in permanent conflict with one another. In Aron's view, however, interpretations of international relations must recognize that there are elements of cooperation as well as conflict in the relations among states. For thousands of years, Aron explained, "each collectivity had to count chiefly on itself to survive, but it also had—or should have had—to contribute to the task common even to enemy cities, exposed to the risk of perishing together by dint of constantly fighting each other" (*PW,* 17). Aron's recognition that there exists some measure of unity or common good among states led him to conclude that "the goal toward which collectivities ought to tend may be determined by rational analysis"—a most un-Weberian conclusion—and thus to adopt as a maxim of statecraft Montesquieu's principle that "different nations ought in times of peace to do one another all the good they can, and in time of war as little injury as possible, without prejudicing their real interests."

Because diplomatic-strategic behavior perpetually oscillates between the poles of conflict and cooperation, theories of international relations cannot be endowed with the same explanatory or predictive power as purely scientific or even economic theories: "As long as each collectivity must think of its own safety at the same time as that of the diplomatic system or of the human race, diplomatic-strategic behavior will never be rationally determined, even in theory." The goals states pursue are too ambiguous and equivocal to be subsumed under a single concept. This is not to say, however, that a theory of international relations is completely devoid of scientific authority. By constructing models of diplomatic systems, or by distinguishing "typical situations on a general level," international relations specialists can introduce a degree of conceptual rigor into their subject matter which elevates analysis beyond simple intuition. This, unfortunately, is all they can do. In the absence of a single goal of diplomatic behavior, social scientists must resign themselves to the fact that "the rational analysis of international relations cannot be developed into an inclusive theory" (*PW*, 17).

Aron now proceeds to bring the field of international relations into sharper focus by constructing a network of concepts extracted from the intelligible structure of diplomatic-strategic behavior. Clausewitz's now classic statements on war serve as the starting point for Aron's efforts: "War . . . is an act of violence intended to compel our opponent to fulfill our will . . . Physical force . . . is therefore the means, the compulsory submission of the enemy to our will is the ultimate object" (*PW*, 22). By this, Aron explained, Clausewitz meant to underscore the simple fact that war serves a purpose; nations do not engage in conflict simply for the sake of victory but for the sake of a certain kind of peace. The course and conduct of a military campaign, then, depends on an existing notion of what good that campaign will serve, and that judgment, Clausewitz asserted, is political judgment par excellence.

Establishing the superiority of political over military judgment is a decisive moment for Aron's theory of international relations because Aron is now in possession of a conceptual tool that can fashion a working compromise between the competing realities of conflict and cooperation. "The primacy of policy," he explained, "permits the control of escalation, the avoidance of an explosion of animosity into passionate and unrestricted brutality. The more the leaders calculate in terms of cost and profit and the less they are inclined to relinquish the pen for the sword, the more they will be content to limit their success and renounce the intoxication of dazzling victories. The reasonable conduct of politics is the only rational one if the goal of the intercourse among states is the survival of all, common prosperity, and the sparing of peoples' blood" (*PW*, 45). The primacy of political judgment here plays much the same conceptual role as Tocqueville's notion of "self-interest, properly understood." Although rooted in self-love, political judgment possesses the wherewithal to encourage the emergence of a certain degree of cooperation and even sacrifice. We are thus confronted with a kind of action that appears to be capable of attaining a "middling standard" of morality, one that recognizes the inescapable facts of power while at the same time holding fast to the possibility that conflict might, over time, be meliorated.

Although the relationship between policy and strategy seems at times to settle into a holding pattern in which the two terms simply revolve around each other—"War is to harmonize entirely with the political views and policy, to accommodate itself to the means available to war"—Clausewitz ultimately awarded pride of place to political judgment. Strategy, as well as diplomacy (which at times in *Peace and War* assumes the role of a conceptual go-between in Aron's discussions of policy and strategy) "will . . . be subordinate to politics, that is, to the conception on the part of the collectivity or its leaders of the 'national interest'" (*PW*, 25, 24).

Despite Aron's repeated and emphatic insistence that war is merely an instrument of policy and not an end in itself, it is difficult to discern the epistemological status of this assertion: Is the primacy of politics a statement of fact or a normative lesson? This question becomes all the more compelling in light of the fact that this is the very question Aron addressed to other theorists of international relations, a question that constitutes, in fact, a litmus test of sorts enabling Aron to discriminate between what he considered to be authentic theory and ideology. Aron's judgment of Hans Morgenthau's doctrine of the national interest offers perhaps the best case in point. Morgenthau's theory, he complained,

> either suggests an idea as undeniable as it is vague—that each actor thinks first of itself—or else tries to oppose itself to other pseudotheories, for example, that the foreign policy of states is dictated by political ideology or moral principles. Each of these pseudotheories means something only in connection with the other. To say that the Soviet Union conducts its foreign affairs on the basis of its "national interests" means that it is not guided exclusively by ideological considerations, by its ambition to spread communism. Such a proposition is undeniable, but to conclude from it that the rulers of a noncommunist Russia would have had the same diplomatic policy between 1917 and 1967 is simply absurd. The purpose of empirical study of international relations consists precisely in determining the historical perceptions that

> control the behavior of collective actors and the decisions of the rulers of these actors.

Whatever policy a regime may pursue, Aron added, "nothing prevents one from asserting after the fact that it was dictated by considerations of 'national interest' as long as 'national interest' has not been strictly defined."[10]

According to Aron, then, Morgenthau's thesis cannot bear the burden of the empirical evidence. Because even the most cursory review of the historical data reveals the fact that different states pursue different goals for different reasons, Morgenthau's concept of the national interest fails as a descriptive account of interstate behavior: "Setting up power . . . as the unique or highest goal of individuals, parties or nations does not constitute a theory in the scientific sense but rather amounts to a philosophy or ideology. In any event, it is not a proposition that can be proven false; thus it cannot be considered a scientific hypothesis."[11]

The question that must be asked at this point is whether Aron's conceptualization of the relation between policy and strategy—which is the cornerstone of his theory of international relations, just as the national interest is the cornerstone of Morgenthau's—fares any better when judged by the same criterion. In *Peace and War* the issue first emerges when Aron comments that Clausewitz's celebrated definition of war ("war is . . . a continuation of political commerce, a carrying-out of the same by other means") did not result from a "bellicose philosophy" but from "a simple observation of fact." "Commerce between nations," Aron explained, "does not cease the day the guns begin to speak; the belligerent phase takes its place in a continuity of relations always controlled by the collectivities' intentions toward each other" (*PW*, 23). By arguing for the next twenty-five pages, however, that strategists and statesmen have all too often overlooked or ignored the proper relation between policy and strategy, and by analyzing the abject failures of political leadership during World War I, World War II, the Korean conflict, and the Vietnam War, Aron leaves the distinct impression that he has reversed himself. Whereas he originally began by grounding his interpretation of the relation between policy and strategy in what he averred was a simple and self-evident statement of fact, Aron later appears to have concluded that this interpretation is a normative one, a prescription deduced from theory and not a description based on experience.

Aron's ambivalence, however, may be more apparent than real. We need only recall his discussion of Montesquieu's use of concepts in order to understand how a concept can be descriptive and prescriptive at the same time: "We know through interpretive analysis what a democracy is, and that in it social inequalities must not be too great; but since men are intelligent they can take decisions or draw up legal codes which are contrary to the character of the regime; in other words, because of their intelligence they can make it impossible for the regime to function."[12]

Like Montesquieu's concept of democracy, Aron's concept of the primacy of politics does not predict the behavior of statesmen but only the probable outcomes of their choice. But, if this is indeed the only way out of the dilemma, it now becomes apparent that the standards by which he judged Morgenthau's concept of the national interest violate the very premises of his epistemology. By complaining that Morgenthau's concept of the national interest ignores the vast differences among foreign policy goals, Aron was effectively demanding that Morgenthau's concept of the national interest do something that, by Aron's own rules, a concept cannot do, namely, account for the contingencies of experience.

Proceeding from his conceptualization of the primacy of politics, Aron tried to solidify his hold on the middle ground by next distinguishing the means of foreign policy, power and force, from the ends of foreign policy—power, security, glory, and idea. Although this schema clearly indicates that power may indeed be the driving force of a foreign policy, it also underscores Aron's belief that other, possibly more humane objectives may also guide policy.

Aron's analysis of the means of foreign policy immediately reveals why *Peace and War* was hailed by Hoffmann as "a triumph of the art of meaningful distinctions."[13] The two primary concepts of power and force are carefully separated out and dissected into several other concepts in order to account for the many different realities that are so frequently and crudely lumped together. The purpose of this conceptual exercise is to highlight the imprecision and uncertainty that attend any effort to calculate power, an uncertainty to which Clausewitz gave eloquent testimony: "War is a peculiar difficulty because all action must, to a certain extent, be planned in a mere twilight, which in addition not infrequently gives to things exaggerated dimensions and an unnatural appearance. What this feeble light leaves indistinct to the sight talent must discover, or else be left to chance" (cited in *PW*, 53–54).

Augmenting this uncertainty is the fact that foreign policy is never determined by the calculations of power alone. The behavior of states, like the behavior of individuals, is at least partly determined by the goals they set for themselves. For Aron these ends are irreducible to one another, a fact that further distinguishes his theory of international relations from those that take their bearings from a rational definition of the national interest. The plurality of foreign policy objectives, Aron maintained, testifies to the impossibility of ascribing a univocal meaning to diplomatic-strategic behavior:

> Not only are the historical objectives of political units not deducible from the relations of forces, but the ultimate objectives of such units are legitimately equivocal. Security, power, glory, idea are essentially heterogeneous objectives which can be reduced to a single term only by distorting the human meaning of diplomatic-strategic action. If the rivalry of states is comparable to a game, what is "at stake" cannot be designated by a single concept, valid for all civilizations at all periods. Diplomacy is a game in which the players sometimes risk losing their lives, sometimes prefer victory itself to the advantages that would result from it. Quantitative expression of the stakes is thereby impossible: not only do we not know in advance what the stake is . . . but, for the warrior, victory suffices in itself. (*PW*, 91)

Aron's dissatisfaction with the concept of the national interest and the concomitant notion that states are everywhere and always engaged in a struggle to maximize their power was not simply a matter of historical judgment. Although he did in fact find fault with these ideas on empirical grounds ("One may recall the Japan of the Tokugawa era: it certainly did not have as its goal the exercise or the capability of exercising increased influence on the other actors or on the international scene"),[14] Aron, it must be remembered, also objected to the concept of the national interest for logical reasons because it is impossible to define the concept rationally ("As long as each collectivity must think of its own safety at the same time as that of the diplomatic system or of the human race, diplomatic-strategic behavior will never be rationally determined, even in theory.") For Aron the antinomies of action betray any effort to ground the theory and practice of international relations in a set of rational standards. If pure thought can recognize but not resolve the dilemmas of statecraft, Aron reasoned, then behavior cannot be explained apart from the value choices that action, by its very nature, demands. For this reason Aron denied "that the national interest might, can, or should be defined apart from the internal regime, the aspirations characteristic of the different classes, the political idea of the state." Conceding that "the collectivity does not always change objectives when it changes its constitution, historical or ruling elite," Aron nevertheless asked, "But how can the political units maintain, through revolutions, the same ambitions and the same methods?" (*PW*, 92). In expressing this conviction, Aron aligned himself with those political thinkers who have seen in the political idea of the state one of the primary determinants of diplomatic-strategic behavior.

The plurality of ends, together with the uncertainty inherent in the calculation of power, thus suggests a reality in constant motion. Perhaps more than any other dimension of human experience, international relations vigorously resists simple, schematic formulations. From this indeterminacy Aron concluded that "There is no general theory of international relations comparable to the general theory of economy. The theory we are sketching here tends to analyze the meaning of diplomatic behavior, to trace its fundamental notions, to specify the variables that must be reviewed in order to understand any one constellation. But it does not suggest an 'eternal diplomacy,' it does not claim to be the reconstruction of a closed system" (*PW*, 93).

With these conceptual building blocks in hand, Aron proceeded to the "theoretician's second and most important task," the construction of systems (*PW*, 13). Systems are, quite simply, those "typical situations" that evince different patterns of behavior. Aron's analysis of international systems in chapters 4 and 5 of *Peace and War* demonstrates the continued relevance of Montesquieu's method for reconstructing social wholes. The same basic elements necessary to reconstruct the intelligible wholes within states are also necessary to reconstruct the intelligible wholes generated by relations among states. In both cases an intentional reality is loosely attached to an empirical one, a synthesis that testifies to Aron's ongoing commitment to human freedom as well as to his effort to transcend the competing alternatives of realism and idealism.

The first characteristic of an international system Aron tabbed the "configuration of the relation of forces." Broadly speaking, there are two typical configurations of forces, multipolar and bipolar. In the first one political rivalry occurs among several states of approximately equal size and strength. In the second configuration two states outstrip the others, "so that equilibrium is possible only in the form of two coalitions, the majority of medium and small states being obliged to join the camp of one great power or the other." Various combinations and patterns of equilibrium are of course possible, reversals of alliances being "a normal process of diplomacy" (*PW*, 98).

But diplomatic-strategic behavior is not controlled by the configuration of forces alone—ideas and emotions are decisive in determining the actions of states. In order to discriminate among international systems, we must reckon with "the nature of the states and the objectives sought by those in power," intentional realities that transcend the purely empirical data of geography and military strength (*PW*, 99). Aron thus presented a second set of systemic categories. "The distinction between homogeneous systems and heterogeneous systems," he wrote, "seems to me fundamental. I call homogeneous systems those in which the states belong to the same type, obey the same conception of policy I call heterogeneous, on the other hand, those systems in which the states are organized according to different principles and appeal contradictory rules" (*PW*, 99–100). In the period between the wars of religion and the French Revolution, Aron explained, the European system was "both multipolar and homogeneous." Since 1945 the international system had become "both bipolar and heterogeneous" (*PW*, 100).

Although Aron commented on certain characteristics of multipolar and bipolar systems, his characterizations are so broad and sketchy that they are of little use in formulating rules for predicting state behavior. This is due to the rather simple fact that actors in a system are not always bent upon preserving a given configuration of forces: "The only universal and formal rule is that of equilibrium in the vague sense that Hume gave it: each actor . . . tries not to be at the mercy of the others." The policy of equilibrium, Aron wrote, "obeys a rule of common sense; it issues from the prudence necessary to the states concerned to preserve their independence and not to be at the mercy of another state possessing irresistible strength." The desire to retain one's autonomy, together with a typical configuration, permits us to sketch models, Aron maintained, but these models are simply too indeterminate "to be able to discover the laws of their functioning and development" (*PW*, 146, 147).

This is a rather striking passage, for it apparently reverses Aron's harsh judgment on the possibility and necessity of national interest thinking delivered just two chapters earlier. To Aron's way of thinking, as we have seen, different regimes pursue such different ends that it makes realism's traditional insistence on a universal will-to-power seem not just implausible but, in Aron's words, "inconceivable" and even "absurd." Statesmen, "inspired by various philosophers," approach their responsibilities in such wildly different ways that it is impossible to define the concept of the national interest with any degree of objectivity.

In evaluating Aron's claim, it must be kept in mind that realism does not insist on a sharp separation between the national interest and the national character; indeed, some realists argue that the moral character of a regime and its people gives the national interest a share of its particular substance and content.[15] What realism does object to, however, is the effort to deduce the national interest from a political ideology, as if the national interest had no objective or independent existence apart from the values held by the regime or individuals in power.

But this is the very proposition Aron dug in to defend. "For most nations in the world," he maintained, "the national interest can no longer be defined apart from ideological preferences; the primacy of foreign policy without any connection with the domestic contests of political parties . . . is no longer a valid postulate when the very principle, on which political units are based are at stake."[16] From this vantage point nothing, not even the urge for simple survival, can take its cue from the laws of objective necessity: "Even if . . . collective servitude were always a means of physical salvation, it [requires] a moral decision to grant precedence to physical salvation."[17] What creates this situation is the unrelenting pressure of ideological conflict. In our time, Aron argued, "a great power is defined by its capacity to show humanity a perspective of stabilization and peace." In fact, after a moment's reflection Aron went so far as to add that a great power "always wants something else and something more than security and power, it wants an Idea."[18] A politics that worked to transcend the tragic facts of necessity was no utopian ideal for Aron. The West, he insisted, must stand for a new idea of the international order if it expected to win over any countries and prevail in the cold war. "The national interest of the United States, or even the collective interest of the Anglo-Saxon minority, will not win over any country nor will it cause any loyalties if it does not appear to be tied to an international order—the order of power as well as the order of law."[19] This, of course, deliberately undoes not only an objective national interest but an orderly and relatively stable pattern of international relations. The whole point of an "Idea," after all, is to mark the escape from necessity, not to dignify its existence.

What remains rather elusive and obscure in all of this is how to account for the universal "rule of equilibrium" which "common sense" and "prudence" are said to discover. If human action is governed not by interest but by "the search for values"—and this search is, Aron makes clear, "part and parcel of human reality, be it individual or collective"[20]—from whence derives the compelling force and power of common sense?

Beyond the theoretical problem of explaining just how it is that statecraft repairs to the rule of equilibrium, however, lies the even thornier practical problem of explaining why it should. If "the strength of a great power is diminished" by refusing "to serve an idea"[21]—Aron's own dictum—then what is it exactly that protects against the sort of crusading, self-destructive moralism Aron repeatedly anguished over and warned against? This problem becomes especially acute when one understands that Aron clearly deplored not simply the hard moralism peculiar to revolutionary utopians but also the "soft" moralism to which liberal democracies are prone. Agreeing with George Kennan—the first head of the State Department's Policy Planning Staff and the author of the famous "Long Telegram" from Moscow in 1946 which mapped out the doctrine of containment—that "vague slogans such as 'to make the world safe for democracy' or 'to insure collective security' often tend to make wars bigger and worse," Aron concluded that "so-called idealistic policies always amount to an attempt to impose a certain conception of social or international organization. Political idealism ends by degenerating into imperialism."[22] How one can "stand for an idea" without at the same time falling victim to "imperialism," or, at the very least, senseless adventurism prompted by national pride, is left for the reader to imagine.

Although the construction of systems is a crucial part of theory construction, it is nevertheless only the beginning. "The models or types of international relations," Aron explained, "must only serve as a preparation for concrete study" (*PW*, 149). The overriding purpose of rational theory, then, is to break ground for empirical analysis. With rational theory in hand Aron is now prepared to engage in a sociological review of constants and determinants.

SOCIOLOGY

In Aron's conceptual empyrean empirical analysis "is an indispensable intermediary between theory and fact" because it attempts to establish causal connections between determinates (those systems or models constructed by rational theory) and determinants (the broader context in which a system is located). The sociologist's peculiar calling, then, is one of establishing "propositions of a certain generality, relative either to the action which a certain cause produces upon power or upon the objectives of the political units, upon the nature of systems, upon the types of peace and war, or to regular series or patterns of development which characterize the situation without the actors necessarily being aware of it" (*PW*, 178). As a moment of analysis located between theory and history, sociology depends on the former, at least in part, to provide it with a systematic list of variables as grist for its mill and anticipates the latter by constructing "the framework within which events occur" (*PW*, 15).

In order for sociology to be useful, Aron explained, the search for determinants must be systematic. Accordingly, just as his analysis of industrial societies grouped determinants into two categories, physical and moral, so too does his analysis of international relations. Physical causes are those that pertain to space (geography), number (demography), and resources (economy). Moral or social causes are also of three kinds but do not "belong to three species as distinct as the three kinds of physical determinants." In the case of social causes, Aron noted, "we are seeking regular relations and above all typical series (if they exist). We are therefore entitled to apportion our inquiry in relation to the historical unities whose development would appear, after the fact, as subject to a general law" (*PW*, 179). In Aron's estimation three historical entities offer this possibility—nations, civilizations, and humanity. Impressing upon his readers just how comprehensive and systematic his determinants are, Aron concluded that "it does not seem to me that any of the problems which the sociologist must ask himself can escape this plan. The first three chapters relate to a spatial consideration, the last three to a temporal one" (*PW*, 180).

Beginning with an analysis of space, Aron explored the degree to which each variable explains the causes of war or, alternately, the causes of peace, an exercise that takes the reader through a breathtaking review of the literature devoted to war and social conflict. Despite his relentless criticism of what seems to be a never-ending stream of theoretical data, Aron by no means intended to leave the impression that the material and moral causes he scrutinized are inconsequential for understanding the course or conduct of international relations. He was, however, most anxious to demonstrate that none of these causes is decisive. By revealing the limits of single-factor analysis, Aron attempted to save the study of international relations from "the illusions of those who hope to put an end to the reign of wars by modifying a single variable."[23] Deriding these simplistic interpretations as "mythologies," Aron explained that "mythologies consist of the substitution of a single factor for the plurality of causes, of lending unconditional value to a desired objective, and of a failure to realize the distance between the dreams of men and the destiny of societies."[24] The most we can expect from critical analysis, then, is a "negative delineation" of reality. A science of human action may not be able to establish the single truth of existence, but it can, if deployed properly, at least eliminate some of the possibilities.

Although Aron's failure to locate either a pattern or a mechanism of progress is discomfiting to idealists, his answer to the closing question of part 2—are we warlike by nature?—is equally unsettling to realists. Turning over a wealth of biological, psychological, and anthropological data, Aron concluded that war has its roots in all of these factors, not just one of them. Human beings are indeed combative and aggressive, Aron observed, but they do not "fight by instinct." War, then,

> is an expression [but] not a necessary expression of human combativity. War has been its constant expression in the course of the historical phase, starting from the moment when societies were organized and armed. It is contrary to the nature of man that the danger of violence be definitely dispelled: in every collectivity misfits will violate the laws and attack persons. It is contrary to the nature of individuals and groups that the conflicts between individuals and groups will disappear. But it is not proved that these conflicts must be manifested in the phenomenon of war, as we have known it for thousands of years, with organized combatants, utilizing increasingly destructive weapons. (*PW,* 365–66)

If war is not a necessary expression of our humanity, then is the end of history, at least as Hegel understood it, finally in sight, or at least somewhere on the horizon? Once again, Aron deflects a direct question: In order to calculate the probabilities of war and peace, we must understand "the world today" (*PW,* 366). It is to this task—understanding the global system in the thermonuclear age—that Aron now turns.

HISTORY

Aron's interpretation of the contemporary political situation put a rather unconventional spin on the notion of historical analysis. The historian, he asserted, "either narrates events or tries to comprehend the uniqueness of a culture, a society, or an international system."[25] In part 3 of *Peace and War* Aron took the latter, less-traveled route. Although it does not narrate historical events, Aron's interpretation of the global system was nevertheless a form of historical analysis: "After seeking generalities or peculiarities, it has a special aim—the extension to the whole globe, for the first time, of a single international system, a system distinguished by its heterogeneity and dominated by the thermonuclear duopoly of the US and the USSR."[26]

More specifically, Aron approached part 3 with two objectives in mind. Bringing the conceptual apparatus he fashioned in parts 1 and 2 to bear on his description of a specific situation, Aron proposed, first, to uncover the original features of strategy and diplomacy in the latter half of the twentieth century and, second, to determine whether the novel conditions of diplomatic-strategic behavior "modify the relations between strategy and diplomacy" (*PW,* 369). In other words, given the current historical landscape, can the threat of war still be a rational expression of policy, or has the "cunning of history" made the threat of war irrational and hence obsolete?

Aron's approach to the contemporary challenges of statecraft was systematic to the point of scholastic: After establishing the original features of diplomatic strategic behavior in the first two chapters of part 3 (nuclear weaponry and ideological heterogeneity), Aron then devoted the next three chapters to reviewing the effects that these features had on the three types of relations that can be deduced from a bipolar configuration of forces (relations within a bloc, between blocs, and between blocs and neutrals).

Anxious to underscore the complexity of choice and the relative indeterminacy of action, Aron's compressed review of the historical landscape reduces to a rather shopworn list of dilemmas and paradoxes. His discussion of deterrence, for example—"the supreme concept of diplomatic strategy in the nuclear age"—repeatedly alludes to the delicacy and complexity of the situation in which the superpowers and their allies find themselves. Bound by a common interest in not destroying each other, the superpowers are nevertheless plagued by a series of tragic dilemmas: In order to reduce the probability of total war, they must move to possess relatively invulnerable second-strike capacities. This reflexive development, however, increases the risk of limited war, a prospect that in its turn again raises the specter of nuclear war. Moreover, because it makes less and less sense for the superpowers to threaten nuclear war in order to deter each other, the credibility of a superpower's commitment to its allies becomes suspect, thus inciting lesser powers to arm themselves with thermonuclear weapons.

The condition of tragic predicament seems to lie at the very heart of almost every issue Aron reviews. In his discussion of U.S.-European relations, for example, Aron observed that Europeans, torn between the fears of a nuclear apocalypse and capitulation, want "the Americans to be either calmer or more combative, either resolved to keep their promises or not to keep them" (*PW*, 482). Of Western relations with the Third World, Aron noted that anticommunist containment forced liberal democracies to prop up authoritarian despots, "a preference as inevitable as it is disagreeable," thus fanning the very flames of discontent which invited communist subversion in the first place. And in his commentary on Western-Soviet bloc relations we read that, "Hostility of position has been aggravated by the technological race that the two superpowers have been drawn into, almost in spite of themselves; by the logic of a rivalry from which neither side was to withdraw" (*PW*, 545).

As Aron's discussion of the challenges confronting statecraft during the cold war so amply demonstrates, the dilemmas that lie at the heart of politics are intractable and, at times, even terrible. But are they, for all that, absolute? Does history or human reason allow for any hope that conflict is being supplanted by cooperation?

These questions were particularly urgent in light of two overriding and interrelated issues—namely, the nuclear threat and the future of Western-Soviet bloc relations. Speaking to the rationality of a nuclear war, Aron concluded that, as terrible as such a war would be, it would not, unfortunately, be terrible enough; the benefits of such a war would still outweigh its costs. "What value can either of the superpowers attribute to the fact of being rid of the threat of the other?" he asked. "What price can a people without space set on the fact of doubling or tripling its territory?" Thus it is that the threat of a war "that no one wants to fight" remains as an indispensable element of diplomatic-strategic behavior. In fact, "this inevitable and rational solidarity of strategy and diplomacy has never been so indissoluble as today, when the thermo-nuclear system on each side is almost continually in a state of alert, aimed at the opposing system even while the leaders of the enemy states are deliberating" (*PW*, 439–40).

Given this hard judgment, the paragraph that immediately follows is rather surprising, seemingly going against the grain of the verdict Aron has just rendered:

> Nonetheless the weapons of mass destruction open the prospect of a historical revolution at the end of which the very essence of the relations between states will be different. Let us imagine each of them possessing an invulnerable capacity for retaliation so that in any circumstances each will be in a position to inflict a mortal punishment

> upon any aggressor. Let us even imagine . . . that each state is in a position to exterminate all humanity, to render the planet uninhabitable. At this moment there will no longer be any difference between "more" and "less," between crime and punishment, between great power and small state. Each state would possess a veto right over the existence of all the others. It is legitimate to presume that the rivalry of political units might continue. But I do not think that this rivalry would remain socially or psychologically possible. No member of the system would agree to be permanently at the mercy of all the others. As humanity approached this system, it would realize that it must renounce either the diplomatic-strategic performance or life itself. Yet the choice it would make between these two alternatives is not predictable. (*PW*, 440)

If the nuclear issue admitted no clear answer to the question of progress, did the broader issue of superpower relations? Was there any reason to hope that tensions between East and West were dissipating? In Aron's analysis superpower relations were tightly constrained by a series of tragic dilemmas. The existence of nuclear weapons, for example, sets in motion a peculiar dynamic that works for both collaboration and competition. Although both sides recognized their common interest in preventing the spread of nuclear weapons, both recognized that a technological breakthrough by one could spell disaster for the other, a recognition that fueled the never-ending arms race between the two.

Augmenting the intensity of the conflict between the United States and the Soviet Union was the fact that this conflict was propelled not by one source of friction but two. At root superpower relations are no different than any other human relation: All action, collective as well as individual, is governed by a complex admixture of intentional realities and historical necessities. In this case conflict stemmed, first, from ideology and, second, from what Aron termed the "hostility of position." The ideological nature of the conflict is obvious; both the United States and the USSR represented two different and even contradictory versions of industrial society. Aron emphatically maintained, however, that even should an era of ideological compatibility come to pass, the power-political dynamics generated by the "hostility of position" would still not make for an automatic or even happy convergence of interests. In every international system, Aron argued, deploying a line of reasoning borrowed freely from the commonsense precepts of realpolitik, friends and enemies are determined by the global demands of equilibrium. Thus, by virtue of nothing more than their size and strength, the United States and the Soviet Union were doomed to clash, and this conflict would have occurred even if Marx had never written his *Manifesto.*

Given the apparently inexpiable hostility between the superpowers, is there any reason to hope that tensions may someday abate or at least become manageable? Surveying the course of superpower relations since the end of World War II, Aron passed some interesting and rather encouraging judgments on the behavior of the two superpowers. If we examine the major international crises since 1947, Aron wrote, we discover that the actions of the superpowers have been "dictated by the firm resolve not to engage in unlimited war" (*PW,* 561). More specifically, "the use of armed force, at least by one of the superpowers against the other, has been increasingly restricted: and the length of each crisis "has been growing shorter." The Berlin blockade, for example, lasted for several months, "as though the Two did not know how to escape unscathed from the trials of strength which they had launched." Although the Korean War lasted for three years, it was prolonged mainly because negotiations repeatedly broke down over the single issue of repatriating Chinese prisoners of war. The Suez-Budapest crises ended after a few days, and the Iraq-Lebanon-Jordan crisis was liquidated within a few weeks. In each case, moreover, "the number and caliber of weapons used diminished" (*PW,* 565).

As Aron himself was willing to admit, however, this is rather scanty evidence on which to base a judgment regarding the future course of Soviet-American relations. Nevertheless, Aron was prepared to declare that the United States and the Soviet Union, "despite the ravings of their propagandists and their Homeric challenges, have learned to know each other and no longer lightly impute bellicose intentions to each other. Even supposing that members of the Presidium feared in the past that the United States might launch a preventative war, they have been reassured on this point for some time now . . . No longer disposed to doubt each other's desire to limit the conflicts, the two superpowers are less inclined to hysteria and panic when, through the fault of an ally or a neutral, a crisis arises in which a country or regime runs the risk of changing allegiance" (*PW,* 566).

Despite this relative stability, we have by no means witnessed the evolution of international relations from a state of nature to a state of peace. In fact, the prospects for peace are directly linked to three historical problems—"the partition of Europe, the arms race, and the fate of the third world" (*PW*, 569). The chances of revolutionary wars, as well as wars pure and simple, will persist as long as these sores continue to fester. In *Peace and War* Aron gave these issues short shrift, seeing little hope that the tensions generated by these three problems would subside in the foreseeable future.

We are thus led to repeat an earlier question: Given this equivocal state of affairs, what must we do? What does progress demand of human effort? Considerations of this sort lead directly to the need for what Aron termed a "praxeology," or a theory of action. Aron's normative reflections constitute the fourth and concluding part of *Peace and War*, the purpose of which is to elucidate the connection between theory and practice. Normative theory thus "relates the understanding of objective conditions and the limits of historical knowledge to the requirements of action" (*PW*, 569).

PRAXEOLOGY

Reduced to its essentials, the question that dominates part 4 of *Peace and War* is this: In a world in which law does not prevail, what kind of strategy is both ethical and effective? Returning to a theme he sounded in the opening pages of *Peace and War*, Aron reminded his audience that diplomatic-strategic behavior retains elements of conflict and cooperation. "As long as international society preserves this mixed and, in a sense, contradictory character," Aron argued, "the morality of international relations will also be equivocal" (*PW*, 608).

And what kind of morality, exactly, is this? "The only morality which transcends the morality of struggle and the morality of law," Aron intoned, "is what I would call the morality of prudence, which attempts not only to consider each case in its concrete particularities, but also not to ignore any of the arguments of principle and opportunity, to forget neither the relation of forces nor the will of peoples." To be prudent, Aron explained, one must "act in accordance with the particular situation and the concrete data, and not in accordance with some system or out of passive obedience to some pseudonorm; it is to prefer the limitation of violence to the punishment of the presumably guilty party to so-called absolute justice; it is to establish concrete accessible objectives conforming to the secular law of international relations and not to limitless and perhaps meaningless objectives, such as 'a world safe for democracy' or 'a world from which power politics have disappeared'" (*PW*,

585). Although prudence does not resolve the antinomies of action, it does attempt to forge a compromise between the competing demands of power and conscience. For this reason the judgments of prudence will satisfy neither the moralist nor the hard realist. Given the complexity of moral judgments, we must learn to be satisfied with proximate solutions to the intractable dilemmas of world politics.

But can we afford so modest a morality in the thermonuclear age? Is it reasonable to sanction a code of behavior which perpetuates the dangerous and bloody game of power politics, especially given that the game is now played with atomic bombs? To those who maintained that unilateral disarmament was the only rational alternative to certain disaster, Aron responded, first, by arguing that not every war necessarily leads to "genetic destruction" and, second, by asserting that such a proposal rests on the shortsighted assumption that "a people which lays down its arms will be neither deported nor reduced to slavery nor simply exterminated." We need only recall the wholesale extermination of six million Jews, Aron wrote, "to conclude that the cost of enslavement, for a people and a culture, can be higher than the cost of war, even atomic war" (*PW,* 631).

Aron found the other strategic extreme, peace by fear, no more plausible than unilateral disarmament. Equipping all states with nuclear weapons increases the instability of the international system exponentially; the larger the number of nuclear states, the greater the chances that these weapons will fall into the hands of an irrational and genocidal regime The major powers would rightfully regard this prospect as intolerable, Aron added, and would agree "to prevent the small states from jeopardizing their superiority." Thus, "no international system has ever been, or can ever be, equalitarian. In the absence of a single authority, a reduction of the number of principal actors is indispensable to a minimum of order and predictability" (*PW,* 641).

If unilateral disarmament is suicidal and if peace by fear is impossible, what about the more modest and incremental attempts to negotiate arms control agreements? Although this proposal edged strategic policy closer to the moderate middle, Aron nevertheless placed little, if any, confidence in the prospects or possibilities of bilateral reductions. Not only are the barriers to verification and inspection virtually insurmountable, but the hostility generated by the dynamic logic of a bipolar and heterogeneous international system rules out explicit agreements between the superpowers, except on issues of relatively minor importance. "No one trusts a rival's honesty," Aron observed, "if the reward for breaking one's word can be world dominion" (*PW,* 646). What, then, is left?

"The traditional arms policy," Aron lectured, "sometimes sought to prevent war, but it always sought to win that war if it broke out in spite of everything" (*PW,* 658). What Aron found so objectionable about the strategic posture of the West was the fact that it seemed to have no other objective than the perpetuation of the present state of nonwar: "To the extent that deterrence completely replaces defense, everything proceeds as if the actors were identifying peace with victory and were unconcerned with the future in the event that deterrence should fail. But no one would say that this strategy is reasonable; in fact, the arms policy should tend to reduce the volume of violence, even or especially if war breaks out" (*PW,* 648). Insofar as the threat of war continues to be a hallmark of international relations, a policy that relies on the threat of destruction alone to deter aggression is absurd, for it condemns states to utter annihilation should it fail. Although refusing to rely on the threat of immediate and total destruction increases the risk of limited war, this position is preferable in Aron's opinion to relying on a strategy in which the consequences of failure spell certain disaster. The trick, then, is to fashion a strategy "according to which superpowers would reduce to a minimum the risk of being involved in spite of themselves in a war they do not want to wage, without either of the two being favored in the prosecution of cold war" (*PW,* 649).

To this end Aron called upon the West to reduce the role of deterrence and reinforce the means of defense. The balance of terror can be better stabilized, he asserted, "through the defense policies adopted unilaterally by each of the big powers, without any bilateral agreement" (*PW,* 660). Aside from a few broad, even skimpy, strategic recommendations—increase the level of conventional forces, encourage civil defense programs, insure the invulnerability of strategic forces—Aron gave his readers very little to go on. It may happen, Aron concluded, that in the near future technological advances will stabilize mutual deterrence. This development would be for the good, he added, because "we must not count on the diplomats" to do so (*PW,* 664).

In addition to this general strategic posture, prudence counseled patience. Unlike the forward strategy of "rollback," which Aron dismissed as aggressive to the point of suicidal, a prudent strategy for the Western world sought nothing more—and certainly nothing less—than "peaceful coexistence" with the communist bloc. Coexistence, in fact, "would . . . mean the victory of the

West, for the latter would have convinced its enemy to give up the idea of destroying it, a renunciation which in its turn is possible only by the conversion of the Marxists-Leninists to a more modest and more truthful self-interpretation. The day this conversion is achieved, we should be victorious without our enemies being therefore conquered; of all victories, the most fruitful, since it would have been obtained without bloodshed and would pave the way to reconciliation" (*PW*, 667–68).

Much like George Kennan, whom Aron greatly respected but often disagreed with, Aron argued that "surviving in peace" meant that some global regions were simply not worth American blood and treasure. The one region clearly worth it, however, was Western Europe. It is impossible to overestimate the importance of Western Europe to the United States. "As long as Atlantic unity is preserved," Aron declared, "all can still be saved; if Atlantic unity were shaken, all the West's other positions would be endangered" (*PW*, 693). In order to strengthen the bonds within the West, Aron counseled that the Atlantic pact become an Atlantic community. And, for this to occur, "leaders in Washington [must] realize that the time of the American . . . directorate is past" (*PW*, 699). Americans must reassure their allies that they are indeed committed to the protection of Europe while simultaneously offering them a meaningful role in the strategic decision-making process. Envisioning the formation of a European force, Aron hoped that a recovery of European military strength would attenuate the inequality between the United States and Europe, thereby transforming the Alliance from an American protectorate into "a common undertaking" (*PW*, 694).

Just what the West should fight for beyond the boundaries of Western Europe, however, Aron left unclear. In the short run, he maintained, should most of the countries in Africa and Asia shift their allegiance, it would alter the balance of resources and power between the blocs only slightly. For that reason the West can afford to respond to its "losses" in the Third World with a measure of detachment. Instead of believing that Western security was endangered "each time 'Ruritania' declares its allegiance to Moscow, it would be better to show . . . a certain indifference, to expose in advance the communist blackmail to which incompetent rulers are too frequently prone, wrongly convinced that Americans would be damaged more than they themselves by a victory for Moscow" (*PW*, 696). This does not mean that American leaders could freely ignore political developments in Asia or Africa; Aron, in fact, urged the West to step up its developmental assistance and counter-subversive efforts for those regimes threatened by communist insurgency movements. It does mean, however, that in the event these efforts should fail—and in many cases, Aron added, they most certainly will—these leaders should never *panic.*

Maintaining the military balance between the two blocs was also of paramount importance to the West. Should the Soviets be led to believe that they hold an incontestable superiority "either as regards passive or active instruments of deterrence or as regards military means in general," Aron argued, "the danger would risk being fatal; the Kremlin leaders would feel that the time for the final struggle had come or, more probably, they would press their adversary to the point of forcing the West to choose between capitulation and war" (*PW,* 691). At what point will the West be atomically outclassed by the East? In *Peace and War* Aron refused to speculate, saying only that it is possible "to form an approximate idea" about the disposition of military force. Was the West militarily vulnerable? "If there is a danger," Aron mused, "it is at the moment, and for many years to come it will remain, more psychological than material, more political than military" (*PW,* 688). Although maintaining a military equilibrium did not require the West to match the East bomb for bomb, stability also meant that the free world could not afford "a radical inferiority in any category" of military power, especially conventional categories (*PW,* 698).

We will save a discussion of the final chapters of *Peace and War,* which examine the possibilities of transforming and transcending power politics, for our review of Alexander Wendt's theory of international relations. Up to this point, given all that Aron has written about the importance of prudence in international relations, it seems reasonable to conclude that Aron may be placed in "the prudence tradition" of international politics, as Brian Anderson argues.[27] Beginning from the premise that human nature is flawed, those in the prudence tradition accept the inescapable reality of political conflict and thus seek not to eliminate power politics—an impossible, utopian ambition—but to temper and soften it.[28] Those in agreement with the broad precepts of the prudence tradition, however, may be a bit unsettled by the last two chapters of *Peace and War,* in which Aron entertains notions about the possible future of international politics which seem to be at odds with the prudential politics he had counseled for some six hundred pages. Before we deal with these rather speculative issues, we need to contend with a more concrete one—namely, is there any longer an interest in a theory of the sort outlined in *Peace and War*? Does it hold any relevance for understanding the post–cold war world, or is it simply a product of a bygone era?

HISTORIANS AND THE NEED FOR INTERNATIONAL RELATIONS THEORY

An interesting test of Aron's relevance might be to see how his theory of international relations responds to John Gaddis's call for "historically useful" theories, or theories that can illuminate the reflections of historians as they try to project past patterns into the future, or in this case as they try to rough out the future features of the post–cold war world. Acknowledging that he was not a "producer" but a "consumer" of theories, Gaddis laid down some markers for theorists of international relations to follow if they wanted to produce theories of some practical relevance for historical scholarship. How well does *Peace and War* match up against Gaddis's criteria?

As it turns out, pretty well. Gaddis reviewed five theories that have been put forward to explain the absence of great power war since the close of World War II: nuclear peace, bipolarity, hegemonic stability, "triumphant liberalism," and long cycles. Beginning his analysis by declaring his preference for "utilitarian standards" in explanation, Gaddis, much like Aron, stipulated that historical reality is too diffuse and indeterminate to be encapsulated within the confines of a single theoretical approach. Why, Gaddis asked, "should a historian not take the view that a single international system exists in reality, and that the theorists' conflicting conceptions of it are simply efforts at characterization from varying perspectives and for different purposes?"[29] Hence the five factors: A utilitarian strategy, or what Gaddis occasionally calls a "consumerist approach" (so named for its frank recognition of the role that personal taste plays in selecting from among an almost unlimited array of historical causes), eschews by methodological pronouncement single-factor generalizations or explanations.

In trying to assess how these factors then mix and match—do different explanations of the same thing undercut one another, do they act independently of one another, or do they somehow reinforce one another?—Gaddis engaged in the same sort of loose, open-ended mental gymnastics which Weber practiced. That is, Gaddis took the historical data at hand and subjected them to variations on Weber's question, "What would happen if . . . ?" His admittedly speculative reconstructions were not designed for precision forecasting; Gaddis, like Weber, is content with probability estimates.

Next, Gaddis insisted that theories of international relations must square the theorists' search for predictable regularities—what he termed "cyclicity"—with the historians' focus on "linearity." Here Gaddis says, theorists and historians need to meditate together on a version of Niebuhr's "Serenity Prayer": "We will require the vision to generalize where prediction is possible, the humility to refrain from generalization where it is not, and the wisdom to know the difference."[30] Unfortunately, Gaddis saw very little ecumenism at work here: "The historians, lacking vision, resist linking their work to theory in the first place, while theorists, lacking humility, claim such sweeping applicability for their generalizations as to make virtually unrecognizable the history upon which they are based."[31] Surprisingly enough, Gaddis evinces an appreciation here for what the hard sciences have done, especially in chaos theory, in trying to link regularity and linearity.

Finally, Gaddis closes his essay by declaring that a world of "unsimilatable situations" means that "the behavior of statesmen and not systems will make the critical difference." As Gaddis recognized, in an inherently indeterminate world, we must rely on those "elusively non-theoretical qualities that we associate with statesmanship—patience, courage, common-sense, vision and humility—qualities whose very resistance to precise definition suggests their adaptability in dealing with the unpredictable." And given this indeterminacy, Gaddis concluded, a long peace requires not just "good history and good theory, but good sense (and good luck) as well."[32]

These, then, are the three features of a "responsible" theory for Gaddis: Theory must acknowledge the existence of a gap between concept and existence, it must acknowledge the need for both generalization and narration, and it must acknowledge the need for human judgment in action. What are these if not the three classical moments, or "antitheses," of theory for Aron: "reality and theory, empiricism (historical and sociological) and theory, practice and theory"? Thus it is that Gaddis testifies to the ongoing utility of the historical sociology articulated in *Peace and War.*

CONSTRUCTIVISM

In assessing the originality and significance of *Peace and War,* it is helpful to place it alongside two relatively recent theoretical innovations, namely, constructivism and neorealism. In doing so, we will discover that Aron's theory of international relations may perhaps be best understood as an effort to occupy intellectual territory midway between the two. We begin by comparing Aron's political sociology with constructivism, particularly as it manifests itself in the work of Alexander Wendt.

Although a new wave of constructivist theories seems to be cresting in international relations, it does not seem to be assuming any immediately recognizable form. The problem of identifying even the most basic elements of this approach, variously referred to as "constructivism," "relativism," or "reflectivism," are legion. Maja Zehfuss, for example, recites a long litany of definitional difficulties, ranging from its place in the conceptual hierarchy—Is it a theory, a methodology, or a philosophy?—to its place within a theoretical spectrum: Is it an alternative to neorealism and neoliberalism or a bridge between them and other, more radical approaches to the discipline?[33]

In the absence of a clear idea or definition of constructivism, Zehfuss adopts the not unreasonable strategy of deciding what it is by first deciding who it is. In other words, Zehfuss locates the first cluster of scholars to identify themselves as "constructivists" and then proceeds to extract some common meaning or shared field of concern from their scholarship, an approach that led Zehfuss to concentrate on the works of Friedrich Kratochwil, Nicholas Onuf, and Alexander Wendt in her own study of constructivism. Of these three I here focus on the work of Alexander Wendt, among the most prolific and theoretically far-ranging of the constructivists. Much like Aron, Wendt is engaged in rethinking the foundations of international relations theory. Accordingly, a comparison between Aron and Wendt is a useful and instructive exercise.

At the heart of Wendt's constructivism is this proposition: "Statism, like the state, can be historically progressive."[34] Beginning from the realist premise that states find themselves in a primordial condition of anarchy, Wendt nevertheless reaches the rather un-realist conclusion that states can learn to swear off violence and work for peace. This stance is possible, Wendt insists, because states are creatures not of interests but ideas. States can therefore be whatever they choose to be; their behavior need not be constrained or hamstrung by a preexistent set of "objective conditions" such as anarchy because anarchy, like any social fact, has only as much power and force as states allow it to have. If they so choose, states could make anarchy a force for peaceful collaboration or collective security just as readily as they have made it a call to arms.

Wendt, then, takes as a central fact of international relations an existential datum that many dismiss as irrelevant, namely, the collective identities of states. Because regimes, leaders, and citizens are so thickly embedded in a political culture, he argues, it is theoretically reckless to assume that their actions are governed simply by the mechanical application of self-interest. Far richer explanations of political behavior begin from the premise that states, like individuals, are social beings that attribute significance to their environments. "A fundamental principle of constructivist social theory," Wendt explains, "is that people act toward objects, including other actors, on the basis of the meaning that the objects have for them."[35] All states, for example, reckon with a given configuration of power, but how they do so depends "on the intersubjective understandings and expectations, on the 'distribution of knowledge,' that constitute their conception of self and other."[36]

Wendt's interest in social meaning and identity formation is hardly original in international relations theory. Two working hypotheses, however, distinguish his constructivism from the "strong liberalism" of thinkers such as Stanley Hoffmann and Joseph Nye, thinkers who, like Wendt, believe that states can learn to overcome their egoism for the sake of collaboration and cooperation. First, Wendt insists that state identity can be profoundly affected, even transformed, by interaction with other states and global institutions. Although neoliberals, too, believe that states can respond favorably to agreeable systemic forces, Wendt believes that neoliberals do not go far enough in recognizing the potential for international political change. Beginning from the unwarranted assumption that there are limits to the changes that states will endure for the sake of a better world, Wendt complains, neoliberals generally end up insisting that "the most we can expect is behavioral cooperation, not community."[37] Wendt, it seems, expects more than functional cooperation among nation-states: He is apparently working not for perpetual peace based on confederation and cooperation but for a perpetual peace based on what can perhaps best be described as a "reconciled humanity."

Second, Wendt insists that "the key structures in the states system are intersubjective, rather than material."[38] By this he means that international structures "are always being reproduced or transformed by practice and thus are not static background conditions for collective identity formation."[39] A structural constraint such as power, then, is not a material reality for Wendt but an intentional one. "The key," he explains, "is to reclaim power and interest from materialism by showing how their content and meaning are constituted by ideas and culture."[40] A systemic environment, therefore, no less than an actor's identity, is forever "in process," sustained or transformed by the beliefs of those who constitute a given system. As Wendt puts it, "Institutions are fundamentally cognitive entities that do not exist apart from actors' ideas about how the world works."[41] Assuming otherwise reifies these institutions and lends to them a sort of permanence or external force that they do not really have.

By viewing state actors and their systemic environments as dynamic, intentional realities created and shaped by those who inhabit them, Wendt hopes "to overcome any false sense of determinism" (*ST*, 375). In doing so, he hopes to unlock the potential for reform in the international system by suggesting that seemingly intractable problems may be amenable to human contrivance after all. "By reconceptualizing the structure of the system in holistic and especially idealist terms," Wendt argues, "we make it possible to ask constitutive questions that might lead to progress in the system's evolution" (*ST*, 376). Perpetual peace, it seems, is not something to be hoped for but something to be willed.

For all of his insistence that the human world is an intentional one fraught with meaning and significance, Wendt still clings to a belief in an "objective" world, a world of stubborn facts and harsh realities capable of resisting our best efforts to make it otherwise. For that reason there are limits to the malleability of power politics and the international system, limits that have their origins in what Wendt terms "systemic" and "psychological" realities. Despite its intentional origins, Wendt writes, a system of any sort is really a very powerful thing. "Once constituted, any social system confronts its members as an objective social fact that reinforces certain behaviors and discourages others."[42] Some reflexive behaviors, it seems, are not easily unlearned; in fact, some expectations may be so powerfully ingrained in a collective identity that there is virtually no room "for actions that deviate from the prescribed script."[43] And, psychologically, some states may resist any change that threatens to undo "any relatively role identities." Leaping into an uncertain future to play an unknown role may generate so much anxiety that states simply refuse to countenance any alternative to the status quo.

This understanding prompts Wendt to reach a rather astonishing conclusion, given all he has said before. Even though states are continuously "producing and reproducing identities and interests, continuously 'choosing now the interests they will have later,'" their choices may not necessarily "be experienced with meaningful degrees of freedom."[44] It seems that realists have a point after all: "This could be a constructivist justification for the realist position that only simple learning is possible in self-help systems. The realist might concede that such systems are socially constructed and still argue that after the corresponding identities and interests have become institutionalized they are almost impossible to transform."[45]

Because ideas apparently do not "go all the way down," in Wendt's suggestive phrase, states still find themselves responding in some measure to material forces such as power. Even in Wendt's intentional universe "brute facts have ontological priority over institutional facts" (*ST,* 110). Wendt identifies three categories of facts and forces that bear directly on political and diplomatic calculation: military forces, technology, and natural resources. These three categories of immovable objects, Wendt maintains, generally stand firm against the irresistible force of subjective intention. No matter how desperately one may wish it otherwise, "armies with tanks will usually defeat armies with spears" (*ST,* 111). For all of its emphasis on human intentionality or subjectivity, Wendt grumbles, his idealism "is that of Durkheim and Mead, not Pollyanna or Peter Pan."[46] The important point here is that material conditions may be expansive or restrictive: the independent power of material forces will vary with circumstances. Anarchy may be what states make of it, but anarchy nevertheless remains.

The similarity between Aron's starting point and Wendt's is striking. Wendt's insistence that states confront one another in a condition of anarchy is no different than Aron's insistence that all international relations take place in the shadow of war. Because Aron and Wendt hold fast to the importance of ideas and intentions in human action, however, both agree that the meaning of anarchy or threat is largely a social one, constructed and interpreted by those who confront it. Moreover, both Wendt and Aron are in fundamental agreement over what Aron termed the "indeterminacy of action." Given the fact that statesmen and diplomats pursue a variety of goals ranging from power to glory to ideas, it is impossible to construct a general theory of international relations comparable to a general theory of the economy. Both Aron and Wendt insist, in other words, that there are limits to rational explanations of political or collective behavior. Wendt takes aim at every manner of rational choice theory, as Aron took aim at Weber's doctrine of zweckrational action. Both agree that the simple schema of calculating ends and means is overly simple: For Aron and for Wendt ideas are in many ways more decisive than interests in directing, and hence explaining, human action.

Aron and Wendt also place the object of international relations in similar systemic environments. Wendt's elaboration of the three forms of anarchy—the Hobbesian, Lockean, and Kantian (or enemy, rival, friend)—only slightly modifies Aron's distinction between homogeneous and heterogeneous systems, while Wendt also subjects his theoretical constructs to many of the same structural or sociological determinants as Aron, such as biology and culture (although Aron's list seems to be more exhaustive and systematic than Wendt's). Finally, Wendt, like Aron, refuses to detach normative issues in international relations theory from theoretical ones, calling at one point for "a dialogue between IR [international relations] and the fields of Political Theory and Normative IR," an appeal that echoes Aron's call for "praxeology."

There is one other area of broad agreement here worth noting, namely, methodology. Again, the similarities between Aron and Wendt are striking. Because Wendt begins from the premise that the object of international relations is both material and ideal, it is not too surprising that, like Aron, he calls for a methodology that combines explanation and understanding. Causal analysis, which takes its cue from a world "out there," or a world that exists independently of human intention, is both possible and necessary to Wendt. "The state and state system are real structures whose nature can be approximated through science," he argues (*ST,* 47). Nevertheless, Wendt insists that there are limits to the objectivity and utility of causal analysis, limits that are revealed the moment one stops to think about exactly what is being explained in the first place. These "what questions" are the questions of "constitutive theorizing," or the propositions of "understanding," in Aronian parlance. "Rather than asking how or why a temporally prior *x* produced an independently existing *y*," Wendt explains, "how-possible and what-questions are requests for explications of the structures that constitute *x* and *y* in the first place" (*ST,* 83). Moreover, constitutive theorizing not only defines the objects of analysis but may in fact connect intentional or ideational realities to some sort of comprehensive, intelligible whole as well. "To understand the difference that ideas and social structures make in international politics," Wendt maintains, "we need to recognize the existence of constitutive effects. Ideas or social structures have constitutive effects when they create phenomena . . . that are conceptually or logically dependent on those ideas or structures, that exist only 'in virtue' of them" (*ST,* 87–88).

In all of this, Wendt seems to hold to a theory of concept formation which closely resembles Aron's. Like Aron, Wendt allows for some slippage between conceptual constructs and reality. Acknowledging that "the boundaries of many natural kinds are hard to specify," Wendt nevertheless refuses to draw the postmodernist conclusion that there are therefore no boundaries to draw in the first place, or that natural and social kinds "do not have any essential properties at all" (*ST*, 59). Not all interpretations or constitutive theories are equally valid, Wendt avers; bad ones must be weeded out and good ones confirmed by a process of verification, a process made possible, at least in principle, by the existence of a world beyond subjective intentions and interpretations.

Despite these similarities, there is one significant difference between Aron's approach to international relations theory and Wendt's, a theoretical difference that may account for a striking practical one. The theoretical difference is that nowhere in Wendt's approach to international relations does there seem to be any room for what Aron termed "history." Nowhere in Wendt's *Social Theory of International Politics* do we encounter an extended discussion of the kinds of causality (sociological and historical) which so preoccupied Aron in the *Introduction to the Philosophy of History.* And nowhere in *Social Theory of International Politics* is there an extended discussion of the current international scene, as there is in *Peace and War,* a discussion "of a concrete situation," as Aron put it, "enlightened by the previous study of concepts and determinants."

Now, on the one hand, there is nothing in Wendt's methodology or in his approach to international relations theorizing which is incompatible with Aron's interest in history. Like Aron, Wendt apparently believes that general sociological determinants are refracted through the historical circumstances of time and place, a fact that explains how collective identities come to display such remarkable variety. On the other hand, it is precisely because Wendt believes so strongly in the power of circumstances that his indifference to history is striking. This lack of interest, however, is no theoretical oversight: Wendt's indifference to history is accounted for by the fact that he and Aron have two very different praxeologies. These differences are differences in degree, not kind, but the difference here in normative conviction may make all the difference in the world.

In order to compare the normative commitments of Aron and Wendt, it is helpful to put to Aron the same question that is at the heart of Wendt's constructivism—namely, can the state be historically progressive? Is there reason to hope not only for perpetual peace based on a confederation of states but for a perpetual peace predicated on a reconciled humanity, one in which new forms of democratic accountability may be envisioned on a global scale? This is, in fact, the very question Aron raised at the end of *Peace and War,* in which he explored the possibility of transcending or transforming the violent character of power politics. His introduction to the issue is worth quoting at length because it reveals the depth of his interest in the issue. "The horrors of twentieth century war and the thermonuclear threat," Aron wrote, "have given the rejection of power politics not only an actuality and an urgency, but also a kind of obviousness. History must no longer be a succession of bloody conflicts if humanity is to pursue its adventure. Never have the disproportion appeared so striking, so tragic, between the possible catastrophe and stakes of inter-state rivalries. All classical strategy—including that which has been sketched in the preceding pages—appears lamentably inadequate, measured by the demands of peace and the dangers of war." "I do not protest against these sentiments," Aron added, "I share them. Men aspire to a historical transformation of states and their transformation" (*PW*, 703). In assessing the likelihood of peace through transformation, Aron picked his way through a seemingly endless thicket of arguments clustered around two broad possibilities, peace through law and peace through federation and empire.

In considering the case for peace through law, Aron reviewed a wealth of ideas and historical data stretching from Hans Kelsen's attempt to ground a system of international law to the founding of the League of Nations. As one would expect, Aron is pessimistic about the prospects for creating an international juridical order, one in which states and other major actors would willingly surrender their sovereign judgments to an international tribunal of some sort. Not only is Aron unable to locate an "originating norm" or a "normative fact" capable of commanding universal assent, he simply does not believe that states currently have the political will to assent to such a system should one prove to be theoretically possible. "When the jurist asserts that 'the will of the international community must be obeyed,'" Aron declared, "it is too easy to reply that the will common to the sovereign states exists only in the imagination of the theoretician" (*PW*, 719).

Aron then proceeded to slam the door shut on any future hopes for a fundamental transformation of the international system by pointing to the grim record of past historical experience. Conceding that there are moments when human beings experience a sense of common humanity—during a natural catastrophe, for example—Aron nevertheless exclaimed, "But how rare and weak are those shared emotions which unite or blocs and divide humanity!" (*PW*, 722). Never, he wrote, "in any limited system—that of the Greek city-states, that of the Christian community, or that of the European Concert—

have the values of common interest controlled the conduct of the actors in major circumstances. In peacetime, to settle secondary problems, the semi-consciousness of a common civilization was not without an influence. It was immediately repressed by passions when the call to arms was sounded." "One does not judge international law," he concluded "by peaceful periods and secondary problems" (*PW*, 732, 733).

And then the door opens, even if but a crack and if only to admit nothing more than an idea of reason. Wondering if peace by law is a chimera, or "a false idea, contradictory to the nature of man and societies," Aron stipulated to three quite Kantian conditions in order for peace by law to prevail: States must be republican in form, aware of their mutual interests, and willing "to say 'farewell to arms,'" agreeing "without anxiety to submit their disputes to a tribunal" (*PW*, 734–35). Are such conditions possible, even imaginable, given the violent and bloody legacy of international relations? Only if states themselves first undergo some sort of transformation: "The end of the arms race requires that states no longer suspect each other of the worst intentions; it also requires that states no longer desire force in order to impose their will upon the others." Should all of these conditions obtain, "who could fail to see that all humanities, pacified by law, would resemble those national communities in which the competition of individuals and interests now only rarely resembles a character of violence?" And here Aron arrives at the question that preoccupies Wendt: "But would such a world . . . still be divided into states, or would it unite humanity into a worldwide federation, if not into a universal empire" (*PW*, 735–36)? Is it possible to believe states will someday wither away, launching a political makeover on a grand, global scale? Are states, in other words, historically progressive?

Aron began by wondering if an international system stripped of sovereign nation-states was even desirable in the first place. Reflecting on the possibility of a "Common Market" creating, "by the tap of a magic wand," a united Europe, Aron declared that "we have . . . lost the essential thing: the community power, animated by a community desire, the state and the nation, the human collectivity, conscious of its uniqueness determined to assert and affirm it in the face of all other collectivities" (*PW*, 747). In other words, economic progress, in and of itself, does not create political will, which is something altogether different. In fact, Aron charged that the "hope that the European federation will gradually and inevitably emerge from the Common Market is based on a great illusion of our times: the illusion that economic and technological interdependence among the various factions of humanity has definitively devalued the fact of 'political sovereignties,' the existence of distinct states which wish to be autonomous" (*PW,* 748). This is not necessarily a bad thing. Indeed, Aron argued that national sovereignties contribute significantly to human moral development. As he explained it, "The ideal of a humanity conscious of its own solidarity does not contradict the fact of a humanity divided into nations conscious of their uniqueness and of the value of their uniqueness." How is it, Aron wondered, that an individual could be "obligated to all of humanity without being so with regard to the nation that made him what he is?" (*PW,* 751). A world drained or stripped of national identities and sovereignties would thus be an "impoverished" world.

This does not mean, however, that nationalisms are therefore "justified." Here, Aron argued, is "the final antinomy of man's political destiny." It is not "more satisfying for consciousness to deny than it is to sanctify nations, to refuse them the right to determine their own destiny than to grant them the right to determine without appeal their own justice" (*PW,* 752). The theoretical solution to this antinomy is federalism, "a civilized or voluntary version of empire," whereby one's national culture is preserved but not the political power to protect it, sovereignty having been turned over to a higher authority. The obstacle to federation of this sort, of course, is precisely the same as the obstacle to peace through law: In both cases states would have to abandon their claims to sovereignty, or their "right of determining justice without appeal." And that, Aron flatly asserted, is most unlikely: "The progress of rational organization, in labor and administration, has made neither individuals nor collectivities reasonable" (*PW,* 754). And peace by empire is neither more likely nor more desirable than peace by law or federation. It requires a rather "robust confidence" in human nature, Aron insisted, "to imagine victors 'surmounting their victory' and sacrificing the pride of triumph to the reconciliation of all" (*PW,* 760).

Yes, but for all of that, is peace by law, federation, or empire impossible? Well before the end of his praxeology, it becomes clear that Aron will not offer a categorical answer to this question. Aron's speculations about the future of interstate relations were rife with uncertainty and hedged about by qualifications. His ambivalence is perhaps best captured in a sentence devoted to the possibility of resolving the antinomy between national sovereignty and global reconciliation. This antinomy, Aron wrote, "is not necessarily eternal, but it is not yet resolved, *supposing of course that it can be*" (*PW,* 752; emphasis added). This is a far cry from Wendt's insistence that even a "strong" liberalism needs to be even more doggedly attached to a program of international reform and reconciliation. Compared to Wendt's American optimism, Aron's Old World weariness is rather striking. Would Aron have been open to greater optimism had he witnessed the collapse of the Soviet Union? Probably not. He seems to believe that, whatever the formal political condition or organization of human beings, enmity will always be present, for enmity seems to be natural to humans. And Aron certainly never suggested that peace lay just beyond the cold war, as if the collapse of the Soviet Empire would usher in a golden age and put an end to all the tensions that plague humanity. Of all the historical and normative scenarios Aron reviewed in his praxeology, none could be imagined to be free from violence and conflict.

It seems, then, that Aron and Wendt part company on an important normative issue—namely, the possibility of creating not a functioning international community but a genuinely sovereign one. Both Wendt and Aron seem to be mirror images of the other on this score: Wendt gives a nod in the direction of the prudence tradition with as much vigor and enthusiasm as Aron nodded in the direction of Kantian idealism. It is important to note that Aron's penchant for pessimism was reinforced by his willingness to place himself on the level of historical fact, or by his willingness to adopt the position of statesman when judging historical and normative possibilities. The importance of this perspective to Aron's thinking is made evident in a story Aron loved to tell about an experience he had during his graduate student days in Weimar Germany. In 1932 Aron's older brother, Adrien, had arranged for Aron to meet a friend of his, Joseph Pagnon, who was an undersecretary in the French Foreign Ministry. Eager to let the undersecretary know exactly what was happening in Germany, Aron leaped at the chance to meet Monsieur Pagnon and describe in detail the threat confronting France. Aron later rather dryly recalled that the lecture he gave the undersecretary upon meeting him was indeed an exceptional one, "brilliant, I suppose, in the pure style of a student from the ENS." When Aron had finished his lecture, the undersecretary, who had been listening with close attention, put a simple question to Aron, one that hit him with such force that it stayed with Aron for the rest of his life. "What would you do," Pagnon asked, "if you were in [the foreign minister's] place?" Aron later wrote that he could not remember what he said: "I am sure that it was embarrassed, unless I kept silent."[47] Viewing events from this perspective tends to underscore the constraints of action, a point that Aron once made in discussing the government of Léon Blum and the war in Spain. "Even though, in André Malraux's circle, Léon Blum's policy was more frequently criticized than excused," Aron wrote, "I put myself in the prime minister's place, following the lesson given to me by Joseph Pagnon, and I came to the same conclusion as he did. Can the leader of a democratic government commit his country to an action that involves a risk of war and that half the country does not consider to be in the national interest?"[48]

Anderson is quite right, then, to claim Aron as a fellow traveler in the prudence tradition. Given Aron's unflagging dedication to the idea of reason, however, those who uphold prudence as the supreme virtue of statesmanship may be a bit unsettled by the uncomfortably large opening in Aron's theory of international relations—especially in his methodology—toward constructivism, especially of the sort advocated by Alexander Wendt. There are differences between Aron and Wendt, to be sure, but, given Aron's dialectical temperament, those differences are certainly not absolute; both thinkers clearly share the hope for a reasonable politics and a reconciled humanity. "Tragedy would be the final judgment," Aron wrote near the end of his life, "only if a fortunate conclusion, beyond tragedy, was not even conceivable. I continue to think a happy end possible, far beyond the political horizon, an Idea of Reason."[49]

THE NEOREALISM OF KENNETH WALTZ

In turning from constructivism to neorealism, we leave behind a world of progressive goodwill and enter a darker, more Machiavellian universe. At first glance it would seem that this is a world in which Aron could think and move rather comfortably. After all, both Aron and Kenneth Waltz—perhaps the chief intellectual architect of neorealism—assert that power and conflict are defining features of international politics. Beyond this shared belief, however, the differences between Aron's realism and Waltz's neorealism are so significant that approaching them as simply two variations on the same gloomy worldview is probably more misleading than helpful. In the end the distance between Waltz's realism and Aron's is perhaps just as great as the distance between Aron's liberalism and Wendt's.

For our purposes perhaps the most striking theoretical difference between Waltz and Aron is Waltz's indifference to some dimensions of what Aron called "sociological causality." Just as Wendt's streak of optimism accounts for his relative indifference to the constraining forces of historical necessity, so too does Waltz's pessimism explain his rather constricted interest in those forms of causality attached to human will and intentionality. Compared to

Aron, then, Wendt works with theoretical tools that exaggerate the possibilities for change and political reform, while Waltz develops a theory of international relations which unduly minimizes them.

Like Aron, Waltz sets out to ground his theory of international relations in a host of preexisting conceptual distinctions. Unlike Aron, however, Waltz attends to this exercise with meticulous precision. One of the problems that usually plagues more traditional approaches to international relations theory, Waltz complains, is that international relations scholars have played a bit too fast and loose with the word *theory,* frequently using it "to cover any work that departs from mere description and seldom to refer only to works that meet philosophy-of-science standards."[50] His theory of international relations, however, would eschew such sloppiness in favor of an approach marked out by clear conceptual boundaries. The anticipated payoff here is that Waltz hopes to have at his disposal a theoretical instrument that can lay claim only to such knowledge as has been tested and verified. As Waltz repeatedly reminds his readers, the problem with most theories of international relations is that few define their terms carefully enough to generate propositions fit for empirical testing. The challenge, then, "is to link theoretical concepts with a few variables in order to construe explanations from which hypotheses can be inferred and tested" (*T,* 17). If a theory of international relations could do so, then such a theory might finally overcome the discipline's rather "depressing" tendency to pass off as knowledge an almost endless parade of studies that are, in the end, almost entirely devoid of explanatory and predictive power.

Perhaps the chief obstacle to a genuine theory of international relations is the taste among social scientists for what Waltz calls "reductionism," or the tendency to explain international political events by referring to "psychological factors or national political and economic characteristics" (*T,* 19). The great shortcoming of this approach is its insistence that a whole is known only by dissecting and peering into its parts, as if "wholes" had no independent identity of their own. The problem with these sorts of "inside out" explanations, Waltz argues, is that they tend to be heavily descriptive and impressionistic, oversensitive as they are to the sudden changes and momentary reversals of international politics. Reductionist approaches thus fail to account for the continuities of international political behavior or for the fact that outcomes in international relations "seldom correspond to the intentions of actors" (*T,* 65).

Aron comes in for some rather heavy criticism from Waltz on this score, as does one of Aron's most celebrated students, Stanley Hoffmann. Analysts such as Aron and Hoffmann "who confine their attention to interacting units, without recognizing that systemic causes are in play," Waltz complains, "compensate for the omissions by assigning such causes arbitrarily to the level of interacting units and parceling them out among actors" (*T*, 62). This analytical habit of Aron's and Hoffmann's has important practical consequences. If domestic factors are seen to be the driving force between and among states, Waltz argues, then "domestic politics are made into matters of direct international concern." This is precisely what happened during the pursuit of détente between the United States and the Soviet Union in the 1970s. Analysts who believed that the balance of power must be buttressed by a common moral framework in order to function effectively also generally tended to believe that American diplomats and policy makers had to lean on Soviet leaders and urge them to govern the Soviet Union "a little more liberally" if the Soviets wanted détente to succeed. If we believe that political outcomes are directly tied to the intentions or character of nation-states, Waltz writes, "then we must be concerned with, and if necessary do something to change, the internal dispositions of the internationally important ones" (*T*, 62). Waltz has also taken Aron to task for upholding the "complexity" of international politics as a deterrent to theoretical precision and for confusing conditions in the testing of theory with difficulties in constructing a theory.[51]

In order to account for the regularities and similarities of international political behavior, Waltz proposes to analyze not the internal characteristics of regimes or the motivations of their designated representatives but the systemic interactions of nation-states, which he takes to be the central actors in international relations. "Since the variety of actors and the variations in their actions are not motivated by the variety of outcomes," Waltz maintains, "we know that systemic causes are in play" (*T*, 69). A systemic perspective might not explain everything, but it explains enough. "Structural concepts," Waltz writes, "although they lack detailed content, help to explain some big, important and enduring patterns" (*T*, 70). This point is of fundamental significance for Waltz. "The problem seen in the light of the theory," he maintains, "is not to say how to manage the world, including its great powers, but to say how the possibility that great powers will constructively manage international affairs varies as the systems change" (*T*, 210). Although he agrees that nation-states may respond to structural or systemic constraints in unpredictable ways, Waltz nevertheless argues that, for analytical purposes, a theory of international relations begins by uncoupling the internal qualities of states from their environment and considering only the systemic environment and its interactions.

The conceptual force at the heart of Waltz's theory of international relations is set in motion simply by detaching the two halves of Aron's elemental construct—the diplomat and the soldier—and then declaring one component (the soldier) to be weightier than the other. By effectively discarding half of Aron's working model, Waltz begins from a vastly more simplified representation of human behavior, one that quite consciously imitates economists' efforts to explain behavior by grounding human rationality in the simple, stripped-down impulse of self-interest. Translating the economic language of self-interest into the political vernacular of international relations, Waltz thus declares that international political behavior is governed by the principle of self-help, a principle or form of behavior made necessary by the anarchy that reigns in the world of nation-states.

By stripping human action of its psychological paraphernalia, Waltz has created a model of human behavior which possesses nothing more than a formal validity; his ideal actor is every bit the empty construct that *Homo economicus* is intended to be. "In a macrotheory," Waltz explains, "the motivations of the actors is assumed rather than realistically described." If theoretical models are not somehow matched against actual behavior—and Waltz emphatically insists that they are not—then exactly how one goes about assessing the adequacy of such theoretical constructs is not altogether clear.[52] On this crucial point Waltz simply advances the notion that theoretical models of human action are never true but are, rather, "sensible" or "useful." A theory's utility "depends on whether a theory based on the assumption can be contrived, a theory from which important consequences not otherwise obvious can be affirmed." And a theory's sensibility is something that "can be directly discussed" (*T*, 91).

In constructing his theory of international relations, Waltz places great store in the constraining effect that systems and structures have on behavior. As a matter of principle, he has to: Otherwise, if Waltz admits that human behavior can resist the canalizing effects of an external environment, then little hope remains that action will congeal into regular patterns of theoretically predictable behavior. "Structural constraints cannot be wished away," Waltz writes, adding almost under his breath, "although many fail to understand this" (*T*, 109). Again, there is a modicum of indeterminacy in human affairs from Waltz's perspective but not much. In opposition to most constructivists

—who seem to believe that, if the state can think it, the state can become it—Waltz insists that "states facing global problems are like individual consumers trapped by the 'tyranny of small decisions.' States, like consumers, can get out of the trap only by changing the structure of their field of activity" (*T*, 110–11). The intractability of systems and structures explains why wishing and working with all one's might will never be enough in international relations: "In a self-help system, each of the units spends a portion of its effort, not in forwarding its own good but in providing the means of protecting itself against others" (*T*, 105). The power of structural constraints explains why outcomes so often run contrary to intentions. Even though Winston Churchill recognized that the naval race between Britain and Germany at the turn of the century would prove to be ruinous, Waltz points out, Churchill knew that Britain had no choice but to run it.

From the twin principles of self-help and anarchy, Waltz then deduces the basic proposition of his theory of international relations—namely, that states invariably attempt to check and balance one another in order to maximize their security. "If there is any distinctively political theory of international politics," Waltz declares, "balance-of-power theory is it." Putting this principle quite so baldly, however, is not terribly helpful. "To infer that expectation from the theory," Waltz explains, "is not impressive if balancing is a universal pattern of political behavior, as is sometimes claimed. It is not." Theorists must also contend with the phenomenon of "bandwagoning," or the tendency of weaker states to ally themselves with stronger states rather than to oppose them. "Whether political actors balance each other or climb on the bandwagon depends on the system structure" (*T*, 117). The next task for Waltz, then, is to construct a complete range of systemic scenarios, a task, as we have seen, of critical significance to Aron.

Given his methodological aversion to reckoning with psychological or intentional determinants, Waltz sets out to create a "purely positional" representation of international relations. Accordingly, Waltz classifies international systems on the basis of their "ordering principle" (anarchy or hierarchy), the character of the units (nation-states), and the capabilities of those units (power). In defining international political structures, Waltz explains, it is important to remember that one must "abstract from every attribute of states except their capability." Waltz then proceeds to rough out "what range of expectations arises merely from looking at the type of order that prevails among [states] and at the distribution of capabilities within that order." In the end, Waltz declares, what should emerge "is a positional picture, a general description of the ordered overall arrangement of a society written in terms of the placement of units rather than in terms of their qualities" (*T,* 99).

After mapping out his theory, Waltz then probes the systemic consequences of carefully specified systemic changes. More specifically, Waltz speculates about the consequences that changes in capability would have on the system as a whole, assuming that the international organizing principle (anarchy) remains constant. This analytical exercise leads Waltz to explore the stability of different sort of systems (bipolar or multipolar) and to analyze just how it is that one estimates a slippery term such as *power,* especially when intentionality has been so thoroughly discounted. Here Waltz is particularly anxious to undercut those who believe that economic interdependence has dramatically reconfigured the international landscape. Analysts of that sort, Waltz suggests, have put the analytical cart before the horse: "They are concerned with interdependence as a unit-level phenomenon, as is to be expected since reduction dominates the field. Those who confine their analyses to the unit level infer from the growth of international business and the increased intensity of international activity that 'interdependence' has risen" (*T,* 145).

In matching Waltz's theory of international relations with Aron's, we notice that both Waltz and Aron share a common appreciation for historical analysis. As an attachment to a theory of international relations, history for both thinkers can be a realm of theoretical inquiry dedicated to confirming theory, although, as Waltz hastens to point out, not without a measure of uncertainty and ambiguity. Conspicuously absent in Waltz's theory of international relations, however, is any sort of sociological plane, or an analytical dimension that lists and reviews the influence of broad causal factors or categories. Aron's theory of international relations, we will recall, incorporated two fields of causal determinants into its conceptual structure, namely, physical and moral determinants. Waltz, for his part, makes it clear that his sort of theorizing is flatly opposed to the introduction of any factor that deflects attention from a consideration of systemic properties and turns analysis inward toward a consideration of national styles or characteristics. By declaring moral or psychological properties fit subjects for analysis, Aron is signaling his determination to do precisely that. Indeed, Aron hastens to point out that the sociological section of *Peace and War* was written to counter the "inexorable determinism" of systemic or single-factor explanations (*PW,* 279).

The reasons for Waltz's reflexive dismissal of this type of sociological analysis become clearer when we notice the complete absence of another theoretical compartment of Aron's theory of international relations, namely, praxeology. Here we reach the nub of the difference between Waltz and Aron. For Aron moral choice in international relations is at least theoretically conceivable, if not always historically possible. For Waltz genuine moral choice is simply out of the question. In addressing the way in which great powers manage global affairs, for example, Waltz points out that states "do not act only for their own sakes. They also act for the world's common good." But, Waltz immediately adds, "the common good is defined by each of them for all of us, and the definitions conflict." Under those conditions "one may fear the arrogance of the global burden-bearers more than the selfishness of those who tend to their own narrowly defined interests" (*T*, 205).

This is why Waltz simply shrugs off normative problems in *Theory of International Politics.* As a political realist, Waltz is more anxious to underscore the limits of collaborative behavior rather than its possibilities, while, as a political scientist, Waltz declares moral issues to be beyond the purview of empirical analysis altogether. In other words, choice, especially moral choice, is so constrained by necessity that it is impossible for Waltz to believe that human action can ever rise above the exigencies of self-preservation. Accordingly, then, to Waltz's way of thinking there is no need for a level of analysis such as sociology which can allow for a modicum of self-determination or for a realm of analysis such as praxeology which allows for a measure of genuine moral judgment.

We have already encountered a social science of this sort in the person and work of Max Weber. Like Weber, Waltz assumes that reason is purely instrumental, or zweckrational. Consequently, political actors are presumed to be, above all else, "interest maximizers," which means that in the international arena the interest that diplomats and political leaders are assumed to be maximizing is security. As we have seen, however, Aron finds this assumption overly restrictive and artificial; even in economics, the discipline from which Waltz draws so much of his own logic and inspiration, Aron warns against the temptation to reduce all human action to a "sole criterion" or to a single quantifiable motivation.[53] Aron's commentary on Weber makes it clear that the great shortcoming of this approach is that it fails to capture or account for the full range of human actions or motivations. Waltz's theory of international relations is thus so highly stylized and abstract that it is not too much to say that for Aron it is virtually pointless.

Virtually but not completely. At the close of *Peace and War,* in a remarkably prescient analysis of game theory and international relations, Aron highlights a few contributions that this sort of economically inspired theory can make. The matrices of game theory, he argues, can render three services to political scientists:

> They oblige them to accept a kind of discipline of thought, to analyze and enumerate all possible eventualities in a given situation. They help them to construct ideal types of circumstances of conflict (games with two players, *N* players, zero-sum games, non-zero-sum games). They permit the abstract formulation of the dialectic of antagonism: decisions are not taken with regard to a future about which we know nothing, nor with regard to a future in which each event is unknown to us, but in which the approximate frequency of the various classes of events is known to us. The strategic decisions constitute a chain, each decision provokes the following and the latter tends to counteract the preceding one. The chess player moves a pawn in response to the movement of an adverse pawn: the strategist opposes his enemy similarly.

Beyond these rather schematic contributions, however, analysts must at some point "focus on the differences between the simplified models that lent themselves to mathematical treatment and the concrete situations" (*PW,* 772). More specifically, Aron worried that, when faced with the need to assess a rival's intentions or reaction, the abstruse calculations of game theory can become "more dangerous than useful." The mental contortions of economic game theory "give an appearance of rigor to decisions which are at best the result of reflection, and above all they falsify the nature and the development of the deliberation." This is due to the fact that "the stake is never definite because it is not separable from the total conflict and because the very stake of the total conflict is not and cannot be known to the strategists" (*PW,* 777).

In the end, then, political theories derived from rational choice may indeed be elegant, parsimonious, and logical; they may, from time to time, even prove to be of great heuristic benefit to political scientists. Nevertheless, to Aron's way of thinking, because rational choice theories abstract *too* much from concrete circumstances, they cannot serve as the sort of social science that matters most, namely, as "a science for the politician."

Some twenty-five years after the appearance of *Peace and War,* it is clear that both maxims of Aron's praxeology—a certain indifference toward communist insurgency movements in the Third World and a commitment to a massive buildup of military strength—were systematically ignored or violated by American leaders, the first in the 1960s during the intervention in Vietnam, the second in the 1970s during the dramatic reduction of U.S. military power.[54] The tragedy of the 1960s, Aron believed, resulted from American hubris, while the event of the 1970s stemmed from a failure of nerve. Neither decade, however, prompted Aron to consider whether American democracy could have long endured the contrary pulls and pressures generated by the two diplomatic-strategic precepts contained in his praxeology. As we will see, a policy that encourages massive increases in military power while simultaneously urging indifference to communist gains and advances in the Third World whipsaws national leaders and their publics between an urgent call to arms and a frequent appeal to reason. This unhappy situation is not simply a speculative possibility contrived by pure reason; as the next two chapters make clear, this dilemma describes a very real foreign policy predicament that Aron, as well as the Kennedy administration, had to contend with.

In Aron's case this dilemma has its origins in what is perhaps the most glaring weakness of *Peace and War,* namely, its inability or refusal to address the creative possibilities of diplomacy. Aron's repeated insistence that political ideologies drive foreign policy has this great drawback—it rules out the possibility of communication between nations governed by incompatible ideas of justice. Because Aron was disposed to regard politics as an essentially moral or intentional phenomenon, he greatly narrowed the range of interests that could be subject to negotiated settlements, hence his call for a military buildup. And, because allies added little, if anything, to the strategic equilibrium in a nuclear age, Aron saw no need for a "Pax Americana," hence his call for global restraint.

The test of scientific theory is conventionally said to lie in its capacity for bringing order and meaning to a mass of data that would otherwise remain unrelated. *Peace and War,* however, makes no such claim. On what basis can it then be judged? At a minimum it should be judged by its self-proclaimed capacity for promoting measured, moderate, and consistent judgments. How well *Peace and War* holds up against this criterion cannot be determined apart from Aron's reaction to the unfolding of events in the 1970s and beyond.

4 Clausewitz and the Art of War

ARON'S STRATEGIC REFLECTIONS ARE by no means confined to the broad, sweeping recommendations found in *Peace and War.* Indeed, deeply interested in the phenomenon of modern warfare, Aron wrote several major works on war and strategy which range in scope and complexity from a strangely impressionistic study of war in the twentieth century (a book Hans Morgenthau once described as having "no beginning, no middle and no end") to a critically acclaimed analysis of the great Prussian military strategist, Carl von Clausewitz.[1]

Of central importance to this chapter is the book many feel to be Aron's best, *Clausewitz: Philosopher of War.*[2] The significance of this book for our analysis of Aron's strategic thought lies in the fact that *Clausewitz,* like *Peace and War,* contains a theory of human action. As works of theory, however, the two books are marked by a fundamental difference: Whereas *Peace and War* is an original work of theoretical construction, *Clausewitz* is, in effect, a work of theoretical renovation. *Clausewitz,* in other words, is an interpretive commentary on the strategic thought of the Prussian general; it does not elaborate an original theory.

Despite the fact that Aron did not begin to work on his two-volume study of Clausewitz until many years after the vast majority of his works on war and strategy had already been published and despite the fact that Clausewitz obviously knew nothing of thermonuclear warheads, we have chosen to introduce Aron's strategic thought as a whole by beginning with his interpretation of Clausewitz for the simple reason that this manner of presentation is in keeping with our method of proceeding from the general to the particular. Because we will place Aron's more substantive analyses of contemporary strategic problems in the broader context of a theory of action, the order of analysis in this chapter is modeled after the order of analysis in the previous one.

This chapter has two main goals, the first being to demonstrate that the model of the self and self-knowledge continues to be a useful guide for presenting Aron's thought. In *Clausewitz,* for example, three moments of analysis are once again matched with three modes of action. In fact, the manner in which Aron mapped out Clausewitz's theory of action so closely approximates the manner in which Aron outlined his own theory of action in *Peace and War* that the similarity immediately calls to mind Heidegger's appraisal of his own commentary on Kant: "I don't know if it's good Kant," Heidegger allegedly quipped, "but its excellent Heidegger."

The second goal here is to underscore the connection between strategic theory and practice by searching for the ways in which Aron applied Clausewitzian precepts to military-strategic problems in the twentieth century. Although this exercise requires a review of *Clausewitz,* we will not enter into the searching philological and historical issues that Aron brought to bear on his interpretation of Clausewitz; neither will we touch on many of the substantive strategic or tactical matters that Clausewitz and Aron discussed at length. Our primary interest is in the logical form of *Clausewitz,* in the conceptual apparatus that Clausewitz fashioned in order to think clearly about war and military strategy, and in the relevance of this conceptual tool for understanding the strategic predicaments of our own age.

By concentrating on matters of logic and form, we can see that Aron's strategic reflections are characterized by the same dialectical stops and starts that mark his theory of international relations. At issue, once again, is the location of political reason. Although Aron consistently maintained that the most reasonable strategic posture is one that aims for some sort of military equilibrium, he hesitated when forced to account for the conditions of equilibrium. Does a moderate military posture rest on the free play of diplomatic communication between rivals—especially during the heat of battle—or is diplomatic reason effective only when braced by strategic superiority? Aron seems to have toyed with both possibilities at times, leaving his readers unsure just where the balance of reason resides.

CLAUSEWITZ

Clausewitz is perhaps Aron's most formidable work. Although not as long as *Peace and War,* it is just as complex and difficult to follow. Written primarily for Clausewitz specialists, *Clausewitz* assumes not only that one has read the works of Clausewitz but that one is familiar with the different schools of interpretation surrounding his work as well. Adding to the difficulty is the fact that the book is poorly translated. *Clausewitz,* one reviewer commented, is a great book; it is not, however, "a great read."[3]

What attracted Aron to Clausewitz was the fact that Clausewitz—like Montesquieu, Tocqueville, and Weber—was a "theorist of uncertainty," a thinker who vigorously resisted any form of dogmatism. In strategic matters, Aron wrote, Clausewitz took dogmatists to be those who "put forward strict rules and claim to have discovered one rule amongst them all which is responsible for victory or defeat" (*C,* 5). Impatient with thinkers such as Heinrich von Bülow and Antoine de Jomini, contemporaries of his who believed that the entire science of war could be deduced from a handful of first principles, Clausewitz sought to mark the *limits* within which theory could operate. The kind of theory Clausewitz hoped to construct, Axon explained, gave human freedom its due; it indicated, in other words, "that the responsibility for decision is thrown back on the man of action" (*C,* 55).

Clausewitz also rejected the contrary thesis, the crudely pragmatic belief that most military problems (excepting the purely technical ones) can be solved with little more than courage, common sense, and some luck. Although he had more sympathy with this outlook than with that of von Bülow or de Jomini, Clausewitz believed that the unqualified denigration of theory was only slightly less mistaken than its unqualified elevation. Clausewitz, Aron wrote, thus fought on two fronts: "On the one hand against the pseudo-rationalists who claim to reduce strategy, in theory and in practice, to a strictly rational exercise; on the other, against the saber-rattling hussars who, scorning science, distrust any officer immersed in books" (*C,* 133). Between these extremes, Aron added, lies the possibility "of cultivating the capacity to judge by means of a double culture, philosophical and historical: through the first, learning to think about the war; through the second, learning by means of study and criticisms of historical examples (the case study method), to make the appropriate decision in a situation whose exact equivalent can never be found, but in which regularities, brought to light by the study of the past, may be apprehended."[4] In Clausewitz's mind, then, theory was connected to action only as preparation for it; strategic theory could not dictate solutions to the man of action but served instead to make action more rational by clarifying the range of choices that can be realistically pursued in a given situation.

The fundamental theoretical problem that preoccupied Clausewitz, Aron observed, was, "Under what conditions and in what manner is it possible to subsume the concrete varieties of war under one concept?"[5] This question suggested itself after Clausewitz had witnessed the revolutionary changes in warfare wrought by the "God of War" himself, Napoléon Bonaparte. The army in which Clausewitz had enlisted as a youth (he was, remarkably enough, only twelve years old when he joined) was the small, professional army of Frederick the Great. Consequently, Clausewitz's early military experience had been in eighteenth-century campaigns of maneuver and siege. The Battle of Auerstadt in 1806, however, gave Clausewitz his first bitter taste of Napoleonic warfare. The catastrophic retreat of the German forces which resulted was so vastly different from the tedious marches and maneuvers of Clausewitz's youth that it was difficult to comprehend both experiences as belonging to the same phenomenon of war. Napoléon had in fact changed the whole tempo of warfare—he waged campaigns with a ferocity that far outstripped the experience of earlier generations. The eighteenth century, Michael Howard explained, "might have reduced warfare to a matter of absurd, rococo formality, but in its essence war was something very different. Napoléon had made this clear for all to see; Clausewitz set himself to explain it."[6]

In explaining how Clausewitz related the concept of war to the historical diversity of wars, Aron noted that Montesquieu's *Spirit of the Laws* had been "something of a model" for Clausewitz. More specifically, Clausewitz's aim, "like Montesquieu's or all sociologists', was to make history intelligible and action rational by adapting means to ends. This intelligibility is to emerge from a constant cross reference from abstraction to history, or from concept to experience, which is typical of the Clausewitzian method" (*C*, 231). In fact, the same three steps that mark Montesquieu's method also mark Clausewitz's: The construction of different types of systems of behavior is followed by an enumeration of constants and determinants which in its turn sets the stage for concrete historical analysis.

These three steps explain Aron's systematic division of Clausewitz's great masterpiece, *On War,* into three main sections or ideas. The first part, "The Means and the Ends," defines the implicit rationality of war and constructs the different systems or types of war. The second part, "The Moral and the Physical," sketches the determinants that influence the course and conduct of campaigns. Finally, the third part, "Defense and Attack," examines specific strategic and tactical scenarios. For reasons that will become clear as our analysis unfolds, we will not begin at the beginning, with a discussion of means and ends; rather, we begin at the end, with a discussion of combat and campaigns.

The third antithesis, defense and attack, is located at a lower level of abstraction than the other two. The first two antitheses, Aron explained, relate to the character and nature of war. The distinction between defense and attack, however, "results from the spatio-temporal conditions in which the struggle unfolds" (*C,* 91). Because this distinction "governs the entire range of war," it is here that we find the prescriptive elements of Clausewitz's work, or the specific proposals for the conduct of campaigns" (*C,* 145).

Two great strategic principles are contained in Clausewitz's analysis of defense and attack. The first is that defense is the stronger form of war. *Beati sunt possidentes*—blessed are those in possession, in war as in law. The second is that strategic action always involves a small number of what Clausewitz termed "centers of gravity." In war, as in mechanics, Aron explained, "there are centers of gravity 'whose movement and direction govern other parts.'" From this it follows that, "just as in the world of inert bodies action against the center of gravity is measured and limited by the composition of the parts, so can it be in war: here and there, one blow can easily have more force than is needed to overcome resistance. The result is a waste of force" (*C,* 158).

The limits of the latter principle as a guide for action are immediately revealed by the light of a simple question: How can one be sure that one is striking at a center of gravity? The short answer is, one cannot. Regarding the time, place, and the method of such a maneuver, Aron wrote that "it depends on the many circumstances, material and moral, which theory may consider in the abstract. Only judgment on the spot can and should appreciate the relative importance of these in given circumstances in order to choose the most appropriate method" (*C,* 157). The same kind of qualification is attached to Clausewitz's strictures on the strength of the defense. "The propositions which we reached at the end of these analyses," Aron explained,

> are not only generally true, "all things being otherwise equal," but even in isolation. The defender normally has the advantage of terrain since he has chosen it, but the decision and the timing from then on belong to the attacker. It can happen that the attacker besieges fortresses and thereby forces the sending of a relief army and this passes over into positive action. In other words, we must always beware of consider-

> ing analyses as valid bases for precepts when they are based both on concepts and historical examples but only partially. The theoretical analysis of defense and attack is by itself no more praxological than the economic analysis of supply and demand. (*C*, 153)

Neither of these precepts, then, constitutes a principle of action. They do, however,

> contain instruction for the commander to the extent that he thinks of the field of battle and of the war commander with the help of major concepts: centres of gravity, destruction of the enemy forces, strength of the defensive, attrition of the offensive, the total character of the battle or campaign, etc. Compared with the maxims of the military theoreticians of his time or of ours, these propositions are of such an abstract character that they seem to belong to another world, and they earned Clausewitz his reputation as a philosopher or metaphysician. (*C*, 195)

It was in the course of writing the lengthy section on defense and attack that Clausewitz reformulated his theoretical propositions, a change that forced him to begin revising the entire work. Briefly, the problem Clausewitz encountered was this: After the initial attack by an aggressor has been repelled, what must the commander do? Is repelling or parrying the blow sufficient, or is the goal of the defensive war "no different from the goal of every war, namely, the destruction of the enemy forces" (*C*, 161)? The commander, in other words, must know at some point what kind of war is going to have to be fought. Would it be a "greater or lesser approximation to a war of observation," or, on the contrary, would it be one "completely governed and saturated" by the urge for a resolution?

It was this question that led Clausewitz to a better understanding not only of the relation between military strategy and political leadership but of the different types of war as well. And it was in the course of exploring the dependence of strategy on politics that Clausewitz hit upon the distinction between war in the abstract and wars in reality, a distinction that is of crucial importance, as we have seen, to Aron's own theory of international relations. Theoretically, Clausewitz reasoned, all conflict should escalate into a total struggle; if security for one implies insecurity for the other, then combatants must outdo one another "until they come to extremes" (*C*, 63). The intrinsic nature of war, then, is total—adversaries cannot rest until one has rendered the other helpless. Yet, as soon as real wars are considered, "the possibility of descent determines or should (*soll*) determine conduct just as much as the abstract possibility determines a rise" (*C*, 65). Clausewitz offered two reasons why this must be so, one intrinsic to the nature of war, the other extrinsic.

Unlike war in the abstract—or, as Clausewitz put it, "war on paper"—real war is an exercise in suffering, exhaustion, and terror. Shocked by the searing heat of warfare, Clausewitz observed, combatants tend to move more deliberately. Fear and uncertainty, in other words, act as a drag on action and constitute what Clausewitz termed a "moral force of gravity," a force that weighs down decision making and drains the ardor from most military campaigns. Thus, it is the inherent "friction" of war that often acts as a brake on escalation and keeps war from expanding into an all-consuming explosion of violence.

Not only is war subject to the intrinsic limitation of friction, but it is also subject to the restraining influence of an external force, namely, political judgment. Here we see the importance of policy. War, Aron wrote, "projects into the activity of interstate relations . . . The belligerents know each other, they know approximately what to fear or hope from the other." By this route we descend "from the absolute concept to the probabilities of the real world and, accordingly, are obliged to follow a policy giving the reasons for the conflict, defining precisely the role of its desired end" (*C*, 64). The reintroduction of policy does not make de-escalation inevitable; it does, however, make it possible.

If they are to be properly understood, then, real wars, like regimes, must not be separated from their origins and their ends. In fact, just as different political imperatives arise from the different kinds of regimes (as well as from historical circumstances), so too do different military imperatives arise from the different kinds of war. Thus, the strategy suitable to fight one type of war could prove to be disastrous if applied to another.

Unlike Montesquieu's typology of regimes, however, Clausewitz's typology of wars recognizes two and only two types. These two types of war, Clausewitz wrote, "are, on the one hand, that in which the object is to overthrow the enemy . . . either with a view to annihilating him politically or to disarming him . . . and thus compelling him to accept any conditions of peace; and, on the other hand, that in which one only wants to make conquests at the frontiers of one's own state with a view to keeping them or using them as a means of exchange at the time of peace. The intermediate stages between one type and the other should remain, but the entirely different nature of the two undertakings should penetrate everywhere and separate the irreconcilable" (*C*, 57). Because the ends of war cannot be separated from a certain type of peace, the manner of the return to peace determines the categorical alternatives: "In the case of 'knockout,' the winner imposes on the prostrate enemy any conditions, including even the disappearance of the state, indeed the physical elimination of the population; in the other case, he treats with an enemy who agrees to abandon one province . . . or he exchanges the province which he has occupied for another" (*C*, 57). The two types of warfare, then, involve imposed peace on the one hand and negotiated peace on the other.

Herein lies Clausewitz's contribution to a theory of war: Despite the vast differences between a limited war and an unlimited one, both types of war must be understood as essentially *political* acts. To Clausewitz's way of thinking, Aron explained, wars have their origins in what are ultimately political intentions. "Whether Marshall Saxe often avoids battle or whether Napoleon always seeks it, war remains war because, in both cases, the states act politically by violence, whatever the methods might be." Despite the diversity of wars and the duality of types, this is the idea that unifies the concept of war. "It is not the initial conception of absolute war which allows the historical diversity of wars to be subsumed under a single concept," Aron added, "but the intrinsically political nature of war" (*C*, 81). Thus the origin of what is perhaps Clausewitz's most celebrated (and most misunderstood) dictum: "War is the continuation of politics by other means."

Why is Clausewitz so insistent that political logic govern the "grammar" of warfare? Because in his view, "*political logic . . . always obeys a tendency toward equilibrium*."[7] In chapter 6 of book 6, Aron observed, Clausewitz discussed what he considered to be the last resort of defensive action—the accumulation of allies. Even a hasty reading of the text, Aron argued, reveals that for Clausewitz "relations among states tend to maintain a particular state system rather than provoke changes. Something like a common interest prevails in the system; it has not sufficient force to guarantee a given state against the loss of a province or a relative diminution of strength, but, ordinarily favors actions oriented toward equilibrium and discourages action that would jeopardize it."[8] This is the image of Clausewitz which Aron hoped to restore and refurbish. Far from being an unqualified advocate of total war, as some of his interpreters have suggested, Aron's Clausewitz emerges as a thinker of moderation and restraint, a theoretician who, like Aron, "could analyze coolly all the factors that often push war toward the extreme, yet whose own prescription was moderation and the deliberate victory of the rational element."[9]

From this idea of the supremacy of politics Clausewitz developed the notion that war is composed of three elements, which Aron presented as "original violence (people), free activity of the spirit (war leaders), supremacy of understanding." Taken together, these three elements form what Clausewitz called "the strange trinity" of war. These three elements are present in every war and determine "by their respective force and their relations" each war's particular character (*C*, 85). Sometimes, Aron wrote, "policy uneasily channels popular passions in order to make them conform to what is at stake. Sometimes it experiences difficulty in inflaming popular passions which the safety of the nation justifies and requires. Sometimes the hostility reaches a point where policy seems to disappear and hostilities resemble a blind clash of unleashed forces; at other times, on the contrary, political considerations—the limitations of the stake, or rivalry between allies—permeate the course of operations." At all times, however, the people play a role, either by participation or indifference, the military leaders make decisions fraught with danger and uncertainty, and, "by gambling, the head of state always bears the higher responsibility, that of appraising the true character of the particular war" (*C*, 119).

Because this is virtually the same conceptual scheme Aron employed in order to account for the intelligibility of diplomatic-strategic behavior, we need not repeat our earlier discussion describing the relations between and among the various components of this "strange trinity." We note only in passing that the structure of warfare as described by Clausewitz conforms to the structure of the self as described by Aron—the intentional reality of political leadership is both conditioned by and independent of military strategy: "The political end governs the war, but it is not a 'despotic lawgiver, it must adapt itself to the nature of the means, and is often modified'" (*C*, 134).

In itself, however, knowledge of the ends of war is insufficient to understand or explain either the development of a specific war or the historical diversity of wars. Real wars are determined not only by the intentions of the combatants but by historical conditions as well. On the one hand, Aron explained, "politics—the brain of the personified state—determines the military objectives in terms of the end of war; on the other hand, circumstances determine the historical diversity of wars. Politics only adequately determine the end provided that the nature of the war is exactly appreciated in terms of the circumstances which condition it" (*C*, 59). What kinds of circumstances, then, explain the transition from one type of war to the other or a particular war's specific character?

Clausewitz—again like Montesquieu—clearly divided the determinants that shape a war's character into two kinds, physical and moral. Indeed, his emphasis on the moral factors of war is precisely what distinguished Clausewitz's work from the work of his contemporaries, most notably von Bülow and de Jomini. Aron observed that in their works on strategy and tactics, von Bülow and de Jomini dealt primarily with the movements of armies, the lines of communication and retreat, and the location of bases. Clausewitz, however, "deals above all with moral forces . . . The rest, including the geometry of campaigns or battles, does not disappear but passes to a secondary level and becomes a subordinate method of consideration" (*C*, 121). Briefly, the three dimensions of moral forces which Clausewitz reckoned with were the spirit and moral qualities of the army, military leaders, and governments; the emotional state of those in the provinces where a war was being fought; and the psychological effects of a victory or defeat.

To what are these moral factors opposed? "Without a doubt, to numbers" (*C*, 125). The size or quantity of troops and material were for Clausewitz "the material element *par excellence*" (*C*, 120). Although Clausewitz never discounted the importance of material factors, he steadfastly refused to assign the sole responsibility for victory or defeat to numbers: "No proposition relating to physical force can be asserted which deliberately disregards what, to simplify matters, we shall call morale. The requirement of totality does not exclude analytical distinctions, but forbids rules or precepts which are based on one element alone and ignores the essential, namely, the activity of the spirit. Clausewitz uses the word *Geist* in its widest meaning, incorporating various faculties or qualities: affection, understanding, courage. What he never ceases to say is that everything emanates from man and everything comes back to man" (*C*, 121). Thus, the theoretician conceptualizes, enumerates, and compares various factors but does not award to them, once and forever more, a given weight of importance. This historical variability, Aron added, "is too often forgotten by interpreters, particularly with regard to numbers" (*C*, 123).

STRACHAN'S CRITIQUE

Widely heralded as a significant accomplishment in Clausewitz scholarship, Aron's reading of Clausewitz has nevertheless been criticized in recent years by the eminent military historian Hew Strachan of Oxford University. Although commending Aron for his erudition and patient analysis, Strachan took Aron to task for reading more into the text of *On War* than what Strachan insists the text can bear. The result, Strachan complained, is that Aron "transmogrified" the "warmongering Prussian" into a "liberal theorist of international relations."[10]

Aron's chief textual mistake, Strachan argues, lay in underestimating the significance of book 8 in *On War* for the development of Clausewitz's later thought. After a detailed historical analysis of the relation between book 8, in which Clausewitz explored the notion of total or absolute war, and book1, in which Clausewitz analyzed the moderating influence of politics or policy on warfare, Strachan declared book 8 to be more definitive for understanding Clausewitz's thinking than book 1. Unlike Aron, Strachan believes that the differences between the two books signal the fact that Clausewitz failed to resolve the types of war into a coherent definition of war. In fact, both books present profoundly different approaches to war. According to Strachan, book 1 regards war as an "instrumental" reality, or something controllable by human will, while book 8 regards war as akin to an explosion beyond human control, or as a reality that can engulf and overwhelm rational human agency.[11]

War resists rational control, Strachan argues, because at its very center is the phenomenon of what Clausewitz called "reciprocity," or the tendency of the elements of war—danger, exertion, uncertainty, and chance—to feed off one another in unpredictable ways. For Clausewitz, Strachan explains, "three quarters of war was wrapped in fog, and events therefore had a tendency to work against the grain of expectation," the upshot being that war has its own inner logic, or dynamic, which exists independently of the actors waging it.[12] If that is true, then what war is *not,* at least by its inner makeup, is a political instrument. Strachan returns to this point repeatedly, arguing that in book 8 "the dynamics of war . . . could make the policy which had given rise to war inoperative, forcing the policy, not the war, to change direction."[13]

In fact, Strachan argues, Clausewitz, as evidenced by his reaction to the French Revolution, thought that politics had the potential to make war even more destructive, not less. In book 8 Clausewitz came to see that for the first time in history the French Revolution made war a matter not just of cabinets and governments but of an entire people. Consequently, the effect of policy on war in this case was not to limit war "as liberal interpreters might wish the text to read" but to expand it by removing all restraint. "The Napoleonic wars revealed the nature of absolute war," Strachan wrote, "because [here] policy was in harmony with war's true nature."[14]

In tandem with misjudging the significance of book 8, Aron's other mistake consisted of mishandling the trinity constituting the character of war. At the end of book 1, chapter1, Strachan argues, Clausewitz presented a trinity of war's characteristics—hate, chance, and reason—which works in different and variable combinations at different moments in history. The important point here is that the relation between these three elements is unpredictable; none of the three is continually dominant, Strachan argues, not even policy. Clausewitz then proceeded to associate each of these three moments with three different attributes, or components, of the state at war, a move that prompted later generations of commentators (such as Aron) to freeze the free-floating variables of war into relatively fixed ones. Hate, chance, and reason thus correlated with the passions of the people, the moral qualities of military commanders, and the political direction of the government. Yet, in drawing those connections, Strachan hastens to point out, Clausewitz was moving from a description of the trinity itself to one of its applications: "The people, the army, and the government are elements of the state, not elements of war."[15] Until 1976, Strachan notes, few commentators made much of this brief and underdeveloped transition in Clausewitz's thinking. Aron, however, made it central to his analysis. In doing so, Strachan suggests, Aron was attempting to reassure his readers that a state-centered international order, one in which the leading actors possessed nuclear weapons, could still be a rational one, even when gripped by a cold war. Indeed, in Aron's reading, Strachan declares, Clausewitz, far from being an old "warmonger," was on his way to developing a theory of conflict resolution.

The interpretive differences between Aron and Strachan have significant practical consequences. Strachan, for his part, fears that an improper reading of Clausewitz may result in an improper understanding of the relation between military and political leadership, and that, in its turn, may lead to dreadful misunderstandings about the nature of a given conflict. More specifically, Strachan argues, an overly exaggerated subordination of war to policy may trigger two unhappy outcomes. First, it leads to the conviction that success in war rests on the establishment of clear aims and the application of overwhelming force to achieve those aims. As a requirement of policy, Strachan observes, that premise may be reasonable enough. As a statement about the nature of war, however, "it is demonstrably false."[16] Second, an elevated regard for political judgment may force one to accept what Strachan avers is the "un-Clausewitzian" assumption that "the army should be left, unfettered by politicians, to deliver the policy objectives that those politicians have set for it." An uncritical acceptance of a debatable Clausewitzian principle, then, "has not only distorted our understanding of war's true nature, but it has erected a barrier to the re-engagement of politicians and soldiers with each other at just the moment when policy and war need to be brought most assiduously into step."[17]

Aron's Clausewitz, at least by Strachan's reckoning, thus expects too much of politics and reason. By contrast, Strachan's Clausewitz is a thinker who grew increasingly anxious about the constraints of action, unnerved as he was by the irrational and uncontrollable forces that Napoléon had apparently unleashed. In fact, Strachan's Clausewitz saw war as ineradicably embedded in the very fabric of human existence. As Strachan writes, Clausewitz believed that "war was a form of human intercourse, 'part of man's social existence,' like commerce or politics, but unlike them it was resolved by bloodshed."[18]

Aron anticipated the sort of substantive (as opposed to textual) criticism launched by Strachan and responded to it, at least in broad outline, near the end of his own commentary on Clausewitz. The most significant and far-reaching issue here revolves around the nature of war: How *should* one understand or define war, especially in the nuclear age? Given the terrible consequences of a nuclear exchange, can war still be a useful instrument of policy? Observing that analysts writing about nuclear war (most notably Thomas Schelling) consciously began from Clausewitz's premise that "violence resembles not the explosion of a mine . . . but a tool that the human will can use after reflection toward attaining its goals," Aron asked whether assuming such a starting point tends to "falsify reality" or accurately depict it. "I am tempted to ask," Aron responded, answering a question with a question, "which other premise do we use?" To reject the "fiction" of the "rational participant," Aron argued, "is to condemn oneself to despair." If one assumes that individuals are simply "the playthings of mysterious or profound forces" or if one believes that war is the byproduct of certain causes immanent to the structure of all societies, then "what do we do while we wait for salvation through revolution or death by nuclear apocalypse?" Thus, "the doctrine of subordinating the military being to political understanding, which I discern in Clausewitz's testament," Aron declared, "becomes necessary and even indispensable in the age of nuclear weapons." After all, he asked, somewhat plaintively, "If we do not wager on reason, what do we wager on?"[19]

Aron's assumption of rationality may keep despair at bay, but his question immediately begs another: Does this premise square with the historical realities of warfare, especially as warfare has been practiced in the twentieth century? Is the insistence on the instrumentality of warfare in keeping with either the inner logic of war or its actual conduct? Is it not evident that the realities of "absolute" or "revolutionary" war fly in the face of reason, given that the goal of both is not the creation of some sort of equilibrium but the utter annihilation of the vanquished? Conceding that "absolute hostility" is indeed a reality, Aron nevertheless argued that absolute hostility is relatively rare, reserving the concept primarily for the war that Nazi Germany waged against the Jews. Even revolutionary wars inspired by the class hatreds of Marxism had demonstrable limits, Aron maintained. In theory, to be sure, revolutionary leaders such as Lenin bore an implacable hatred for the enemies of revolution. But, as Aron pointed out, many Marxists (such as the Chinese) "thought they could redeem their adversaries," although Aron did wonder how humane "conversion after brainwashing" could be (*C*, 369). Moreover, Aron added, "Clausewitz, Marx, Lenin and Mao agree in their view that war only becomes meaningful in the light of politics and policy, in the circumstances that cause war and the intentions of the combatants" (*C*, 350). Even the wars of "national feeling" which Napoléon had unleashed left room for reason. "As interpreted by Colmar von der Goltz and Marshal Foch," Aron argued, "absolute war was a contradictory concept. Both the German and the Frenchman believed that great conquests were impossible in Europe because of the very strength of the national feeling, this same national feeling that . . . set people against one another." Both men imagined a "sort of fight of the Horatii and Curatii" in which delegates and not citizens would fight, the outcome representing the judgment of God on the combatants. Yet "the consequence of the postulate of absolute hostility (and to be paid for very highly)," Aron declared, "was the common will to dictate peace" (*C*, 368).

WAR AND STRATEGY IN THE NUCLEAR AGE

Far from being made obsolete by the advent of nuclear weapons, Clausewitz is in many ways more relevant than ever. At the very least Clausewitz's concept of absolute war serves a normative function—it reminds adversaries that they run the risk of committing suicide together. Because absolute war is no longer an abstract notion but a physical possibility, prudence and moderation are even more important today than in Clausewitz's era. "In the nuclear age," Michael Howard has observed, "the political object has to be kept in mind in order to impose limits on an activity whose destructiveness, left to itself, will rapidly escalate to extremes of a kind such as Clausewitz had never conceived."[20] Or, as Aron put it, "the spirit of reasoned intent that informs policy must not be allowed to evaporate the moment the first bombs start exploding; intelligent national policy must to the very end make a determined effort simultaneously to *safeguard the national interest* and to *prevent escalation to the extremes of violence.*"[21]

It was on the basis of this fundamental Clausewitzian principle—preserving the "spirit of reasoned intent"—that Aron judged the doctrine of massive retaliation and found it wanting. It is here, in Aron's rejection of massive retaliation, that we see the first and most direct connection between Clausewitz's approach to military strategy and Aron's. Noting the conventional superiority of the Soviet Union and fearful of becoming bogged down in another limited war like the Korean conflict, officials in the Eisenhower administration declared that the United States would respond with nuclear weapons to communist aggression against it or its allies. Yet, as Aron and a host of other commentators were quick to point out, relatively minor or limited acts of aggression would lead the United States to run the risk either of not acting at all or of responding at levels beyond the original provocation. Massive retaliation thus violates a cardinal tenant of Clausewitzian strategy: One must strike a balance between the interests at stake and the effort required to protect them. What kind of strategy in the nuclear age meets this test?

Aron's response is immediate and unequivocal: "Precautions against misunderstanding and escalation require *scuttling the doctrine massive retaliation* and replacing it by *the doctrine of graduated response.*" The danger of fighting a war that no one wants to fight "can be reduced to a minimum only if the oversimplified and lethal all-or-nothing concept is buried once and for all" (*C*, 67). By placing an emphasis on calibration, or "fine-tuning"—ensuring that one's response is appropriate to the situation—graduated response enables national leaders to apply a wide range of military instruments to the task at hand, thus allowing them to exercise a greater degree of control over escalation than was possible under the doctrine of massive retaliation. "We believe in maintaining effective deterrent strength," President Kennedy declared in explaining his administration's new strategic doctrine, "but we also believe in making it do what we wish, neither more nor less."[22]

In lavishing praise on the Kennedy administration's choice of strategic doctrine, Aron stressed the importance of Secretary of Defense Robert McNamara's call for a strategic counterforce capability to complement the strategic counter-city capability already in place. If the Soviet Union ever attacked the entire complex of American military power, including government and production centers, McNamara explained, "we would of course have no alternative but to retaliate in kind." But, McNamara reasoned, "we have no way of knowing whether they would actually do so. It would certainly be in their interests as well as ours to try to limit the terrible consequences of a nuclear exchange" (*GD*, 72). In other words, Aron hastened to explain, "the concept of a separate phase of counterforce strategy, preceding the countercity strategy of an all-out war, does not rest on the illusion that the United States would be able to wipe out the entire Soviet retaliatory capability. Rather the concept was introduced, in the resolute hope of preserving up to the very end whatever chances reason and mankind may still have, of acknowledging differences in degree even of nuclear exchanges, and of never unleashing the full fury of homicidal madness before being forced to do so" (*GD*, 73).

Aron's enthusiasm for the McNamara doctrine, however, was not widely shared by other Europeans. Indeed, many were rather unnerved and even horrified by the Kennedy administration's strategic doctrine. To most Europeans the doctrine of flexible response signaled the "disatomization" of Europe; it was commonly regarded as a ham-handed attempt to reduce the risk of involving the United States in nuclear destruction while exposing Europe to the risk of a conventional war. In fact, Europeans were worried that they would be forced to bear not only the brunt of a conventional attack but, because the Kennedy administration sought to establish a continuity in explosive power between thermonuclear and conventional arms by refusing to rule out the use of tactical nuclear weapons to secure the defense of the Continent, many Europeans feared that they would have to bear the brunt of a nuclear disaster as well. Unconvinced by McNamara's assertion that limited wars could be kept limited, Europeans believed that escalation was virtually inevitable and that they, not the United States, would pay the price.

It was also believed that graduated or flexible response weakened deterrence. "Europeans," Aron wrote, "discovered that their security was no longer based on an automatic American nuclear response to any Soviet violation of the military line of demarcation but rather on Russia's uncertainty about United States reaction to an aggressive move on their part" (*GD*, 75). Our allies now feared that the subtle sophistry of a graduated response might tempt the Russians into a partial attack below the atomic threshold.

These concerns, Aron admitted, were not altogether groundless. In fact, resurrecting a rather Weberian principle of analysis, he noted that "nuclear strategy . . . involves intrinsic antinomies. It is *impossible, by definition, to ward off one danger without thereby automatically increasing another*" (*GD,* 81). Abstractly considered, graduated response "may seem eminently reasonable, but considered in its proper historic and geographic context it appears to be a sort of insurance policy. As such, it may be understandable and legitimate from the American point of view but it does not necessarily coincide with the national interests of Frenchmen and Germans because the primary purpose of the policy is to minimize the risk of a big war that might involve the continental United States at the price of putting up with little wars . . . in which only Europeans would be killed" (*GD,* 78). Without minimizing the risk or costs of graduated response, Aron nevertheless insisted that *from a global perspective* the risks of graduated response are smaller—and thus more rational—than those of massive retaliation.

Europeans must first understand, Aron argued, that the disparity of risks between the old and new continents "should be blamed on geography rather than on the president of the United States; for even in the thermonuclear age distance has not been entirely eliminated as a factor, except in the imagination of so-called experts inclined to confuse strategy with science fiction" (*GD,* 77). This is one of those cold, hard facts of world politics which Europeans must simply learn to accept. It took the McNamara doctrine "to force Europeans into realizing that their situation was ultimately not identical with the United States and that there was less truth than wishful thinking to the old bromide about all of us being in the same boat" (*GD,* 76). Because the United States is separated from its chief rival by a span of several thousand miles, American territory cannot be subject to "minor" or "local" aggression in the same way that Europe can.

Aron wielded this simple fact with great effect against those Europeans (especially the French) who detected sinister and chauvinistic motives behind the McNamara doctrine's implicit distinction between the American mainland, now regarded as a "sanctuary," and the territory of its allies. To those who clamored for national nuclear forces to compensate for the vulnerability of Europe, Aron posed a simple question: "Will the French sacrifice Paris for Hamburg or, for that matter, all of France for the sake of one city or province?" (*GD,* 90). "I am convinced," Aron wrote,

> that if France or continental Europe were to acquire atomic or thermonuclear arms tomorrow, a school of analysts attacking the theory of massive retaliation would immediately arise. They would stress the dangers of getting trapped in an all-or-nothing situation and point out that, with both sides in possession of invulnerable deterrents, each threat would elicit a comparable counter threat. Would the enemy in such circumstances let himself be deterred from limited aggression by an apocalyptic threat that he has every reason to regard as an empty bluff? In other words, any country contiguous to a potential aggressor will have to provide for a series of contingencies even if it does not possess nuclear arms, unless it has all by itself, the ability to wipe out the adversary's retaliatory force. (*GD,* 129)

This, then, is the great virtue of graduated response—by enabling statesmen to tailor a proportionate response to an act of aggression, it enables them "to practice what they preach." Then and only then, Aron explained, will there exist a strategy that reduces the element of bluff implicit in all thermonuclear deterrence; then and only then will threats be interpreted "not as an expression of fear but as proof of rational resolve" (*GD,* 133). A nation that has a wide range of possible strategic choices at its disposal is far more likely to be believed by potential aggressors, especially those that are considering limited or local acts of aggression. Thus, the increased capacity to conduct combat operations without having to employ nuclear weapons should also be regarded as a deterrent, "indeed as the means of deterring local aggression against which the threat of massive retaliation might prove futile" (*GD,* 68). Surely it is the "height of paradox," Aron argued, to assert that "the West *would weaken its deterrent capability in relation to local aggression by acquiring the means to repel such aggression without recourse to nuclear weapons*" (*GD,* 92).

We now approach what for many is the touchstone of a reasonable strategic doctrine—the possibility that a specific posture offers for keeping a limited war, especially one fought with tactical nuclear weapons, from escalating into an all-out conflagration. Unlike other strategic analysts such as Herman Kahn, Thomas Schelling, or even Henry Kissinger, Aron nowhere analyzed an extended range of concrete scenarios in order to assess the specific risks of escalation inherent in the use of nuclear weapons. In fact, Aron showed some disdain for purely theoretical studies of strategic issues. "I confess," he once wrote, "that in spite of the intellectual satisfaction it often gives me this literature makes me uneasy."[23] Citing the work of Herman Kahn as an example, Aron complained that Kahn "imagines, invents, and describes with a minuteness bordering on unreality, dozens of situations of conflict reduced to simplified schemes and the decisions that suit these situations." Although Kahn's scholarship is not "science fiction," Aron added, "what other name but 'strategy fiction' could one give to this form of literature?"[24] The great danger of overly theoretical analyses is that they may lead policy makers to overestimate "the technical aspect of diplomatic or military problems" and to underestimate "the importance of given psychological, moral and political factors, which are different in each situation."[25] Aron, for his part, preferred to treat strategic issues—especially the problem of escalation—as historically or as concretely as possible. "When it is a question of . . . the use of force or escalation," Aron mused, "the analyst who wishes to be the Prince's adviser must dirty his hands; I mean he has to come down from the ethereal level of models and plans and get to know in their totality the elements that make up the situation and in terms of which the statesman will have to make his decision."[26]

In discussing the problem of escalation, Aron underscored the dilemma that plagues defense and deterrence in the nuclear age. On the one hand, "reducing the risk of escalation increases the temptation to use conventional weapons as a 'sword' under the cover of a thermonuclear 'shield' (or under the protection of reciprocally paralyzed thermonuclear systems)." On the other hand, Aron immediately added, "If no distinctions are made between initial operations and ultimate weapons, there is a risk of ultimate escalation by accident or misunderstanding." In other words, "*escalation is at once a danger that needs to be met and a threat that could not and should not be surrendered*" (*GD*, 216).

It was for this reason that Aron refused to speak of deterrence in the abstract. The "eternal question" of deterrence for Aron was, "Who can deter whom, from what? in what circumstances? and how?" (*GD*, 163). Although the determination to raise the level of violence is essential to the efficacy of deterrence, Aron argued, one should never assume that escalation is *automatic*. Clausewitz immediately comes to mind—a specific military decision "depends on the many circumstances, material and moral, which theory may consider in the abstract. Only judgment on the spot can and should appreciate the relative importance of these in given circumstances in order to choose the most appropriate method."

Considering the use of tactical nuclear weapons becomes particularly compelling if parity at the conventional level is unattainable. If NATO troops continue to be overmatched by the conventional forces of the Warsaw Pact, then it becomes utterly pointless to refuse to employ tactical atomic weapons either for deterrence or attack. Given the West's conventional inferiority, a tactical nuclear threat "does not add substantially to the risk of their actual use . . . because use of these weapons is in any event, highly probable." Moreover, Aron reasoned, such a threat may help to prevent a possible misunderstanding on the part of the aggressor, "who might misinterpret all the multitudinous and subtle precautions taken against an almost inevitable course of events as simple lack of fiber and determination" (*GD*, 174).

The contradiction inherent in deterrence, Aron concluded, "has led us to the strategy of graduated response which, however, is as much a part of *arms control* as it is of the *theory of stability*. Arms control, in the widest sense of the term, refers to the total effort aimed at preventing recourse to force and, failing this, at limiting the scope of the resulting violence. The strategy of graduated response may therefore be interpreted as *arms control during a crisis*" (*GD*, 174).

All of this raises a crucial question: Exactly whose finger is or should be on the nuclear trigger? "In theory, perhaps," Aron wrote, "it might have been preferable to limit to the United States possession and disposition of nuclear weapons within the Alliance." Although entrusting the control of nuclear weapons to a single power does not guarantee that these weapons will be rationally deployed, Aron suggested, it certainly improves the odds. Yet, as he also noted, given the nature of international political behavior and the "age-old aspirations" of states, it would be unreasonable to expect that those who do not possess nuclear weapons would willingly forgo the opportunity to acquire them. Thus, the problem today "is less to ascertain what formula would be best in itself than to avoid certain ill-fated consequences of the multiplication of costly national forces, which are of scant effectiveness and quickly outmoded by technological progress" (*PW*, 693). What must be done, then, to accomplish this end?

Aron's answer is not altogether clear. In *Peace and War* he apparently envisioned the formation of a European deterrent force that, "without officially depending on the American deterrent, would act only in cooperation with it" (694). In a later work, however, he hedged on his call for a European deterrent, uncertain about the institutional or operational forms that "cooperation" would entail. As he observed, "The question of the control of the trigger arises in connection with the European deterrent just as it does with the Atlantic one" (*GD*, 187). Nevertheless, convinced that "the time of the American (or Anglo-American) directorate is past," Aron very much hoped that the West (especially the United States) would do more to change NATO from a strictly military alliance into an "authentic Atlantic community" (*PW*, 693).

Broadly speaking, the solution to the problem of command and community rests on the United States' willingness "to understand the mentality of the Europeans" and on Europe's willingness "to trust the principles of American doctrine" (*GD*, 181). More concretely, Americans must give Europeans a greater sense of participation in formulating Atlantic strategy. There is no good reason, Aron insisted, for excluding Europeans from the conception, formulation, or elaboration of military strategy. Relying freely on arguments developed by Alastair Buchan, Aron argued that, once Europeans "had made a genuine contribution to the strategic concepts and operational plans, they would be willing to leave operational responsibility to the American leaders" (*GD*, 184). In this plan, then, the United States would retain control of the nuclear trigger, but the elaboration of an overall military posture and division of labor would be the joint responsibility of the Americans and Europeans.

If the French government accepted this proposal, Aron mused, then the United States and Great Britain would probably do the same. There was, of course, a rather large obstacle standing in the way of an agreement of this sort, namely, Charles de Gaulle. De Gaulle's demand for military independence, so essential to his vision of national grandeur, could be satisfied only by the creation of an exclusively national nuclear force. Aron, however, vacillated between two familiar impulses. On the one hand, he was supportive—at least in principle—of a politics of grandeur.[27] As we have seen, Aron believed that a vision of moral greatness was essential not only to France's recovery of its national self-confidence but also to the conduct of Western foreign policy during the cold war. For this reason, perhaps, Aron applauded France's efforts to develop a nuclear capability of its own during the 1950s. The French, he observed, were "overjoyed" by the explosion of a bomb over the Sahara because it meant that "their scientists have shown themselves equal to those of other countries."[28] The burst of national pride that attended the event was, in fact, "normal, inevitable and legitimate."[29] Even though the utility of a French nuclear force was limited, it would be valuable to France for three reasons. First, it was "the supreme defence against blackmail or aggression" because France could now inflict substantial losses on a potential aggressor, losses that would "appear out of proportion to the gains." Second, even a modest nuclear force could serve "as a diplomatic trump" in dealing with allies. Finally, even though it would be less costly for France if the Atlantic Alliance would come to share its nuclear weaponry, it must nevertheless be admitted that the "French production of atomic bombs is more helpful in stimulating the sharing of knowledge and of equipment than the most eloquent pleas have proven to be." All things considered, Aron concluded, the worst that could happen to France is that it would "bear the inconvenience of greatness without possessing its reality."[30]

On the other hand, Aron became increasingly impatient over time with the idea of an independent French deterrent: The "force de frappe" was too small, too vulnerable, and too expensive to be of much strategic significance. As we saw in *Peace and War,* Aron did not doubt that a country can exert some degree of deterrent power once it acquires a nuclear retaliatory capability. By the 1980s, however, what he did doubt was that "in a test of nerves the leaders of a country risking total annihilation are the equals of those whose country would merely sustain some losses" (*GD,* 138). In Aron's opinion France would be better served if it submitted to a common discipline and integrated its military forces into the command structure of NATO. "To value the power of independent choice between war and peace above national security may once have been a sign of greatness," Aron wrote, "but I do not believe that in the thermonuclear age this should be considered an appropriate goal for the national ambition of a country such as France" (*GD,* 265). Given the terrible possibilities of a nuclear war, everything, including the eternal political desire for independence, must be subordinated to the contemporary needs of security. Whatever pretensions to greatness may have accrued to France through its possession of nuclear weapons have thus been completely subordinated to the facts of military, economic, and political necessity.

Aron took up the problem of escalation once again when McGeorge Bundy, George Kennan, Robert McNamara, and Gerard Smith publicly urged the United States to adopt the policy of "no first use" in 1982. Unlike some members of the "band of four," however, Aron had not changed his mind regarding the possible use of tactical and strategic weapons to defend Europe from military aggression. The case for no first use, Aron observed, rests on "an essential idea that [Bundy, Kennan, McNamara, and Smith] do not demonstrate but affirm, here and there, as self-evident: any use of nuclear arms, tactical or strategic, provokes uncontrolled escalation."[31] To Aron a vastly different scenario was every bit as imaginable as the one postulated by Kennan and his colleagues. The overwhelming fear and dread that would inevitably grip the leaders of those states contemplating a nuclear strike make it reasonable to assume that those leaders would, "by the intermediary of the hot line," make contact with the enemy, resume the dialogue, and stop the escalation.[32] This is not to say that such a scenario is more likely; it is, however, no less improbable than the one suggested by Bundy, Kennan, McNamara, and Smith.

Aron also refused to subscribe to the notion that all escalation necessarily ends in mutual destruction. A nuclear exchange would certainly leave untold death and destruction in its wake, Aron wrote, but it would not necessarily reduce both the United States and the Soviet Union to radioactive rubble; neither would it "condemn millions of children to genetic destruction."[33]

The plea for a no-first-use policy, prompted by the decision to station mid-range missiles (the Pershing 2) on European soil, also led Aron to review his own call, delivered some twenty years earlier, for a strategy of graduated response. More specifically, Aron sought to understand the effect that the growth of Soviet nuclear power had had on the American defense posture. Did the loss of American nuclear superiority in recent years make the policy of flexible response an anachronism? "In a sense," Aron answered, "yes." "The original idea of escalation—or, in Clausewitzian language, of the ascension to extremes—was sustained, if not created, by the implicit hypothesis of American superiority at the highest levels." Aron immediately pointed out, however, that, given the growth of the Soviet nuclear arsenal, there is no longer any reason "to conserve this illusion." The decisive question, then, is "Does the intervention of 'engine de la balance centrale' [Pershing 2 missiles] restore the credibility of the Western deterrent?"[34]

The fundamental significance of the Euromissiles, Aron argued, does *not* lie in the fact that they contribute to the reestablishment of a numerical equilibrium that had been upset by the Soviet introduction of the SS-20. "The notion of equilibrium hardly has any meaning in matters of nuclear arms. That the medium-range missiles are as numerous on one side as the other matters little."[35] What does matter is that the Euromissiles can strike at targets deep inside Soviet territory, a fact that immediately dispels the notion that a limited war will be confined to European soil, thus sparing the superpowers. In the event that a Pershing 2 is launched in self-defense, does this mean that the Soviet Union will then respond by launching its missiles against the United States? If they should do so, then the Soviet Union "risks enlarging the range of battle and entering into direct conflict with the power of the outer Atlantic."[36] An attack against Western Europe would thus "in all probability" lead to American participation. "In strategic jargon, the Pershing Twos have for their mission the task of keeping a limited war from being confined to the boundaries of the Old Continent," thereby preventing the decoupling of the United States from Europe.[37]

But does this situation not set in motion the possibility of an ascension to extremes that Bundy, Kennan, Bundy, McNamara, and Smith protested so vigorously against? It does indeed. Aron, however, was willing to take his chances: "If the menace of a nuclear threat is taken seriously, non-war becomes more probable; but if it is not taken seriously, if we proceed to applying the threat, catastrophe engulfs us all. This is a valid objection, but one which responds to an antinomy that has been recognized and commented upon indefinitely for the past forty years: the greater the horror threat banished, the greater the horror of its execution."[38]

The decision to station Pershing 2 missiles on European soil was one of the very few strategic decisions by the West which Aron had warmly applauded. Alarmed by the growth of Soviet military power, Aron repeatedly voiced his concern that détente and the Strategic Arms Limitation Talks (SALT) had lulled the West into a false sense of security. By any standard of judgment, Aron argued, all attempts at bilateral arms control (most notably the SALT agreements) have been abject failures:

> We recall the official goals of arms control. Reduce the risk of war: I see no improvement. Reduce the destruction if, in spite of everything, a war should occur: the destruction would perhaps be worse because the superpowers have eliminated the means of defense and increased the means of offense—the number of warheads and the throw-weight of the heavy missiles. Reduction of military spending: since SALT I, both sides have increased their budgets for strategic weapons, the Soviet Union much more than the United States. Jimmy Carter had promised a massive increase of spending on the MX and the Trident if SALT II were not ratified. Ronald Reagan will do it with or without ratification.[39]

In fact, Aron maintained, "arms control has assisted in the decline of American power and helped to conceal it."[40] Although the Soviet Union spared neither money nor brainpower in its quest for "military absolutes," it was equally true that the United States' "obsession with arms control caused the American leaders to forget the balance of power and remain passive in the face of the Soviet threat."[41] Unmoved by the assertion that dialogue between the superpowers was desirable in itself, Aron flatly declared that no meaningful agreement about the relationship of military forces could ever result from a dialogue between two states so implacably hostile toward each other.

Given this situation, there is simply no alternative to safeguarding deterrence and defense than by stockpiling American-controlled nuclear weapons in Europe. What other prospect is there, Aron asked, once disarmament is ruled out? Dismissing George Kennan's proposal for a mutual withdrawal of military forces from the European theater as naive and far-fetched, Aron maintained that Moscow and Washington prefer a situation that is deplorable but stable to "the unpredictability of the process which a military disengagement would set in motion."[42] What would the United States do, for example, in the event of a new repression in Hungary after Russian troops have been withdrawn and Western relations with Hungary normalized? However unfortunate the division of Europe may be, the dividing line is at least "known and respected."[43]

Aron, then, unlike Kennan, regarded the militarization of containment in Europe as an almost inevitable consequence of the ideological split between the United States and the Soviet Union. The cold war, he wrote, means that "the world is living in a limited war. A semi-war requires semi-mobilization. Intercontinental equilibrium dictates additional duties. We must resign ourselves either to losing valuable territories in the early weeks of the fighting [in Europe] or to keeping up a sufficient number of divisions in time of peace."[44] In order to fill the void created by World War II, Americans have no alternative but to station troops in Europe. But, Aron added, intervention would be "of no use" if Europeans resigned themselves to accepting a precarious security based on American protection alone. "In the long run," Aron observed, "it is the work of the Europeans to fill the European void. If they do not decide to do it, one day or another the United States will resign itself to a strategy of intercontinental war—in reply to European defeatism."[45]

Whatever the merits of Aron's arguments here, the important point is that we are now far from the cool confidence in political rationality that commended Clausewitz to Aron in the first place. Implicit in this interpretation of events is the notion that diplomacy can do little to alter or ease the conventions of the cold war. In light of the Soviet Union's sworn hostility to the West, Aron reasoned, diplomatic negotiations, which by definition "suppose that we give as much as we receive," would only be an act of craven acquiescence or appeasement.[46] Aron was particularly disturbed by Morgenthau's claim that the cold war would inevitably become a hot one if the superpowers failed to negotiate a settlement dividing the world into spheres of influence. Although it was to Morgenthau's credit that his political realism "invites us to keep our heads cool, to be suspicious of abstractions, [and] to look at the world as it is instead of imagining it to be what we would like it to be," Morgenthau nevertheless tended "to mistake traditional diplomacy . . . for eternal diplomacy."[47] Morgenthau may very well be correct in maintaining that the intense rivalry between the Soviet Union and the United States must end in either war or compromise, Aron declared, but "it is wrong to believe that compromise must take the form of a negotiated settlement. Usually, in the history of the world or at least of the Western world opposing states have negotiated agreements whenever they did not want to fight any longer. But states can reach compromises other than negotiated deals. Between the Parthians and the Romans . . . semi-permanent wars did take place without any formal peace treaties putting an end to these wars, or without a death struggle evolving from them."[48]

Germany was perhaps the best modern case in point. Even though each of the superpowers would obviously have preferred to see a united Germany integrated into its own military bloc, both were nevertheless willing to tolerate the existing partition indefinitely. Nonnegotiated settlements, in other words, were an inevitable and tolerable by-product of the cold war, a fact that Aron regarded as proving the limited utility of the traditional maxims of statecraft, especially when these maxims are tested by a revolutionary power such as the Soviet Union.

Aron was also profoundly unhappy with George Kennan's willingness to embrace diplomatic negotiations as a means of relieving some of the pressure generated by the mistrust and hostility between the United States and the Soviet Union. Although he had greatly admired Kennan's public service and scholarship earlier in his life, Aron was bitterly disappointed by what he perceived to be a change of heart on Kennan's part during the late 1960s. After thirteen years of diplomatic service, Aron wrote, "Mr. X" had rightfully denounced the illusions of the American Left, incapable as it was of comprehending the method and the manner of Soviet thinking. Unfortunately, some thirty years later Kennan "had lost his learning and his convictions."[49] What Aron found to be utterly incomprehensible was Kennan's conviction that the death of Joseph Stalin had altered the nature of the Soviet regime. Even though Leonid Brezhnev exhibited none of Stalin's paranoia and even though the Soviet leadership was in all probability not plotting to launch a surprise attack against Europe, it simply does not follow that the Soviet Union had become more politically agreeable, concerned primarily with improving its agricultural productivity, as Kennan maintained.

Particularly regrettable, in Aron's opinion, was Kennan's failure to see any significance in the changing balance of power between the United States and the Soviet Union. The Soviet Union had not only surpassed the United States in nuclear strength but had at the same time developed the capacity to project its power globally; for the first time since 1945 the Soviets had begun to use military force outside the zones occupied by their army. To Aron it seemed that Kennan had chosen an odd historical moment to declare that the analysis of Soviet foreign policy he had offered in 1946–47 was no longer valid. How, Aron wondered, could Kennan argue that, at the very moment when Soviet military power and activity had increased, Soviet political ambitions had declined? Thus one of Aron's rare and uncharacteristic outbursts: "I say to Kennan: what world are you living in? Why have you lost contact with reality?"[50]

Aron's reading of Kennan and the sources of Soviet conduct aside, it must be admitted that his attitude toward negotiating with the Soviet Union appears to be more logically satisfying than Kennan's in one fundamental respect: Given the goal of containing the Soviet Union, the United States would do considerable damage to its credibility both at home and abroad if it initiated negotiations with the Russians. "How could the American commitment to resist aggression be believed," John Gaddis has asked in this context, "if at the same time the United States was engaged in negotiations with the most likely aggressor? It [is] simply easier not to negotiate."[51] Perhaps, but, as Gaddis also recognized, the price of consistency can be strategic shortsightedness. If one's immediate goal is to maintain economic and military strength to counter the Soviet threat, then one must be very careful not to lose sight of the objective that strength is supposed to serve—ending the cold war.

Properly approached, with an eye to the identification of convergent interests as well as the open recognition of irreconcilable differences, negotiations can contribute to the creation of a stable world order. Otherwise, if one negotiates only with those whom one trusts, diplomacy becomes a luxury to be enjoyed only after stability has been achieved. Moreover, as Henry Kissinger has so often pointed out, discovering what the Soviets would agree to and abide by could not be determined in the abstract; if the Soviets wanted a genuine settlement, negotiations would reveal this. Surely it is no contradiction to assert, as Kennan did, that, although the United States and the Soviet Union may not have been able to sustain a long-term partnership, limited agreements based on mutual interest could prove to be possible and even profitable.

A discussion of Aron's strategic thought would be incomplete if it did not include his reflections on the two most important military engagements since World War II, the conflicts in Korea and Vietnam. Aron regarded the Korean War as a major turning point in the history of the twentieth century.

> In thirty years, from 1914 to 1944, humanity had passed from horses to internal combustion engines, from rifles to atomic bombs. In 1918 the Second Reich had laid down its arms but had not ceased to exist as a state. In 1944 the war had been brought to an end only by the junction of the Anglo-American and Russian armies in the center of Germany, the total destruction of the army of the Third Reich, and the temporary disappearance of the German state itself. To what orgies of violence would a third world war lend? In Korea, the two great powers made it abundantly clear that, for the time being at least, they did not want to wage a third world war.[52]

Thus, a negotiated peace was the outcome of the restrictions that the combatants had placed on themselves. What was not inevitable, however, was the American willingness to return to the status quo ante. Had the Americans voluntarily halted at the 38th parallel after landing at Inchon and destroying the North Korean army, they would have been able to claim that they were the victors and been acknowledged as such "by chancelleries and men-in-the-street all over the world." But, because the American effort to reunite Korea by military force had failed, "America's non-victory was a defeat, as the Chinese non-defeat was a victory."[53]

In retrospect, Aron wrote, one is tempted to conclude that neither General Douglas MacArthur's supporters nor his adversaries were entirely in the right. MacArthur's famous slogan "There is no substitute for victory" is either "a truism or a dangerous error, according to the meaning one gives it."[54] If it means that nothing can replace the need to destroy the enemy's armed forces, then the slogan "merely revives the conception unfortunately adopted by Roosevelt during the Second World War."[55] If it means that the objective of any war is simply to create a situation more favorable than that which existed before hostilities began, then the proposition simply becomes a tautology. In Aron's opinion MacArthur's mistake was to identify total victory as the only form of victory. His opponents, however, erred in the opposite direction—by confusing the renunciation of total victory with any victory at all, they posed the overly simple option between total war or a draw. The return to the status quo ante, then, "was the inevitable consequence not of the limitation of the conflict but of the refusal to engage the forces necessary to a partial and local victory."[56] A more skillful conduct of the campaign, Aron argued—if the Eighth Army had been reinforced by two or three more divisions and not been stopped by the armistice negotiations, for example—would have enabled the United States to push the enemy back beyond Pyongyang and so obtain more favorable armistice terms.

The United States's mistakes in Vietnam, however, were of an altogether different order. Aron faulted the American military and political leadership during the war in Southeast Asia not for its indecisiveness but for its hubris. Not only did Washington refuse to believe the reports of its own intelligence communities emphasizing the link between Vietnamese communism and nationalism, but it also evinced "a simpleminded trust in the efficacy of turning the techniques of subversion against the Communist enemy."[57] Like the French colonels in Algeria, the president's advisors believed that the techniques of subversion and persuasion were effective in any circumstance whatsoever. Returning to a fundamental theme of Clausewitz's, Aron observed that the American reliance on bombing to break the will of the North Vietnamese violated "the lessons learned in previous wars and the rule propounded in the Treatise, namely that the same step can produce contrary results according to the nature of the enemy. The Communists do not allow themselves to be intimidated by threats of escalating to extremes, which in any case were not very effective. Because of its relatively primitively nature their economy survived destruction. The war fought according to the principles of political annihilation was forced to fail by the war that obeyed only political intelligence" (*C*, 360). Aron also criticized American policy makers for their conviction—"genuine in many cases"—that the United States would "*jeopardize its role throughout the world if it accepted defeat anywhere,* a conviction strengthened by the course of events, a sort of self-fulfilling prophecy."[58] This attitude, in fact, had proved to be the undoing of French foreign policy in Vietnam. The French statesman Georges Bidault had believed that surrender in Southeast Asia would precipitate surrender in Africa. To Bidault's way of thinking, the French Union could not survive "the strain of the crumbling of a single of its pillars—a prophecy that had inherent in it the prerequisites for self-fulfillment."[59]

Finally, Aron condemned American leadership for the "corruption" of those who conduct foreign policy. The president and his advisors were at heart men of decency and goodwill, Aron maintained, but they ended up reviewing military situations and formulating policy options "as if they were dealing with pawns on a chessboard or material in a factory." "To give orders for such large-scale, cold-blooded bombing and then sleep at night," Aron wrote, "requires a personality transformation the need for which I do not deny; but I am troubled by the ease with which it occurs in men whom I knew before they entered the realm of [public] affairs."[60] There were thus three fundamental factors that finally rendered the war in Vietnam odious and intolerable—first, the inordinate violence done to the very people whom the United States was trying to protect; second, the American interference in the internal politics of a country that the United States was trying to defend; and, finally, the disparity between what the American leaders said and what the American forces did, "between an interminable war and the new climate of inter-state relations."[61]

If the means of fighting the war were flawed, the ends for which it was being fought were not. Aron was adamant on this point: "American policy in Vietnam, *legitimate in its intention,* became apparently immoral because of the destruction it entailed without attaining its objective."[62] Aron's reasoning was straightforward—if one accepts the proposition that the South Vietnamese were not waiting for the northerners to "liberate" them, then the aim of American foreign policy was not in itself unethical or immoral. In this instance, in fact, American foreign policy not only "conformed to accepted practice in the rivalry between superpowers," but it also "protected a country (or half-country) from the rigors of the Hanoi regime."[63] Throughout his life Aron steadfastly refused to label the American involvement in Vietnam as imperialist; American involvement in Vietnam could be explained by the simple application of the doctrine of containment.

Could the United States have won the war by reinforcing the South Vietnamese army and government while gradually withdrawing its own troops, or was the effort to create South Vietnamese nationalism doomed from the beginning, compromising as it did the independence of the Saigon government?

Aron was inclined to favor the first hypothesis, noting that "General Thieu seemed to be able provisionally to maintain his authority over a large part of the Vietnamese population and sustain a war that the Vietcong intended to wage until they achieved a final victory." The events of 1975, he immediately added, by no means "prove that this undertaking was condemned from the start" (*C*, 360). Did the atrocities committed by the Vietnamese and the Cambodians after the war justify the American engagement? Do those crimes, in fact, not reprove the American retreat? Not necessarily, for as critics of the United States hasten to point out, "the Khmer Rouge would never have come to power if the Nixon-Kissinger policy had not devastated the country." [64] The historical debate, then, remains as heated and as passionate as the original one, "the worst of it being that each group in a way possesses a part of the truth." [65]

Near the end of his life Aron asked, "Who can now recall the Indochinese war with a clear conscience?" [66] Neither those who unconditionally supported the Vietminh and the Khmer Rouge nor those who propelled the United States into the war and swept Cambodia into the resulting sound and fury "can congratulate themselves or be proud of their actions." [67] To have peace of mind these days, Aron wrote, "one would need the faith of a perfect Manichaean, capable of seeing where the good is and where the evil. And that Manichaean would require also a virtue rarely in harmony with his faith: the transfer of values, with good becoming evil and evil becoming good. Between Moscow and Peking, between Peking and Hanoi, how are these roles distributed?" [68]

Aron's concluding paragraph to a small volume of essays on war in the twentieth century provides a fitting conclusion to this chapter. In bringing his study to a close, Aron asked whether it was prudent to peer into the future in order to divine the course of politico-strategic events. True to form, he refused to speculate: "What would be the point, unless to ward off the temptation to despair?" [69] Instead of conjecture, Aron offered only the following observation: "The men and the nations are divided chiefly by ideological prejudice and human passions. The power of false ideas condemns all hope of world unity in the immediate future, but not the hope of a gradual, ultimate reconciliation of the human race." [70]

5 Critical Confrontation

IT WAS NOT UNTIL the mid-1970s, a period that marks the beginning of a growing disenchantment with radical thought in France, that Aron began to receive the recognition he so justly deserved. Although Aron was well-known to his colleagues and countrymen—his books and columns were read throughout all of France—he never received the same measure of public acclaim as his more radical peers. Thinkers such as Merleau-Ponty, Sartre, and, among the younger generation, Michel Foucault were the intellectual trendsetters, while Aron was something of a solitary thinker, an intellectual outsider whose stolid liberalism was eclipsed by the exotic but unstable synthesis of Marxism and existentialism made fashionable by the Left.

Ironically, the declining intellectual appeal of the radical Left in France owed less to the efforts of Aron than to the work of another thinker who had never set foot in France—the Soviet writer Aleksandr Solzhenitsyn. Solzhenitsyn's graphic revelations of Stalin's atrocities sent shock waves through the French intellectual community. Whereas Aron's *Opium of the Intellectuals* had provoked the Left to fury, Solzhenitsyn's *Gulag Archipelago,* written by an eyewitness, reduced it to silence. This confrontation with Marxist totalitarianism, one political scientist has written, eventually gave "a new and vibrant moral impetus to [French] thinking," one that was strengthened as the French watched the unfolding of the Solidarity struggle in Poland.[1] An increasing contempt for communism in general and the Soviet Union in particular manifested itself in student protests against the Soviet Union's treatment of dissidents, its invasion of Afghanistan, and the execution of political prisoners by the Vietnamese. By the 1980s the cycle was complete. Sartre, one European commentator reported, was passé—the mantle of intellectual leadership had passed to Raymond Aron.[2]

Given Aron's wide if somewhat belated popularity, it comes as no surprise that all of France mourned his death in 1983. Although he was buried quietly—in marked contrast to the huge crowds and emotional outbursts that had accompanied Sartre's burial in 1980—Aron's memory and legacy were honored by scholars and public figures alike from around the world. All paid homage to Aron's courage, his integrity, and, of course, his great learning (even the Left paid a rather grudging tribute in the pages of *Libération*). M. J. Lasky's tribute, "Death of a Giant," is particularly moving and fitting:

> Raymond Aron is gone. He was heir, for all his skepticism, to the best traditions of European Judaism and the French Enlightenment. A committed democrat in the spirit of John Stuart Mill and Tocqueville, and a political scientist and sociologist with the sharpness of a Marx and a Max Weber, he was a cosmopolitan publicist, with a familiar by-line in the world press, and at home in three or four languages and political cultures. He was a liberal who had only one single libertarian standard when it came to issues of censorship, dogmatism, labour camps, and any other form of tyrannical or totalitarian excess. A man of ringing eloquence who kept his speech and his style free from rhetoric and the cant of conventional sloganeering, he remained an inspiring teacher who offered no intellectual tricks, no utopian optimism, no impassioned panaceas, only a modest and earnest concern with the human condition, the spiritual need to understand it and the ethical devotion to save it from needless troubles and tragedies . . . When will Europe produce his like again?[3]

That Aron was a genius cannot be doubted. His genius, however, was of a peculiar order. Unlike Sartre, whose effortless creativity Aron deeply admired (and even envied), Aron by his own admission wrote very little that was original. In judging the significance of Aron's scholarship, Stanley Hoffmann wrote that Aron "always put 'creators' above 'critics': Sartre, for all his political divagations, was a creator; Aron, for all his lucidity, was only a critic. His conception of man and of history made him impatient with what he called half-truths, prophecies based on a powerful but partial central intuition, such as Marx's or Freud's. But he admired most those who had changed man's way of thinking in this fashion, and he knew he was not one of them."[4] Of what he regarded as his four best works, for example—*Introduction to the Philosophy of History, Opium of the Intellectuals, History and the Dialectic of Violence,* and *Clausewitz*—the latter two were commentaries, while one, *Opium of the*

Intellectuals, was meant for popular rather than scholarly consumption. That leaves a single book, *Introduction to the Philosophy of History,* as Aron's signal contribution to scholarship.

Before we proceed to a critical evaluation of Aron's thought, we would do well to place him among some of his contemporaries, particularly the "American realists," of whom Aron was at times so very critical. Because we have already noted some of the fundamental differences between Aron and George Kennan, we here turn to two other leading figures in American realism, Reinhold Niebuhr and Hans Morgenthau.

Certain similarities between Aron and Niebuhr immediately suggest themselves. Recognizing that friction and struggle are universal features of the human condition, neither Aron nor Niebuhr softened the hard, tragic facts of power politics. At the same time, however, both men refused to take their normative bearings from the realities of conflict; both agreed that, if one regards the selfish qualities of human nature as a final imperative, then one will suffer the debilitating consequences of nihilism. For Niebuhr, Kenneth W. Thompson has written, the law of Christian love "was the sole proof against this peril."[5] For Aron the laws of logic and human reason were proof enough. For both Aron and Niebuhr justice must temper power: Both believed that government is the expression of a community's need for justice as well as the reflection of an oligarchy's will-to-power.

Because both men recognized that justice and power stand in a relation of tension, both underscored the contingent nature of knowledge. It was on this basis that Aron and Niebuhr rejected the dogmatic philosophy of Marxism, a system of thought that lays claim to a complete knowledge of the motive force of history. Impatient with any doctrine that claims to offer a final solution to what are essentially never-ending problems, Niebuhr and Aron asserted that men and women must strive for justice with the full knowledge that justice may never be achieved. Thus, both men accepted a fundamental paradox of the human condition: "Man is most free in the discovery that he is not free."[6]

Also like Aron, Niebuhr questioned whether the national interest and the balance of power were sufficient guides for the conduct of American foreign policy. In a review of George Kennan's book *American Diplomacy: 1900–1950,* Niebuhr wrote that "the cure for a pretentious idealism, which claims to know more about the future and other men is given to mortal man to know, is not egotism. It is concern for both the self and the other in which the self, whether individual or collective, preserves a 'decent respect for the opinions of mankind,' derived from a modest awareness of the limits of its own knowledge and power."[7] For Niebuhr "proximate justice" included not only the notion of equilibrium among or between powers but the notion of a moral consensus as well. Devoid of such a consensus, the balance of power is a "potential anarchy which becomes actual anarchy in the long run."[8] Niebuhr would most certainly have agreed with Aron that a sound foreign policy must not ignore "the arguments of principle and opportunity, to forget neither the relation of forces nor the will of peoples."

On a less abstract level of analysis both Aron and Niebuhr displayed profound misgivings about the character and objectives of the Soviet Union. In 1946 Niebuhr had written that "Russian truculence cannot be mitigated by further concessions. Russia hopes to conquer the whole of Europe strategically and ideologically . . . Russia's policy is much too hard-boiled and has too many prospects of success to be diverted by softness on our part."[9] Anticipating as it does Kennan's call for a policy of containment directed against the Soviet Union, this passage could very well have been written by Aron. Unlike Kennan, who opposed the military aspects of containment, Niebuhr believed that American military might was a necessary element of containment, at least in Europe. When the North Atlantic Treaty was signed in 1949, Niebuhr, like Aron, recognized it as the cornerstone of American postwar policy, declaring that it linked the United States's new sense of responsibility for the international community with its position as head of the Western world.

Beyond these general points of agreement, however, lie rather substantial differences. Perhaps the most significant difference between Niebuhr and Aron centers upon their attitude toward power. Although both men understood and accepted the necessity of power politics, Niebuhr tended to inveigh against the *temptations* of power, whereas Aron tended to underscore the *responsibilities* of power. Niebuhr's pleas for greater political realism in the conduct of U.S. foreign policy were invariably accompanied by a warning—power corrupts and absolute power corrupts absolutely. Consequently, it was the task of "prophetic religion" to unmask the sins of pride and self-righteousness which so often attend the exercise of great power. Prophetic judgments thus remind leaders and citizens alike that there are limits to power, or to their ability to mold the world after their own image. For Aron, however, it was "moral lethargy" or "failure of nerve" that was of the gravest concern; his deepest fear was that the United States would fail to recognize the historic and global obligations of great power leadership. "I have always been troubled less by the excessive power of the United States," Aron wrote, "than by the instability of a continent-nation, cast by the fortunes of war into world politics, whose leaders, most of them unaware of the historical fate of the Republic, are driven by the changing currents of world opinion."[10]

If Aron's realism compares favorably at times with Reinhold Niebuhr's, it stands in sharp contrast on most points to the realpolitik of another American thinker, namely, Hans Morgenthau. As we have observed in the course of our study, Aron's rather trenchant criticism of Morgenthau's political thought extends to a wide range of issues including the logic of theory, the nature of politics, and the criteria for a sound foreign policy. What accounts for these differences? Is there a fundamental point of disagreement between Aron and Morgenthau from which all else—or at least most else—follows? These questions become all the more compelling in light of the fact that Aron and Morgenthau appear to hold fast to a common set of first principles. Both men, for example, stressed the limited utility of theory for practice and so counseled a politics of prudence, or a politics of incremental adjustment wrought by the slow, hard work of compromise and negotiation. Where, then, do their differences lie, and at what point do these differences first begin to emerge?

Comparing the intellectual styles and legacies of Morgenthau and Aron, Hoffmann offers a sweeping observation: "One of the many reasons why Raymond Aron's *Peace and War*—a book far more ambitious in its scope and far more sophisticated in its analyses than *Politics among Nations*—incited no comparable reaction from scholarly readers may well have been the greater judiciousness and modesty of Aron's normative conclusions. Humane skeptics invite nods and sighs, not sound and fury; and sound and fury are good for creative scholarship. Moreover, Aron's own scholarship was overwhelming enough to be discouraging; Morgenthau's was just shaky enough to inspire improvements."[11] Whatever the merits of Hoffmann's observations, his comparison does not really get us very far in discovering the roots of the difference between Aron and Morgenthau. Our comparison takes a different tack: We begin with a brief but systematic summary of Morgenthau's introduction to political realism as expressed in *Politics among Nations*. By so doing, we will discover that an inversion in theoretical starting points—and not "sound" or "shaky" scholarship—accounts for much of the difference between these two leading exponents of realism.

Of the six principles of political realism which Morgenthau reviews in the first chapter of *Politics among Nations,* the first is of greatest importance here. "Political realism," Morgenthau wrote, "believes that politics, like society in general, is governed by objective laws that have their roots in human nature. In order to improve our society it is first necessary to understand the laws by which society lives. The operation of these laws being impervious to our preferences, men will challenge them only at the risk of failure." To this point Morgenthau added that "realism, believing as it does in the objectivity of the laws of politics, must also believe in the possibility of developing a rational theory that reflects, however imperfectly and one-sidedly, these objective laws. It believes also, then, in the possibility of distinguishing in politics between truth and opinion—between what is true objectively and rationally, supported by evidence and illuminated by reason, and what is only a subjective judgment, divorced from the facts as they are and informed by prejudice and wishful thinking." [12]

Aron will have none of this. His neo-Kantian insistence that theoretical thought cannot gasp the essence of anything compels him to reject any talk of a human "nature." Because the power of abstract reasoning does not extend to the discovery of essential unity, conceptualization cannot penetrate to what philosophers have commonly referred to as "the thing itself." So limited, theoretical thought discovers only opposites-in-relation, or pairs of polar opposites bound together by an unknowable substance. Aron, for example, did not define the self by referring to one fundamental property such as the will-to-power but by postulating a dialectical relation between two properties, namely, *motifs* and *mobiles.*

From this starting point virtually all else follows. If theoretical thought is incapable of disclosing a stable, invariant object of analysis, then the concomitant notion of "objective laws" governing the behavior of these objects becomes exceedingly problematic. Although Aron did not dismiss Morgenthau's search for the theoretical order as necessarily misguided, he did, as we have seen, regard it as insufficient. Given the indeterminacy of human action—given, in other words, the dialectical relation between *motifs* and *mobiles*—political behavior can never be rationally determined, even in theory. And, if this is true, then foreign policy cannot take its bearings from a rational definition of the national interest.

Aron thus grounded his conclusions about human action and politics in his existing reflections on the nature and limits of knowledge. For Aron the inherent limits of theoretical thought suggest that we can never know our true self, the self that lies behind our acts of love and self-interest but which can be identified with neither. Viewed from this perspective, Morgenthau's reduction of the human self to little more than a "foul rag-and-bone shop" is pure dogma, a one-sided abstraction that fails to do justice to the full reality of the human condition.

For his part, however, Morgenthau looked upon the relation between knowledge and human nature from an entirely different vantage point. Reason, he declared, "is like a light which by its inner force can move nowhere. It must be carried by the irrational forces of interest and emotion to where these forces want it to move, regardless of what the inner logic of abstract reason would require."[13] By refusing to separate the process of cognition from the inescapable pull of self-love, Morgenthau emphasized the dependence of the epistemological question ("What can I know?") on the anthropological one ("Who am I?"). For Morgenthau reason does not define the self as it does—at least in part—for Aron. Rather, reason reflects or expresses the self. From this perspective it is Aron's willingness to postulate a "gap," or "break," between the intentional and the psychological dimensions of the human personality which constitutes an unjustifiable abstraction. To Morgenthau's way of thinking, rationality and contemplation are not more authentically human than emotion and volition, as Aron's epistemological hierarchy suggests, because the will-to-power—the urge to control both nature and one's fellows—can be pursued by the intellect as well as the passions.

We direct our criticism to this very point, namely, to Aron's insistence that reason can somehow carve out a realm of perfect freedom from within the vortex of historical necessity, a conviction that drove not only Aron's politics but also his theory of knowledge. By creating a categorial framework that acknowledged the reality of both freedom and necessity, Aron was underscoring the fact that our knowledge of history and human action is limited, a fact that in turn underscores the limits of our ability to guide and direct the course of human history. A theory of knowledge that demands humility before the facts thus tends to a politics of similar modesty and prudence. Yet, despite Aron's lifelong efforts to reconcile freedom and necessity—to "touch both ends and fill up the space between," in Pascal's wonderful phrase—his grasp repeatedly fell short, forcing him to shuffle restlessly between one endpoint and the other as he tried to stake out a moderate position somewhere in between.

Aron's preference for the middle ground is certainly reasonable enough.

What is at issue, however, is whether or not his logic allowed him to clear out a middle ground with much clarity or consistency. On the one hand, as we have seen, Aron criticized positivism for its tendency to reify concepts. By postulating a direct correspondence between ideas and the objects that these ideas are called on to represent, positivism suggests that theoretical thought can completely exhaust or conform to its objects. In doing so, however, it treats human reality as an essentially mechanical one and thus fails to account for the experience of human freedom, or for the fact that human action can change the conditions of its existence. Weber, on the other hand, made precisely the opposite mistake—by refusing to acknowledge any substantive correlation between ideas and their objects, Weber's nominalism so greatly exaggerated the reality of human freedom that it reduced the notion of truth to a matter of personal taste.

Searching for a via media between positivism's realism and Weber's nominalism, Aron argued for the necessity of discriminating among different kinds of historical objects. Some historical objects, as we have seen, have different "principles of permanence" than others and thus call into existence different methods of knowing. The interpretation of human "works," for example, requires an altogether different process of understanding than the interpretation of human "acts." From this perspective the interpretive freedom Aron granted to historians and sociologists, as well as the freedom he granted to human subjects generally, was neither absolute nor nonexistent but variable: It changed according to the situation or according to the object(s) under consideration.

What mars this apparently moderate and measured epistemology is that Aron nowhere explained where these principles of permanence come from or, more to the point, how they retain their identity in light of the corrosive effects of interpretation. Understanding, after all, is never a strictly theoretical or rational operation that simply "grasps" its intentional objects in the process of comprehending them. By virtue of its inherent autonomy, understanding is always a practical or projective exercise that "shapes" the objects of experience in the very act of knowing them. Although Aron repeatedly emphasized the independent and preexistent status of historical objects, his refusal to regard concepts as anything other than "working hypotheses" suggests that these objects do not possess an ontic independence but only a believed one. The actual existence of these objects, in other words, seems to be reduced to a belief in their existence. Although Aron was surely correct in maintaining that positivism's impersonal view of knowledge leads to a world without humanity, his own judgment that all historical judgment must draw upon the reserves of faith and personal commitment runs the risk of leaving humanity without a world.

This problem is particularly acute when one tries to discover the nature of those limits that serve to restrain human reason. If the presence of anything beyond the human intellect is not so much proven as affirmed, what then becomes of those standards by which we judge our knowledge and behavior? In considering this problem, Aron opted for the Kantian solution: The only concept of limits which is compatible with the notion of human freedom is one in which limits are self-imposed. As we saw in chapter 1, historical relativism is overcome only when historians "put themselves in a position to recognize the points of view of others." But, as so many critics of Enlightenment rationality have pointed out, limits that are self-imposed can also be self-removed, a point of great significance, as we will see, when we consider Aron's approach to foreign policy.

In the realm of international relations Aron's attempt to preserve the autonomy of reason found expression in his insistence that policy be guided by an "idea," or by a normative principle grounded in reason. Just as knowledge consists of a dialectical relation between intentional and causal realities, or between reason and experience, so too does politics. In Aron's opinion, as we have seen, morally responsible statecraft is that which "attempts not only to consider each case in its concrete particularities, but also not to ignore any of the arguments of principle and opportunity, to forget neither the relation of forces nor the wills of people."

Applying this general precept to foreign policy, Aron argued that what the West needed during the cold war was a diplomacy that defended—and exported whenever possible—liberal democratic values. Much like Paul Nitze, former director of the Policy Planning Staff during the Truman administration and the widely acknowledged elder statesman of defense intellectuals, Aron believed that Americans would retreat into isolationism rather than spill their blood and treasure for the sake of a hard-boiled realism. In order to forestall the possibility of isolationism and at the same time invigorate Western diplomacy with moral purpose, Aron maintained that an international consensus must be constructed on an ethical base, which for him translated into a policy of anticommunist containment.

Few European intellectuals were as vocal as Aron in their denunciation of communism. Yet at no time did Aron call for the kind of moralistic anticommunist crusade sanctioned by thinkers such as William Kintner and Robert Strausz-Hupé. Unlike many such thinkers, Aron believed that American foreign policy should be guided by a situational ethic, one located somewhere between the bloodless calculations of realpolitik and the elevated demands of personal morality. Arguing that the United States alone possessed the military strength to prevent communist tyranny, Aron nevertheless warned that there must be a relationship between morality and action in foreign affairs if the United States was going to be successful in persuading its allies and the nonaligned nations of the world to follow its lead. At the same time, however, Aron admitted that political necessity sometimes forced the United States to act against its higher moral principles. Thus, in order to check the spread of communism without triggering a direct military confrontation, the United States had to prop up authoritarian regimes in the far corners of the world, recognize a Soviet sphere of influence (at least tacitly), and participate in an arms race. These actions, are, admittedly, of dubious morality—indeed, they smack of realpolitik—but to Aron's way of thinking they testify to the possibility of feeling one's way through foreign affairs by the admittedly dim light of a contextual ethic, one that adhered to long-term moral ideals while recognizing that current historical circumstances prevented their immediate realization.

Aron's contextual ethic was intended to check the tendency of anticommunist containment to overreach itself because a contextual morality is by definition a morality of *prudence*. As we saw in chapter 3, prudence demands that one act "in accordance with the particular situation and the concrete data and not in accordance with an ideological imperative" or some "pseudo-norm." In short, prudence means that American policy makers must be selective in deciding where and how to intervene in matters beyond their own borders.

Unfortunately, Aron never considered what a policy or an act of prudential restraint would do to the moral foundations of his foreign policy or to public support for it. "After all," Richard Melanson has written in this context, "could Johnson have refused to intervene in Vietnam and still preserved the Cold War consensus that had legitimated anti-communist containment? And hadn't Eisenhower's 'prudent' decision in 1954 merely laid the entire problem in Kennedy's lap?" [14] It was the Kennedy administration, in fact, which felt the full force of this dilemma. John Gaddis has described the difficulty here. President Kennedy and his advisors, Gaddis wrote,

> were continually torn between urges to arouse and to educate. There was, on the one hand, the belief that Eisenhower had not made the nation face up to the threats confronting it, that the new administration had a duty, accordingly, to awaken the country—shock it if necessary—out of its complacency. On the other hand, there was a comparable sense of obligation to persuade the public to take a calmer and more rational view of the Cold War, to abandon the passions and oversimplifications characteristic of the early years of that conflict. These conflicting impulses colored Kennedy's public explanation of his strategy throughout his term in office.[15]

The same conflicting impulses colored Aron's "public explanations" as well. Despite his condemnation of strident cold war rhetoric, especially President Kennedy's impassioned promise to defend "the frontiers of freedom" everywhere, Aron himself could not resist conjuring up images of falling dominoes in his efforts to goad the United States into accepting its global responsibilities. ("Is it of no consequence to the American republic that the African states are falling one after the other into the Soviet orbit?")[16] Indeed, given his enthusiasm in *Peace and War* for a massive, across-the-board increase in military strength, Aron's complaints about Kennedy's rhetoric are a little surprising. What else did Aron expect? How else *can* an administration convince the public to make the sacrifices necessary to sustain such a buildup save by persuading it that the nation stands in imminent peril? Similarly, his criticism of the American conviction that the United States would jeopardize its role throughout the world if it accepted defeat anywhere is somewhat suspect for the same reason. If the communist threat is of such scope and magnitude that the traditional maxims of statecraft no longer apply—if, in other words, the communist threat is as much ideological and moral as geopolitical—then how can tactical withdrawals, especially those demanded by the dictates of prudence, be construed as anything other than major defeats? Under these conditions how could the United States even appear to withdraw from its admittedly overextended positions without triggering a crisis of confidence which would undermine U.S. interests everywhere?

The same conflicting impulse to "arouse" and to "educate" shows through in Aron's approach to one of the most contentious issues in postwar French politics, Algeria. Although Aron had hoped that French political leaders would strike a sensible balance on the Algerian question between a politics of *grandeur* and a policy attuned to economic and political necessities, he himself struck that balance no better than anyone else, hamstrung as he was by his own logic.

Aron's writings on Algeria can be divided into three blocks of books and articles. The first is made up of four articles written for *Le Figaro* in October 1955, in which Aron analyzed the causes of Algerian unrest and the political choices that France had at its disposal in dealing with the crisis. To Aron's way of thinking the most fundamental source of Algerian unrest was economic. In spite of massive French financial support and investment, he wrote, "the fact remains that in Algeria the standard of living of the mass of the population is extremely low and not rising . . . Hundreds of Algerians without work and without hope for the future are inevitably ripe for revolt." [17] Surveying the range of options, Aron concluded that the only sensible course of action open to the French was to create "an Algerian unity and an Algerian personality." As Robert Colquhoun explained, "Assimilation and association were not enough—Algerian nationalism would have to be recognized." [18] Under these conditions, Aron argued, an "association" with Algeria similar to those that France had established with Tunisia and Morocco was the only manageable solution.

Aron had nothing further to say on the Algerian question until the publication of his little book *La Tragédie algérienne* in 1957.[19] Aron's views on Algeria had been so at odds with the views of the paper's director, Pierre Brisson, that Brisson asked Aron not to write on the topic again. Aron respected the request and mentioned the Algerian problem only in passing in the middle of an article he had written for another paper, arguing that it was the empire as a whole and not simply Algeria which was a bad economic deal for France. Because the comment generated a storm of controversy, Aron believed that the time had come for him to speak out "against the conspiracy of cowardice" and "tell the whole truth, however bitter it may be." Writing directly to the supporters of French Algeria, Aron forcefully declared: "*Algérie française*—all of you who give such moving expressions to the ravings of national vanity, first look at the realities and examine the facts before dreaming about the riches buried in the burning sands." [20] Calling as it did for Algerian independence—not even the Left did that—*La Tragédie algérienne* "went off like a gun shot at high mass."[21] Aron immediately found himself at the center of a political firestorm, even once fearing for his physical safety during a public lecture in

Paris. The attacks on Aron were so bitter and so intensely personal—and so utterly indifferent to the economic and political realities of the situation—that Aron had no appetite for further engagement on the issue.

When Charles de Gaulle assumed power in June 1958, however, Aron believed that the time had come to take up his pen and address the issue a third time. "If the fall of the Fourth Republic has given madmen back their reason and governments the possibility of action," he wrote, "it is worth taking up the argument again. And since no one can say what liberties will still exist in France in six months' time, perhaps my detractors will grant me, this time, in the absence of far-sightedness or patriotism, the merit of non-conformism."[22] Thus it was that Aron came to write *L'Algérie et la république,* a far weightier and more substantive work than *La Tragédie algérienne.*

Aron's arguments for Algerian independence were based, as Judt observed, "on three characteristically Aronian grounds."[23] First, returning to a theme he sounded throughout his writings on the Algerian crisis, Aron argued that the policy of assimilation and integration would be culturally impossible and financially overwhelming. In Aron's mind the French "were deluding themselves, not to speak of misleading the Arabs, when they promised equality and equal representation in the future—having steadfastly refused it in the past."[24] Second, the emotional force of Algerian nationalism was so great that it could be contained only by the application of overwhelming military force, an exercise that Aron did not think the French could afford, either economically or politically. Third, even though Algerian well-being would not be best served by the independence that Algerians fought for, it was in the best interest of both countries that independence happen quickly.

What is most striking about Aron's reasoning, Judt noted, is that, while Aron agreed with almost every other leading intellectual in France on the need for independence, he offered arguments that were derived from principles wholly unlike theirs. Aron, for example, did not attempt

> to show the legitimacy of the Arab claim to independence. He was not interested, for these purposes in the moral debt the French had inherited from their colonial past and which could only be liquidated by the abandonment of colonial power. He never invoked the course of history or the "natural" move to a postcolonial world. And, above all, he did not refer to the emotive issue of French military and police practices in Algeria itself, the use of torture to extract confessions from suspected

> terrorists, and the price that was being paid for these crimes in the soul of the French Republic. The Algerian tragedy, for Aron, lay not in the moral dilemma posed to individuals caught in the "dirty war," but in the absence of a satisfactory third alternative to continuing conflict or a "catastrophic" independence.[25]

Indeed, many charged Aron with overlooking the moral dimensions of the Algerian crisis altogether. When he was confronted with this accusation during his interview with Missika and Wolton and asked why he never joined with those who were speaking out against the use of torture by the French military, Aron responded with characteristic directness: "What would I have achieved by proclaiming my opposition to torture? I have never met anyone who is in favor of torture."[26] Of his refusal to ground his case for Algerian independence in moral criteria, Aron simply shrugged and pointed out that others were already advancing that argument. "The important thing was to convince those who were arguing the opposite position."[27] Or, as he put it in 1954, it was necessary to speak "a language of reason" at a time when so much public discourse was driven by passion and emotion.

But how can one realistically expect a democratic republic to heed the "language of reason" after it has been prodded into believing that it has a mission to "civilize" the rest of the world, or at least North Africa? Aron may have been among the first to call for Algerian independence, but, remarkably enough, he was not opposed to the possession of colonies in principle. Colonies were, in fact, an important element of the "inspiring idea" necessary for French greatness. Indeed, Aron explained in *Le Figaro,* France had a duty to keep North Africa "in the sphere of modern civilization." It is not, he pointed out, "in order to preserve outlets for our products that public opinion is attached to 'la presence française,' so much as to maintain our country's rank and sense of mission in the world."[28] In fact, Aron was angered by the initial American and British failure to help beleaguered French troops in Vietnam because, as Judt explained, he "shared the view widespread in the political class of his time, that France's identity was intimately bound up with her worldwide possessions and influence."[29]

Aron's repeated warning to the French not to dissipate their energies and resources on "sterile adventures" thus rings a bit hollow. His conviction that French democracy needed to be moved or inspired by a measure of *grandeur* seems to have blinded him to the possibility that a democracy is, in George

Kennan's artful description, rather like "one of those prehistoric monsters with a body as long as this room and a brain the size of a pin: he lies there in his comfortable primeval mud and pays little attention to his environment—in fact, you practically have to whack his tail off to make him aware that his interests are being disturbed; but once he grasps this, he lays about him with such blind determination that he not only destroys his adversary but largely wrecks his native habitat" as well.[30] In other words, striking fine balances between competing principles is, for a democratic republic, rather beside the point given the inherent difficulties of the challenge. The job of "educating," then, seems to be made immeasurably more difficult by the inclination to "arouse."

The conflicting principles of arousing and educating are a manifestation of the dilemma that haunts any effort to arm power politics with moral purpose. Those who judge politics by the light of an abstract ideal are driven to feel an ever-increasing sense of responsibility for creating the conditions under which those ideals can be realized. As Kenneth W. Thompson has argued, "Humanity has been endlessly prompted by conscience and insight to visions of perpetual peace . . . such a vision, [however], can be kept alive only when permitted to overreach itself."[31] Although Aron repeatedly emphasized that the universal values that guide our actions are purely formal realities that may never be realized, his policy of anticommunist containment and his notion of grandeur seem to suggest that prudent restraint may at times constitute a form of betrayal. Bequeathing the dilemma of an "inaccessible paradise" to philosophers may be harmless enough; bequeathing it to statesmen, however, may prove fatal indeed.

In Aron's thought we witness a heroic effort to keep the contradictions of the human condition pulled together into some kind of reasonable synthesis. Given the inherent difficulties of the task, it is not surprising that Aron lost his footing at times. Aron's emphasis on reason and moral ideas make his philosophy more appealing than realists such as Weber or Morgenthau, but it also contributes to the confusion and ambiguity in many of his analyses. In order to escape from the morally discouraging implications of political realism, Aron insisted on the existence of a realm of perfect freedom, a world devoid of the contaminating effects of historical necessity and hence knowable only by pure reason. At the same time, Aron tried to procure an accord between historical necessity and moral freedom so that morality can operate within history and so history can be receptive to moral action and even changed by it. Having separated the two worlds of intentionality and necessity, in other words, Aron was then compelled to unite them, which he did by constructing "intermediaries" and "correspondences" between them. Therein lies the origin and logic of his many pluralisms: Conceptual opposites were always held together in his thinking by the force of a middle term that kept the other two terms within range of each other.

Yet, as I have tried to show, the connecting points that Aron attempted to build here are rather wobbly, attached as they are by an unsteady logic that understands intentionality to be simultaneously independent of and anchored in historical necessity. This is the reason for the restless ambiguity of so much of Aron's thinking. Beneath the surface clarity of his writings lies a certain unwillingness or inability to reach many clear or firm conclusions. Despite the confidence of Aron's prose, many commentators have been driven to ask, "Exactly what has Aron said, anyway?"[32] In order to avoid being impaled on the horns of a dilemma, for example, Aron frequently took refuge in an "idea of reason"—that of a "reconciled humanity"—an idea that never knows its full realization. But, as Pierre Hassner observed, "This makes one think a little bit of the 'meager black and gold immortality' of Valéry; its content is vague and its philosophical status, hardly assured, seems vulnerable to the criticisms to which the Kantian idea of indefinite progress has been submitted from Hegel to Strauss."[33]

In assessing Aron's legacy, perhaps Pascal's standard is the most appropriate: "It is on thought that we must depend for our recovery," Pascal wrote, "not on space and time, which we could never fill. Let us strive to think well; that is the basic principle of morality." In striving to think well, we strive for truth. Despite the monstrous deformations of the truth wrought by twentieth-century despotisms, Aron held fast to his lifelong conviction that "the truth is great and will prevail." It is in that light that Aron's work is best understood; it is for that effort that his life deserves to be remembered.

NOTES

INTRODUCTION

1. H. Stuart Hughes, *The Obstructed Path* (New York, 1968), 12.

2. Hughes, *Obstructed Path,* 14.

3. Roy Pierce, *Contemporary French Thought* (London, 1966), 206.

4. Cited in Kenneth W. Thompson, *Masters of International Thought* (Baton Rouge, 1980), 173.

5. Raymond Aron, Introduction, in *Politics and History: Selected Essays by Raymond Aron,* ed. and trans. Miriam B. Conant (New York, 1978), xxiv.

6. Tony Judt, *Past Imperfect: French Intellectuals 1944–1956* (Berkeley, 1992), 239.

7. Talcott Parsons, *The Structure of Social Action* (Glencoe, Ill., 1949), 24.

8. For an analysis of Aron's criticism of radical philosophy, see Brian C. Anderson, *Raymond Aron and the Recovery of the Political* (Lanham, Md., 1997).

9. Raymond Aron, "The Quest for Meaning: A Sociologist's Reflections," *Encounter* 39 (September 1978): 37.

10. Aron, "Quest for Meaning," 45.

11. Stephen Koch, "Jean-Paul Sartre: France's Philosopher-King," *Washington Post,* 21 (21 June 1987), Book World sec., 11.

12. Tony Judt, *The Burden of Responsibility: Blum, Camus, Aron, and the French Twentieth Century* (Chicago, 1998), 138.

13. Raymond Aron, *Memoirs: Fifty Years of Political Reflection,* trans. George Holoch (New York, 1990), 176.

14. Allan Bloom, "Le Dernière des libraux," *Commentaire* 8 (1985): 177.

15. Raymond Aron, "Philosophy and History," in Conant, *Politics and History,* 19.

16. Raymond Aron, *L'Age des empires et l'avenir de la France* (Paris, 1946), 20.

17. Aron, *L'Age des empires,* 20; emphasis added.

18. Raymond Aron, *The Committed Observer: Interviews with Jean-Louis Missika and Dominique Wolton,* trans. James and Marie McIntosh (Chicago, 1983), 267.

19. Raymond Aron, *L'Homme contre les tyrans* (Paris, 1944), 249.

20. Raymond Aron, *Le Grand schisme* (Paris, 1948), 290.

21. Raymond Aron, "Max Weber and Michael Polanyi," in *The Logic of Personal Knowledge: Essays Presented to Michael Polanyi on His Seventieth Birthday* (London, 1961), 105.

22. Raymond Aron, *France Steadfast and Changing: The Fourth to the Fifth Republic,* trans. J. Irwin (Cambridge, 1960), 77.

23. Aron, *Le Grand schisme,* 167.

24. Aron, *Committed Observer,* 110.

25. Raymond Aron, "On Treason," *Confluence* 3 (September 1954): 290.

26. See Roy Pierce, *Contemporary French Political Thought* (London, 1966), 228; Judt, *Burden of Responsibility,* 168.

27. Judt, *Burden of Responsibility,* 168.

28. Aron, *Committed Observer,* 38.

29. Nicolas Baverez, *Raymond Aron: Un Moralist au temps des idéologies* (Paris, 1993), 19.

30. Claude Lévi-Strauss, *Commentaire* 8 (1985): 18.

31. Allan Bloom, *Commentaire,* 8 (1985): 180.

32. Aron, *Memoirs,* 6.

33. Aron, *Memoirs,* 6–7.

34. Baverez, *Raymond Aron,* 33–34.

35. Aron, *Memoirs,* 354.

36. Aron, *Memoirs,* 4.

37. Aron, *Memoirs,* 8.

38. Aron, *Memoirs,* 10.

39. Aron, *Committed Observer,* 24. For an introduction to Brunschvicq's philosophy, see Gary Gutting, *French Philosophy in the Twentieth Century* (Cambridge, 2001), 40–49.

40. Aron, *Committed Observer,* 23.

41. Aron, *Memoirs,* 34.

42. Aron, *Memoirs,* 53.

43. Raymond Aron, "La Philosophie de Léon Brunschvicq," *La France Libre* 44 (1944): 118. Cited in Baverez, *Raymond Aron,* 66.

44. Aron, *Committed Observer,* 26–27.

45. See Raymond Aron, "Monnaie et credit," *Thalès* 4 (1939): 235–53; Raymond Aron, "Remarques sur l'objectivité sciences sociales," *Theoria* (Göteborg) 5 (1939): 161–94; Raymond Aron, "Réflexions sur les problèmes économiques français," *Revue de Metaphysique et de Morale* 44 (1937): 793–822.

46. Raymond Aron, *German Sociology,* trans. Mary and Thomas Bottomore (New York, 1964); Raymond Aron, *Essai sur une théorie de l'histoire dans l'Allemagne contemporaine: La Philosophie critique de l'histoire* (Paris, 1938); Raymond Aron, *Introduction to the Philosophy of History: An Essay on the Limits of Objectivity,* trans. George J. Irwin (Boston, 1961).

47. Cited in Aron, *Memoirs,* 76.

48. Cited in Robert Colquhoun, *Raymond Aron,* vol. 1: *The Philosopher in History, 1905–1955* (London, 1986), 45.

49. Aron, *Memoirs,* 90.

50. Baverez, *Raymond Aron,* 128.

51. Gutting, *French Philosophy in the Twentieth Century,* mentions Aron only in passing, while Christian Yves Dupont, "Receptions of Phenomenology in French Philosophy and Religious Thought, 1889–1939" (Ph.D. diss., University of Notre Dame, 1997), mentions Aron

not at all, despite the fact that the eminent historian of Continental phenomenology Herbert Spiegelberg hailed Aron as "a social scientist of rank." Spiegelberg, *The Phenomenological Movement: A Historical Introduction* (The Hague, 1965), 2:590.

52. Cited in Robert Colquhoun, *Raymond Aron*, vol. 2: *The Sociologist in Society, 1955–1983* (London, 1986), 400.

53. Raymond Aron, *La Tragédie algérienne* (Paris, 1957).

54. Aron, "Réflexions sur les problèmes économiques français," 794.

55. Judt, *Past Imperfect*, 242.

56. Aron, *Memoirs*, 140.

57. Aron, *Memoirs*, 160.

58. Aron, *Memoirs*, 140.

59. Raymond Aron, "The Social Responsibility of the Philosopher," in Conant, *Politics and History*, 258.

60. Aron, *Committed Observer*, 258.

61. Aron, *Committed Observer*, 258, 259.

62. Aron, *Memoirs*, 160. This is why Allan Bloom once observed that Aron felt most comfortable as a journalist and scholar separating these two aspects "rather than fusing them together." Allan Bloom, *Giants and Dwarfs: Essays, 1960–1990* (New York, 1990), 257.

63. See Colquhoun, *Raymond Aron*, 1:319.

64. See, for example, the tributes to Aron from Henry Kissinger and McGeorge Bundy included in the special edition of *Commentaire* dedicated to Aron shortly after his death.

65. Raymond Aron, "L'Editorialiste," in *Fondation Nationale des Sciences Politiques: Problèmes et techniques de la presse* (Paris, 1948), 65–83. Reprinted in *Commentaire* 9 (1985): 387–96.

66. Judt, *Past Imperfect*, 303.

67. Raymond Aron, "Politics and French Intellectuals," *Partisan Review* 17 (1950): 600.

68. Aron, "Politics and French Intellectuals," 600.

69. Aron, "Politics and French Intellectuals," 595.

70. Aron, "Politics and French Intellectuals," 606.

71. Richard Posner, *Public Intellectuals: A Study of Decline* (Cambridge, 2001), 12.

72. Judt, *Past Imperfect*, 318.

73. Aron, *Memoirs*, 230.

74. Aron, *Memoirs*, 243.

75. François Furet, "La Rencontre d'une idée et d'une vie," *Commentaire* 8 (1985): 52.

76. Pierre Viansson-Ponté, "La France s'ennuie," *Le Monde*, 15 March 1968. Cited in Colquhoun, *Raymond Aron*, 2:313.

77. Daniel J. Mahoney, *The Liberal Political Science of Raymond Aron* (Lanham, Md., 1992).

78. Anderson, *Raymond Aron*.

79. See Philip Abrams, *Historical Sociology* (Ithaca, 1982), 16. See also Stephen Hobden and John M. Hobson, *Historical Sociology of International Relations* (Cambridge, 2002).

80. See esp. James Davison Hunter, *Before the Shooting Begins: Searching for Democracy in America's Culture Wars* (New York, 1994).

81. Ralf Dahrendorf, "The Achievements of Raymond Aron," *Encounter* 54 (May 1980): 29.

82. Pierre Manent, "Raymond Aron, Educateur," *Commentaire* 8 (1985): 159.

83. Fred Frohock, *The Nature of Political Inquiry* (Homewood, Ill., 1967), 15.

CHAPTER 1: "TO GRASP TRUTH AND REALITY"

1. Aron, *Memoirs,* 13.

2. Aron, *Memoirs,* 20.

3. Hughes, *Obstructed Path,* 14.

4. Aron, Introduction, in Conant, *Politics and History,* xviii–xix.

5. Cited by Colquhoun, *Raymond Aron,* 1:55.

6. Raymond Aron, *La Sociologie allemande contemporaine* (Paris, 1935). Trans. as *German Sociology* by Mary and Thomas Bottomore (Glencoe, Ill., 1957); Raymond Aron, *Essai sur la théorie de l'histoire dans l'Allemagne contemporaine: La philosophie critique de l'histoire* (Paris, 1938).

7. Raymond Aron, *German Sociology,* 67.

8. Julien Freund, *The Sociology of Max Weber,* trans. Mary Ilford (New York, 1968), 8.

9. Aron, *German Sociology,* 73.

10. Cited in H. Stuart Hughes, *Consciousness and Society: The Reorientation of European Social Thought 1890–1930* (New York, 1958), 312.

11. Aron, *German Sociology,* 72.

12. Aron, *Essai sur la théorie de l'histoire dans l'Allemagne contemporaine,* 242.

13. Aron, *German Sociology,* 78.

14. Raymond Aron, *Main Currents in Sociological Thought,* trans. Richard Howard and Helen Weaver (Garden City, N.Y., 1970), 2:236.

15. Aron, *Main Current in Sociological Thought,* 2:240.

16. Aron, *German Sociology,* 80.

17. Aron, *Main Currents,* 2:239.

18. Aron, *Main Currents,* 2:241.

19. Aron, *German Sociology,* 81.

20. Aron, *Main Currents,* 2:244.

21. Aron, *German Sociology,* 81.

22. Aron, *Main Currents,* 2:238.

23. Carlo Antoni, *From History to Sociology: The Transition in German Historical Thinking,* trans. Hayden V. White (Detroit, 1959), 178.

24. Aron, *Essai sur la théorie de l'histoire dans l'allemagne contemporaine,* 246.

25. Raymond Aron, *Introduction to the Philosophy of History,* 95; hereafter cited parenthetically in the text as *IPH.*

26. Aron, *German Sociology,* 83.

27. Aron, *German Sociology,* 84.

28. Aron, *German Sociology,* 84.

29. Aron, *German Sociology,* 106.

30. Aron, *Main Currents in Sociological Thought,* 2:294.

31. Aron, *Essai sur la théorie de l'histoire dans l'Allemagne contemporaine,* 272.

32. Aron, *Main Currents in Sociological Thought,* 2:302.

33. Raymond Aron, "Max Weber and Modern Social Science," in *History, Truth and Liberty: Selected Writings of Raymond Aron,* ed. Franciszek Draus (Chicago, 1985), 338.

34. Quentin Lauer, Introduction, in Edmund Husserl, *Phenomenology and the Crisis of Philosophy,* trans. Quentin Lauer (New York, 1965), 9.

35. Lauer, Introduction, in Husserl, *Phenomenology and the Crisis of Philosophy,* 21.

36. Lauer, Introduction, in Husserl, *Phenomenology and the Crisis of Philosophy,* 61.

37. Lauer, Introduction, in Husserl, *Phenomenology and the Crisis of Philosophy,* 23.

38. Lauer, Introduction, in Husserl, *Phenomenology and the Crisis of Philosophy,* 47.

39. Leszek Kolakowski, *Husserl and the Search for Certitude* (New Haven, Conn., 1975), 45.

40. Kolakowski, *Husserl and the Search for Certitude,* 51.

41. Lauer, Introduction, in Husserl, *Phenomenology and the Crisis of Philosophy,* 64.

42. Aron, *Memoirs,* 43.

43. Raymond Aron, *Dimensions de la conscience historique* (Paris, 1960), 55.

44. H. Stuart Hughes, *History as Art and Science* (New York, 1964), 11.

45. Raymond Aron, *Opium of the Intellectuals,* trans. Terence Kilmartin (London, 1957), 139.

46. Aron, *Opium of the Intellectuals,* 136.

47. Aron, *Opium of the Intellectuals,* 142.

48. Raymond Aron, "The Philosophy of History," in Conant, *Politics and History,* 14.

49. Aron, "Philosophy of History," 14.

50. Aron, "Philosophy of History," 10.

51. Raymond Aron, "Three Forms of Historical Intelligibility," in Conant, *Politics and History,* 48.

52. Aron, *Opium of the Intellectuals,* 141.

53. Aron, *Opium of the Intellectuals,* 141–42.

54. Aron, *Opium of the Intellectuals,* 141.

55. Raymond Aron, *History and the Dialectic of Violence,* trans. Barry Cooper (New York, 1976), 92.

56. Aron, "Three Forms of Intelligibility," 48.

57. Aron, "Three Forms of Intelligibility," 47–48.

58. Sylvie Mesure, *Raymond Aron et la raison historique* (Paris, 1984), 95.

59. Mesure, *Raymond Aron et la raison historique,* 95–96.

60. Aron, *Dimensions de la conscience historique,* 21.

61. Aron, *Main Currents in Sociological Thought,* 2:331.

62. Aron, "Philosophy of History," 13.

63. Aron, "Philosophy of History," 10.

64. Aron, "Philosophy of History," 10–11.

65. Mesure, *Raymond Aron et la raison historique,* 115.

66. Aron, *Essai de l'histoire sur la théorie dans l'Allemagne contemporaine,* 34

67. Mesure, *Raymond Aron et la raison historique,* 116.

68. Raymond Aron, *Committed Observer,* 267.

69. Aron, *Committed Observer,* 269.

70. Mesure, *Raymond Aron et la raison historique,* 118.
71. Mesure, *Raymond Aron et la raison historique,* 116.
72. Mesure, *Raymond Aron et la raison historique,* 116–17.
73. Cited in Colquhoun, *Raymond Aron,* 1:144.
74. Judt, *Past Imperfect,* 83.
75. Aron, *Opium of the Intellectuals,* 190.
76. Aron, *Committed Observer,* 106.
77. Aron, *Memoirs,* 329.
78. Aron, *Committed Observer,* 152.
79. Aron, *Committed Observer,* 146.
80. Aron, *Committed Observer,* 156.
81. Raymond Aron, *Marxism and the Existentialists* (New York, 1969), 30.
82. Aron, *Marxism and the Existentialists,* 23.
83. Aron, *Marxism and the Existentialists,* 23.
84. Aron, *Marxism and the Existentialists,* 174.
85. Aron, *Marxism and the Existentialists,* 173.
86. Aron, *History and the Dialectic of Violence,* 214.
87. Aron, *Memoirs,* 89–90.
88. Cited in Colquhoun, *Raymond Aron,* 1:144.
89. Aron, *Committed Observer,* 266.
90. Aron, *Committed Observer,* 266.

CHAPTER 2: "THAT COOL DISTILLER OF PASSION AND INTEREST"

1. Raymond Aron, "Conflict and War from the Viewpoint of Historical Sociology," in *Contemporary Theory in International Relations,* ed. Stanley Hoffmann (Englewood Cliffs, N.J., 1960), 200.
2. Raymond Aron, *18 Lectures on Industrial Society,* trans. Mary K. Bottomore (London, 1967); *La Lutte des classes: Nouvelles leçons sur les sociétés industrielles* (Paris, 1964); and *Democracy and Totalitarianism,* trans. Valence Ionescu (New York, 1969).
3. Aron, *18 Lectures on Industrial Society,* 1; hereafter cited in the text as *EL.*
4. Aron, *Memoirs,* 235.
5. Aron, *Memoirs,* 236.
6. Aron, *Memoirs,* 236.
7. The phrase was Herbert Nicolson's. Cited in Kenneth W. Thompson, *Masters of International Thought,* 170.
8. Raymond Aron, "Science and Consciousness of Society," in *History, Truth, Liberty,* 204.
9. Aron, *German Sociology,* 4.
10. Aron, "On the Historical Condition of the Sociologist," in Conant, *Politics and History,* 74.
11. Raymond Aron, *Main Currents in Sociological Thought* (Garden City, N.Y., 1968), 1:14; hereafter cited in the text as *MC.*
12. Aron, "Science and Consciousness of Society," 211.
13. Roy Pierce, *Contemporary French Political Thought,* 238. I am indebted to Professor Pierce's discussion of scientific analysis and moral choice here.

14. Aron, "Science and Consciousness of Society," 220.

15. Aron, "Science and Consciousness of Society," 221.

16. Aron, *Democracy and Totalitarianism,* 11.

17. Aron, *Democracy and Totalitarianism,* 5.

18. Aron, *Democracy and Totalitarianism,* 11.

19. Aron, *Democracy and Totalitarianism,* 24.

20. Raymond Aron, "Remarques sur l'objectivité des sciences sociales," *Theoria* (Göteborg) 5 (1939): 184–85. Cited in Colquhoun, *Raymond Aron,* 1:174.

21. Raymond Aron, *Études politiques* (Paris, 1972), 162.

22. Aron, "On the Historical Condition of the Sociologist," 62.

23. Raymond Aron, *Progress and Disillusion: The Dialectics of Modern Society,* trans. Elaine Halperin (New York, 1968), xii.

24. Aron, *Progress and Disillusion,* xii.

25. Aron, "Science and Consciousness of Society," 205.

26. Raymond Aron, "Social Class, Political Class, and Ruling Class," in *History, Truth, Liberty,* 242.

27. Aron, "Science and Consciousness of Society," 208.

28. Aron, *Democracy and Totalitarianism,* 237.

29. Pierce, *Contemporary French Political Thought,* 236.

30. Aron, *Democracy and Totalitarianism,* 237.

31. Cited in Pierce, *Contemporary French Political Thought,* 237.

32. Pierce, *Contemporary French Political Thought,* 237.

33. Pierce, *Contemporary French Political Thought,* 245.

34. Aron, *Opium of the Intellectuals,* 315.

35. Pierce, *Contemporary French Political Thought,* 246.

36. Raymond Aron, "Max Weber and Power-Politics," in *Max Weber and Power Politics Today,* trans. Kathleen Morris, ed. O. Stammer (Oxford, 1971), 98.

37. Aron, "Max Weber and Power-Politics," 99.

38. Raymond Aron, "Max Weber and Modern Social Science," in *History, Truth, Liberty,* 364.

39. Aron, *Opium of the Intellectuals,* 233.

40. Roy Pierce, "Liberalism and Democracy in the Thought of Raymond Aron," *Journal of Politics* 25 (August 1963): 22.

41. Pierce, "Liberalism and Democracy in the Thought of Raymond Aron," 23.

42. Raymond Aron, *War and Industrial Society,* trans. Mary K. Bottomore (London, 1958), 57.

43. Raymond Aron, "On Treason," *Confluence* 3 (September 1954): 287.

44. Aron, "History and Politics," in Conant, *Politics and History,* 248.

45. Aron, "History and Politics," 248.

46. Aron, *L'Age des empires,* 84.

47. Aron, *L'Age des empires,* 84.

48. Raymond Aron, "The Fifth Republic: Letter from Paris," *Encounter* 11 (December 1958): 12.

49. Aron, *Memoirs,* 260.

50. Aron, "Fifth Republic: Letter from Paris," 10–11.

51. See Aron, "Fifth Republic: Letter from Paris," 10.

52. Aron, *L'Homme contre les tyrans,* 346.

53. Aron, *L'Homme contre les tyrans,* 347.

54. Aron, *L'Homme contre les tyrans,* 352.

55. Aron, *Opium of the Intellectuals,* 324.

56. This was the famous rallying cry of the French Left during the 1960s.

57. Raymond Aron, *Industrial Society: Three Essays on Ideology and Development* (New York, 1967), 169.

58. Aron, *Industrial Society,* 159.

59. Aron, *La Lutte des classes,* 55.

60. Aron, *Opium of the Intellectuals,* 322.

61. Raymond Aron, "The Education of the Citizen in Industrial Society," *Daedalus* 91 (1962): 263.

62. Raymond Aron, *The Dawn of Universal History,* trans. Dorothy Pickles (New York, 1961), 53.

63. Aron, *Dawn of Universal History,* 54.

64. Aron, *Dawn of Universal History,* 55.

65. Aron, *Dawn of Universal History,* 56.

66. Cited in Pierce, *Contemporary French Political Thought,* 249.

67. Pierce, *Contemporary French Political Thought,* 249.

68. Aron, *L'Age des empires,* 47.

69. Cited in Judt, *Past Imperfect,* 239.

70. Aron, *L'Age des empires,* 47.

71. Judt, *Past Imperfect,* 240.

72. Aron, *Opium of the Intellectuals,* 323.

73. Bell, *End of Ideology,* 405.

74. Aron, *Opium of the Intellectuals,* 263.

75. Tracy B. Strong, "History and Choices: The Foundations of the Political Thought of Raymond Aron," *History and Ideas: Studies in the Philosophy of History* 11 (1972): 191. For Aron's affirmation of ideology, see Raymond Aron, "L'Ideologie, support nécessaire de l'action," *Res Publica* 2 (1960).

76. Aron, *Dawn of Universal History,* 63.

77. Aron, *Dawn of Universal History,* 65.

CHAPTER 3: *PEACE AND WAR*

1. Aron, *Memoirs,* 301.

2. Aron, *Memoirs,* 302.

3. Raymond Aron, *Peace and War: A Theory of International Relations,* trans. Richard Howard and Annette Baker Fox (New York, 1966); hereafter cited parenthetically in the text as *PW.*

4. Jean-Baptiste Duroselle, "*Paix et guerre entre les nations:* La Théorie des relations internationals selon Raymond Aron," *Revue Française de Science Politique* 12 (1962): 963. Cited in Colquhoun, *Raymond Aron,* 2:191–92.

5. Stanley Hoffmann, "Minerva and Janus," in *The State of War: Essays on the Theory and Practice of International Relations,* ed. Stanley Hoffmann (New York, 1965), 33.

6. Raymond Aron, "What Is a Theory of International Relations?" in Conant, *Politics and History,* 185.

7. See Hoffmann, "Minerva and Janus," 22–32.

8. Hans Morgenthau, *Politics among Nations: The Struggle for Power and Peace* (New York, 1978), 8.

9. Gustav Bergman, "Purpose, Function, Scientific Explanation," in *Readings in the Philosophy of the Social Sciences,* ed. May Brodbeck (New York, 1968), 220.

10. Aron, "What Is a Theory of International Relations?" 174.

11. Aron, "What Is a Theory of International Relations?" 170.

12. Aron, *18 Lectures on Industrial Society,* 53.

13. Hoffmann, "Minerva and Janus," *State of War,* 35.

14. Raymond Aron, "Macht, Power, Puissance: Democratic Prose or Demonic Poetry?" in Conant, *Politics and History,* 112.

15. See, for example, W. David Clinton, *The Two Faces of National Interest* (Baton Rouge, 1994), esp. 50–70.

16. Raymond Aron, "The Quest for a Philosophy of Foreign Affairs," in *Contemporary Theory in International Relations,* ed. Stanley Hoffmann (Englewood Cliffs, N.J., 1960). 88.

17. Aron, "Quest for a Philosophy of Foreign Affairs," 86.

18. Aron, "Quest for a Philosophy of Foreign Affairs," 87.

19. Aron, "Quest for a Philosophy of Foreign Affairs," 89.

20. Aron, "Quest for a Philosophy of Foreign Affairs," 85.

21. Aron, "Quest for a Philosophy of Foreign Affairs," 87.

22. Aron, "Quest for a Philosophy of Foreign Affairs," 80.

23. Aron, "What Is a Theory of International Relations?" 181.

24. Raymond Aron, *A Century of Total War* (Boston, 1954), 97–98.

25. Aron, "What Is a Theory of International Relations?" 179.

26. Aron, "What Is a Theory of International Relations?" 179.

27. See Anderson, *Raymond Aron and the Recovery of the Political.*

28. For a discussion of the prudence tradition, see Alberto Coll, "Prudence and Foreign Policy," in *Might and Right after the Cold War,* ed. Michael Cromartie (Lanham, Md., 1993).

29. Gaddis, *United States and the End of the Cold War,* 169.

30. Gaddis, *United States and the End of the Cold War,* 190.

31. Gaddis, *United States and the End of the Cold War,* 190.

32. Gaddis, *United States and the End of the Cold War,* 192.

33. Maja Zehfuss, *Constructivism in International Relations: The Politics of Reality* (Cambridge, 2002), 2–9.

34. Alexander Wendt, "Anarchy Is What States Make of It: The Social Construction of Power Politics," *International Organization* 46 (1992): 425.

35. Wendt, "Anarchy Is What States Make of It," 396–97.

36. Wendt, "Anarchy Is What States Make of It," 397.

37. Alexander Wendt, "Collective Identity Formation and the International State," *American Political Science Review* 88 (1994): 284. Wendt complains that supporters of liberal democracy can "celebrate the 'end of history' with hardly a peep about democracy at the international level" (393).

38. Wendt, "Collective Identity Formation and the International State," 385.

39. Wendt, "Collective Identity Formation and the International State," 389.

40. Wendt, *Social Theory of international Politics* (Cambridge, 1999), 371; hereafter cited parenthetically in the text as *ST.*

41. Wendt, "Anarchy Is What States Make of It," 399.

42. Wendt, "Anarchy Is What States Make of It," 411.

43. Wendt, "Anarchy Is What States Make of It," 411.

44. Wendt, "Anarchy Is What States Make of It," 411.

45. Wendt, "Anarchy Is What States Make of It," 412.

46. Wendt, "Collective Identity Formation and the International State," 389.

47. Aron, *Memoirs,* 42.

48. Aron, *Memoirs,* 99.

49. Aron, *Memoirs,* 475.

50. Kenneth Waltz, *Theory of International Politics* (Reading, Mass., 1979), 1; hereafter cited parenthetically in the text as *T.*

51. See Kenneth Waltz, *Realism and International Politics* (New York, 2008), 70–73.

52. This seems to be a common criticism of rational choice theory. On this point, see James Ceaser, *Liberal Democracy and Political Science* (Baltimore, 1990), 78–87.

53. See, for example, Raymond Aron, "On Hayek and Liberalism," in *In Defense of Political Reason: Essays by Raymond Aron,* ed. Daniel J. Mahoney (Lanham, Md., 1994), 89.

54. See Scott McConnell, "Homage to Raymond Aron," *Commentary* (May 1985): 42–44.

CHAPTER 4: CLAUSEWITZ AND THE ART OF WAR

1. Hans Morgenthau, "Foreign Policy: The Conservative School," *World Politics* 2 (January 1955): 285. The book Morgenthau was referring to is Raymond Aron, *The Century of Total War* (Boston, 1955).

2. Raymond Aron, *Clausewitz: Philosopher of War,* trans. Christine Booker and Norman Stone (London, 1983); hereafter cited parenthetically in the text as *C.*

3. C. Douglas-Home, "Master of the Disciplines of War," *Times of London,* 1 December 1983. Cited in Colquhoun, *Raymond Aron,* 2:485.

4. Raymond Aron, "Reason, Passion and Power in the Thought of Clausewitz," *Social Research* 39 (1972): 603.

5. Aron, "Reason, Passion and Power in the Thought of Clausewitz," 602.

6. Michael Howard, *Clausewitz: A Very Short Introduction* (Oxford, 1983), 14.

7. Aron, "Reason, Passion and Power in the Thought of Clausewitz," 610.

8. Aron, "Reason, Passion and Power in the Thought of Clausewitz," 610.

9. Stanley Hoffmann, "The Sword and the Pen," *New Republic,* 4 November 1985, 39.

10. Hew Strachan, *Carl von Clausewitz's* On War: *A Biography* (New York, 2007), 24.

11. Strachan, *Carl von Clausewitz's* On War, 87.

12. Strachan, *Carl von Clausewitz's* On War, 143.

13. Strachan, *Carl von Clausewitz's* On War, 176.

14. Strachan, *Carl von Clausewitz's* On War, 169.

15. Strachan, "A Clausewitz for Every Season," *American Interest* 2 (July–August 2007): 29.

16. Strachan, "Clausewitz for Every Season," 33.

17. Strachan, "Clausewitz for Every Season," 33.

18. Strachan, *Carl von Clausewitz's* On War, 142.

19. Aron, *Clausewitz,* 339.

20. Howard, *Clausewitz,* 71.

21. Raymond Aron, *The Great Debate,* trans. Ernest Pawel (Westport, Conn., 1981), 67; hereafter cited in the text as *GD.*

22. Cited in John Gaddis, *Strategies of Containment: A Critical Appraisal of Postwar American National Security Policy* (New York, 1973), 214–15.

23. Raymond Aron, "The Evolution of Modern Strategic Thought," in Conant, *Politics and History,* 198.

24. Aron, "Evolution of Modern Strategic Thought," 199.

25. Aron, "Evolution of Modern Strategic Thought," 199.

26. Aron, "Evolution of Modern Strategic Thought," 197.

27. The most complete expression of Aron's assessment of the politics of *grandeur* is found in Raymond Aron, "De la politique de grandeur," *Preuves* 105 (November 1959): 3–12.

28. Raymond Aron, "A New Member of the Nuclear Club," *Survival* 1 (1959): 137.

29. Aron, "New Member of the Nuclear Club," 137.

30. Aron, "New Member of the Nuclear Club," 138.

31. Raymond Aron, *Les Dernières années du siècle* (Paris, 1983), 68.

32. Aron, *Les Dernières années du siècle,* 69.

33. Aron, *Les Dernières années du siècle,* 70.

34. Aron, *Les Dernières années du siècle,* 79.

35. Aron, *Les Dernières années du siècle,* 83.

36. Aron, *Les Dernières années du siècle,* 81.

37. Aron, *Les Dernières années du siècle,* 81.

38. Aron, *Les Dernières années du siècle,* 85.

39. Raymond Aron, "Arms Control and Peace Research," Tanner Lectures on Human Values. Cambridge University, 22 November 1979, 2:22.

40. Aron, "Arms Control and Peace Research," 15.

41. Aron, "Arms Control and Peace Research," 15.

42. Raymond Aron, *On War,* trans. Terence Kilmartin (New York, 1968), 133.

43. Aron, *On War,* 133.

44. Aron, *Century of Total War,* 207.

45. Aron, *Century of Total War,* 208.

46. Aron, "Quest for a Philosophy of Foreign Affairs," 83.

47. Aron, "Quest for a Philosophy of Foreign Affairs," 84.

48. Aron, "Quest for a Philosophy of Foreign Affairs," 83.

49. Aron, *Les Dernières années du siècle,* 184.

50. Aron, *Les Dernières années du siècle,* 193.

51. Gaddis, *Strategies of Containment,* 86.

52. Aron, *On War,* 27.

53. Aron, *On War,* 27.

54. Aron, *On War,* 29.

55. Aron, *On War,* 29.

56. Aron, *On War,* 30.

57. Raymond Aron, *The Imperial Republic: The United States and the World, 1954–73,* trans. Frank Jellinek (Englewood Cliffs, N.J., 1974), 106.

58. Aron, *Imperial Republic,* 107.

59. Aron, *Imperial Republic,* 95–96.

60. Aron, *Imperial Republic,* 107.

61. Aron, *Imperial Republic,* 99.

62. Raymond Aron, "On Dubious Battles," *Parameters: Journal of the Army War College* 10 (December 1980): 8.

63. Aron, "On Dubious Battles," 7.

64. Aron, "On Dubious Battles," 9.

65. Aron, "On Dubious Battles," 9.

66. Aron, "On Dubious Battles," 8.

67. Aron, "On Dubious Battles," 9.

68. Aron, "On Dubious Battles," 9.

69. Aron, *On War,* 142

70. Aron, *On War,* 143.

CHAPTER 5: CRITICAL CONFRONTATION

1. Thomas Pangle, "Political Theory in Contemporary France: Towards a Renaissance of Liberal Political Theory," *PS: Political Science and Politics* 20 (Fall 1987): 1000.

2. Michael Dobb, "The Café Counterrevolution: France's Left Turns on Itself," *Washington Post,* 17 February 1985, D1.

3. Cited in Colquhoun, *Raymond Aron,* 2:594.

4. Stanley Hoffmann, "Raymond Aron (1905–1983)," *New York Review of Books,* 8 December 1983.

5. Kenneth W. Thompson, "The Political Philosophy of Reinhold Niebuhr," in *Reinhold Niebuhr: His Religious, Social and Political Thought,* ed. Charles Kegley and R. Bretall (New York, 1956), 241.

6. Reinhold Niebuhr, *The Nature and Destiny of Man: A Christian Interpretation* (New York, 1941), 1:260.

7. Reinhold Niebuhr, *The Irony of American History* (New York, 1952), 89.

8. Reinhold Niebuhr, *The Children of Light and the Children of Darkness: A Vindication of Democracy and a Critique of its Traditional Defense* (New York, 1944), 174.

9. Reinhold Niebuhr, "The Fight for Germany," *Life* 21, 21 October 1946, 56–72. Cited in Michel Joseph Smith, *Realist Thought from Weber to Kissinger* (Baton Rouge, 1986), 119.

10. Aron, *Memoirs,* 300.

11. Stanley Hofmann, *Janus and Minerva: Essays in the Theory and Practice of International Politics* (Boulder, 1987), 7.

12. Han Morgenthau, *Politics among Nations,* 4.

13. Hans Morgenthau, *Scientific Man vs. Power Politics* (Chicago, 1962), 155.

14. Richard Melanson, "Paul H. Nitze to Norman Podhoretz: The Tradition of Anti-Communist Containment," in *Traditions and Values: American Diplomacy, 1945 to the Present,* ed. Kenneth W. Thompson (Lanham, Md., 1984), 166.

15. John Gaddis, *Strategies of Containment,* 232.

16. Raymond Aron, *Les Dernières années de la siècle,* 184.

17. Raymond Aron, "La France joue sa dernière chance en Afrique: Des centaines de milliers de sans-travail disponibles pour la révolte," *Figaro,* 12 October 1955. Cited in Colquhoun, *Raymond Aron,* 2:42.

18. Colquhoun, *Raymond Aron,* 2:44. Colquhoun has written an excellent account of Aron's role in the Algerian debate. See Colquhoun, *Raymond Aron,* 2:41–80. Another very good account of Aron's involvement is M. Winock, "La Tragédie algérienne," *Commentaire* 8 (1985): 269–73.

19. Raymond Aron, *La Tragédie algérienne* (Paris, 1957).

20. Aron, *La Tragédie algérienne,* 40. Cited in Colquhoun, *Raymond Aron,* 2:48.

21. Winock, "La Tragédie algérienne," 270

22. Aron, *L'Algérie et la République* (Paris, 1958), 9. Cited in Colquhoun, *Raymond Aron,* 2:55.

23. Judt, *Burden of Responsibility,* 165.

24. Judt, *Burden of Responsibility,* 166.

25. Judt, *Burden of Responsibility,* 167.

26. Aron, *Committed Observer,* 288.

27. Aron, *Committed Observer,* 289.

28. Raymond Aron, "La France joue sa dernière chance en Afrique: IV. L'Unité française en peril," *Figaro,* 15 October 1955. Cited in Colquhoun, *Raymond Aron,* 2:45.

29. Judt, *Burden of Responsibility,* 165.

30. George Kennan, *American Diplomacy, 1900–1950* (New York, 1951), 59.

31. Kenneth W. Thompson, "The Political Philosophy of Reinhold Niebuhr," in *Reinhold Niebuhr: His Religious, Social and Political Thought,* 244.

32. See, for example, David Thomson, "The Three Worlds of Raymond Aron," *International Affairs* 39 (February 1963): 49–58.

33. Pierre Hassner, "Raymond Aron and the History of the Twentieth Century," *International Studies Quarterly.*

SELECT BIBLIOGRAPHY

BOOKS BY RAYMOND ARON

Aron, Raymond. *Essai sur la théorie de l'histoire dans contemporaine Allemagne: La Philosophie critique de l'histoire.* Paris: Vrin, 1938.

———. *L'Homme contre les tyrans.* New York: Editions de la Maison Française, 1944.

———. *L'Age des empires et l'avenir de la France.* Paris: Défense de la France, 1946.

———. *Le Grand schisme.* Paris: Gallimard, 1948.

———. *The Century of Total War.* Boston: Beacon Press, 1954.

———. *German Sociology.* Translated by Mary K. Bottomore and Thomas Bottomore. Glencoe, Ill.: Free Press, 1957.

———. *The Opium of the Intellectuals.* Translated by Terence L. Kilmartin. London: Secker & Warburg, 1957.

———. *La Tragédie algérienne.* Paris: Plon, 1957.

———. *L'Algérie et la République.* Paris: Plon, 1958.

———. *War and Industrial Society.* Translated by Mary K. Bottomore. London: Oxford University Press, 1958.

———. *Dimensions de la conscience historique.* Paris: Plon, 1960.

———. *France Steadfast and Changing.* Translated by George J. Irwin. Cambridge: Harvard University Press, 1960.

———. *The Dawn of Universal History.* Translated by Dorothy Pickles. New York: Praeger, 1961.

———. *Introduction to the Philosophy of History: An Essay on the Limits of Historical Objectivity.* Translated by George J. Irwin. London: Weidenfeld & Nicolson, 1961.

———. *La Lutte des classes: Nouvelles leçons sur les societies industrielles.* Paris: Gallimard, 1964.

———. *Peace and War: A Theory of International Relations.* Translated by Richard Howard and Annette Baker Fox. Garden City, N.Y.: Doubleday, 1966.

———. *18 Lectures on Industrial Society*. Translated by Mary K. Bottomore. London: Weidenfeld & Nicolson, 1967.
———. *Industrial Society: Three Essays on Ideology and Development*. New York: Praeger, 1967.
———. *On War*. Translated by Terence Kilmartin. New York: Norton, 1968.
———. *Progress and Disillusion: The Dialectics of Modern Society*. Translated by Elaine Halperin. New York: Frederick A. Praeger, 1968.
———. *Democracy and Totalitarianism*. Translated by Valence Ionescu. New York: Praeger, 1969.
———. *Marxism and the Existentialists*. New York: Harper and Row, 1969.
———. *Main Currents in Sociological Thought*. 2 vols. Translated by Richard Howard and Helen Weaver. Garden City, N.Y.: Anchor Books, 1970.
———. *Études politiques*. Paris: Gallimard, 1972.
———. *The Imperial Republic: The United States and the World, 1954–73*. Translated by Frank Jellinek. Englewood Cliffs, N.J.: Prentice-Hall, 1974.
———. *History and the Dialectic of Violence: An Analysis of Sartre's* Critique de la raison dialectique. Translated by Barry Cooper. New York: Harper and Row, 1976.
———. *Politics and History: Selected Essays by Raymond Aron*. Translated and edited by Miriam B. Conant. New York: Free Press, 1978.
———. *The Great Debate: Theories of Nuclear Strategy*. Translated by Ernest Pawel. Westport, Conn.: Greenwood Press, 1981.
———. *Clausewitz: Philosopher of War*. Translated by Christine Booker and Norman Stone. London: Routledge & Kegan Paul, 1983.
———. *The Committed Observer: Interviews with Jean-Louis Missika and Dominique Wolton*. Translated by James and Marie McIntosh. Chicago: Regnery Gateway, 1983.
———. *Les Dernières années du siècle*. Paris: Julliard, 1983.
———. *Memoirs: Fifty Years of Political Reflection*. Translated by George Holoch. New York: Holmes & Meier, 1990.

BOOKS OF COLLECTED ESSAYS BY RAYMOND ARON

Aron, Raymond. *Politics and History: Selected Essays by Raymond Aron*. Edited by Miriam B. Conant. New York: Free Press, 1978.
———. *History, Truth, Liberty: Selected Writings of Raymond Aron*. Edited by Franciszek Draus. Chicago: University of Chicago Press, 1985.
———. *In Defense of Political Reason: Essays by Raymond Aron*. Edited by Daniel J. Mahoney. Lanham, Md.: Rowman and Littlefield, 1994.

CITED ARTICLES AND LECTURES BY RAYMOND ARON

Aron, Raymond. "Réflexions sur les problems économiques français." *Revue de Metaphysique et de Morale* 44 (1937).

———. "Monnaie et credit." *Thales* 4 (1939).

———. "Remarques sur l'objectivité des sciences socials." *Theoria* (Göteborg) 5 (1939).

———. "La Philosophie de Léon Brunschvicq." *La France Libre* 44 (1944).

———. "L'Editorialiste." *Fondation Nationale des Sciènces Politiques: Problèmes et Techniques de la Press* (Paris) (1948).

———. "Politics and French Intellectuals." *Partisan Review* 17 (1950).

———. "On Treason." *Confluence* 3 (1954).

———. "La France joue sa dernière chance en Afrique: Des centaines de milliers de sans-travail disponibles pour la révolte." *Figaro,* 12 October 1955.

———. "La France joue sa dernière chance en Afrique: IV. L'Unité française en peril." *Figaro,* 15 October 1955.

———. "The Fifth Republic: Letter from Paris." *Encounter* 11 (1958).

———. "De la politique de grandeur." *Preuves* 105 (1959).

———. "A New Member of the Nuclear Club." *Survival* 1 (1959).

———. "Conflict and War from the Viewpoint of Historical Sociology." In *Contemporary Theory in International Relations.* Edited by Stanley Hoffmann. Englewood Cliffs, N.J.: Prentice-Hall, 1960.

———. "L'Ideologie, support nécessaire de l'action." *Res Publica* 2 (1960).

———. "The Quest for a Philosophy of Foreign Affairs." In *Contemporary Theory in International Relations.* Edited by Stanley Hoffmann. Englewood Cliffs, N.J.: Prentice-Hall, 1960.

———. "Max Weber and Michael Polanyi." In *The Logic of Personal Knowledge: Essays Presented to Michael Polanyi on His Seventieth Birthday.* Edited by T. A. Langford and W. H. Poteat. London: Routledge & Kegan Paul, 1961.

———. "The Education of the Citizen in Industrial Society." *Daedalus* 91 (1962).

———. "Max Weber and Power-Politics." *Max Weber and Power Politics Today.* Translated by Kathleen Morris and edited by Otto Stammer. Oxford: Basil Blackwell, 1971.

———. "Reason, Passion and Power in the Thought of Clausewitz." *Social Research* 36 (1972).

———. "The Evolution of Modern Strategic Thought." In *Politics and History: Selected Essays by Raymond Aron.* Edited by Miriam B. Conant. New York: Free Press, 1978.

———. "History and Politics." In *Politics and History: Selected Essays by Raymond Aron.* Edited by Miriam B. Conant. New York: Free Press, 1978.

———. Introduction. In *Politics and History: Selected Essays by Raymond Aron.* Edited by Miriam B. Conant. New York: Free Press, 1978.
———. "Macht, Power, Puissance: Democratic Prose or Demonic Poetry." In *Politics and History: Selected Essays by Raymond Aron.* Edited by Miriam B. Conant. New York: Free Press, 1978.
———. "On the Historical Condition of the Sociologist." In *Politics and History: Selected Essays by Raymond Aron.* Edited by Miriam B. Conant. New York: Free Press, 1978.
———. "Philosophy and History." In *Politics and History: Selected Essays by Raymond Aron.* Edited by Miriam B. Conant. New York: Free Press, 1978.
———. "The Philosophy of History." In *Politics and History: Selected Essays by Raymond Aron.* Edited by Miriam B. Conant. New York: Free Press, 1978.
———. "The Social Responsibility of the Philosopher." In *Politics and History: Selected Essays by Raymond Aron.* Edited by Miriam B. Conant. New York: Free Press, 1978.
———. "Three Forms of Historical Intelligibility." In *Politics and History: Selected Essays by Raymond Aron.* Edited by Miriam B. Conant. New York: Free Press, 1978.
———. "What Is a Theory of International Relations?" In *Politics and History: Selected Essays by Raymond Aron.* Edited by Miriam B. Conant. New York: Free Press, 1978.
———. "Arms Control and Peace Research." Tanner Lectures on Human Values. Cambridge University, 22 November 1979.
———. "On Dubious Battles." *Parameters: Journal of the Army War College* 10 (1980).
———. "Max Weber and Modern Social Science." In *History, Truth, Liberty: Selected Writings of Raymond Aron.* Edited by Franciszek Draus. Chicago: University of Chicago Press, 1985.
———. "Science and Consciousness of Society." In *History, Truth, Liberty: Selected Writings of Raymond Aron.* Edited by Franciszek Draus. Chicago: University of Chicago Press, 1985.
———. "Social Class, Political Class, and Ruling Class." In *History, Truth, Liberty: Selected Writings of Raymond Aron.* Edited by Franciszek Draus. Chicago: University of Chicago Press, 1985.
———. "On Hayek and Liberalism." In *In Defense of Political Reason: Essays by Raymond Aron.* Edited by Daniel J. Mahoney. Lanham, Md.: Rowman and Littlefield, 1994.

OTHER REFERENCES

Aiken, Henry. "The Revolt against Ideology." *Commentary* 25 (1958).
Anderson, Brian C. *Raymond Aron and the Recovery of the Political.* Lanham, Md.: Rowman and Littlefield, 1997.

Antoni, Carlo. *From History to Sociology: The Transition on German Historical Thinking.* Translated by Hayden V. White. Detroit: Wayne State University Press, 1959.

Baverez, Nicolas. *Raymond Aron: Un Moralist au temps des idéologies.* Paris: Flammarion, 1993.

Bell, Daniel. *The End of Ideology: On the Exhaustion of Political Ideas in the Fifties.* Glencoe, Ill.: Free Press, 1960.

Bergman, Gustav. "Purpose, Function, Scientific Explanation." In *Readings in the Philosophy of the Social Sciences.* Edited by May Brodbeck. New York: Macmillan, 1968.

Bloom, Allan. *Giants and Dwarfs.* New York: Simon and Schuster, 1990.

———. "Le Dernière des libraux." *Commentaire* 8 (1985).

Ceaser, James. *Liberal Democracy and Political Science.* Baltimore: Johns Hopkins University Press, 1990.

Clinton, W. David. *The Two Faces of National Interest.* Baton Rouge: Louisiana State University Press, 1994.

Coll, Alberto. "Prudence and Foreign Policy." In *Might and Right after the Cold War.* Edited by Michael Cromartie. Lanham, Md.: Rowman and Littlefield, 1993.

Colquhoun, Robert. *Raymond Aron: The Philosopher in History, 1905–1955.* London: Sage Publications, 1986.

———. *Raymond Aron: The Sociologist in Society, 1955–83.* London: Sage Publications, 1986.

Dahrendorf, Ralf. "The Achievements of Raymond Aron." *Encounter* 54 (1980).

Dobb, Michael. "The Café Counterrevolution: France's Left Turns on Itself." *Washington Post,* 17 February 1985.

Freund, Julien. *The Sociology of Max Weber.* Translated by Mary Ilford. New York: Pantheon Books, 1968.

Frohock, Fred. *The Nature of Political Inquiry.* Homewood, Ill.: Dorsey Press, 1967.

Furet, François. "La Rencontre d'une idée et d'une vie." *Commentaire* 8 (1985).

Gaddis, John. *Strategies of Containment: A Critical Appraisal of Postwar American National Security Policy.* New York: Oxford University Press, 1982.

———. *The United States and the End of the Cold War.* New York: Oxford University Press, 1992.

Gutting, Gary. *French Philosophy in the Twentieth Century.* Cambridge: Cambridge University Press, 2001.

Hoffmann, Stanley. *Contemporary Theory in International Relations.* Englewood Cliffs: Prentice-Hall, 1960.

———. "Minerva and Janus." In *The State of War: Essays on the Theory and Practice of International Relations.* Edited by Stanley Hoffmann. New York: Praeger, 1965.

———. *The State of War: Essays in the Theory and Practice of International Politics.* New York: Praeger, 1965.

———. "The Sword and the Pen." *New Republic,* 4 November 1985.

———. *Janus and Minerva: Essays on the Theory and Practice of International Politics.* Boulder: Westview Press, 1987.

Howard, Michael. *Clausewitz: A Very Short Introduction.* Oxford: Oxford University Press, 1983.

Hughes, H. Stuart. *Consciousness and Society: The Reorientation of European Social Thought, 1890–1930.* New York: Alfred Knopf, 1958.

———. *History as Art and as Science: Twin Vistas on the Past.* New York: Harper and Row, 1964.

———. *The Obstructed Path: French Social Thought in the Years of Desperation, 1930–1960.* New York: Harper and Row, 1968.

Husserl, Edmund. *Phenomenology and the Crisis of Philosophy.* Translated by Quentin Lauer. New York: Harper and Row, 1965.

Judt, Tony. *Past Imperfect: French Intellectuals, 1944–1956.* Berkeley: University of California Press, 1992.

———. *The Burden of Responsibility: Blum, Camus, Aron, and the French Twentieth Century.* Chicago: University of Chicago Press, 1998.

Kennan, George. *American Diplomacy: 1900–1950.* New York: New American Library, 1952.

Koch, Stephen. "Jean-Paul Sartre: France's Philosopher-King." *Washington Post* 21, 21 June 1987.

Kolakowski, Leszek. *Husserl and the Search for Certitude.* New Haven: Yale University Press, 1975.

Lichtheim, George. "French Neo-Liberalism." *Commentary* 25 (1958).

Mahoney, Daniel J. *The Liberal Political Science of Raymond Aron.* Lanham, Md.: Rowman and Littlefield, 1992.

Manent, Pierre. "Raymond Aron, educateur." *Commentaire* 8 (1985).

McConnell, Scott. "Homage to Raymond Aron." *Commentary* (1985).

Melanson, Richard. "Paul H. Nitze to Norman Podhoretz: The Tradition of Anti-Communist Containment." In *Traditions and Values: American Diplomacy, 1945 to the Present.* Edited by Kenneth W. Thompson. Lanham, Md.: University Press of America, 1984.

Mesure, Sylvie. *Raymond Aron et la raison historique.* Paris: J. Vrin, 1984.

Morgenthau, Hans. *Scientific Man vs. Power Politics.* Chicago: University of Chicago Press, 1946.

———. "Foreign Policy: The Conservative School." *World Politics* 2 (1955).

———. *Politics among Nations: The Struggle for Power and Peace.* New York: Knopf, 1978.

Niebuhr, Reinhold. *The Nature and Destiny of Man: A Christian Interpretation.* 2 vols. New York: Charles Scribner's Sons, 1941.

———. *The Children of Light and the Children of Darkness: A Vindication of Democracy and a Critique of Its Traditional Defense*. New York: Charles Scribner's Sons, 1944.

———. "The Fight for Germany." *Life* 21, 21 October 1946.

———. *The Irony of American History*. New York: Scribner, 1952.

Pangle, Thomas. "Political Theory in Contemporary France: Towards a Renaissance of Liberal Political Theory." *PS: Political Science and Politics* 20 (1987).

Parsons, Talcott. *The Structure of Social Action*. Glencoe, Ill.: Free Press, 1949.

Pierce, Roy. "Liberalism and Democracy in the Thought of Raymond Aron." *Journal of Politics* 25 (1963).

———. *Contemporary French Political Thought*. New York: Oxford University Press, 1966.

Posner, Richard. *Public Intellectuals: A Study of Decline*. Cambridge: Harvard University Press, 2001.

Smith, Michael Joseph. *Realist Thought from Weber to Kissinger*. Baton Rouge: Louisiana State University Press, 1986.

Speigelberg, Herbert. *The Phenomenological Movement: A Historical Introduction*. 2 vols. The Hague: Nijhoff, 1965–69.

Strachan, Hew. *Carl von Clausewitz's* On War: *A Biography*. New York: Atlantic Monthly Press, 2007.

———. "A Clausewitz for Every Season." *American Interest* 2 (2007).

Thompson, Kenneth W. "The Political Philosophy of Reinhold Niebuhr." In *Reinhold Niebuhr: His Religious, Social and Political Thought*. Edited by Charles Kegley and R. Bretall. New York: Macmillan, 1956.

———. *Masters of International Thought*. Baton Rouge: Louisiana State University Press, 1980.

Viansson-Ponté, Pierre. "La France s'ennuie." *Le Monde*, 15 March 1968.

Waltz, Kenneth. *Theory of International Politics*. Reading, Pa.: Addison-Wesley, 1979.

———. *Realism and International Politics*. New York: Routledge, 2008.

Wendt, Alexander. "Anarchy Is What States Make of It: The Social Construction of Power Politics." *International Organization* 46 (1992).

———. "Collective Identity Formation and the International State." *American Political Science Review* 88 (1994).

———. *Social Theory of International Politics*. Cambridge: Cambridge University Press, 1999.

Winock, M. "La Tragédie algérienne." *Commentaire* 8 (1985).

Zehfuss, Maja. *Constructivism in International Relations: The Politics of Reality*. Cambridge: Cambridge University Press, 2002.

INDEX